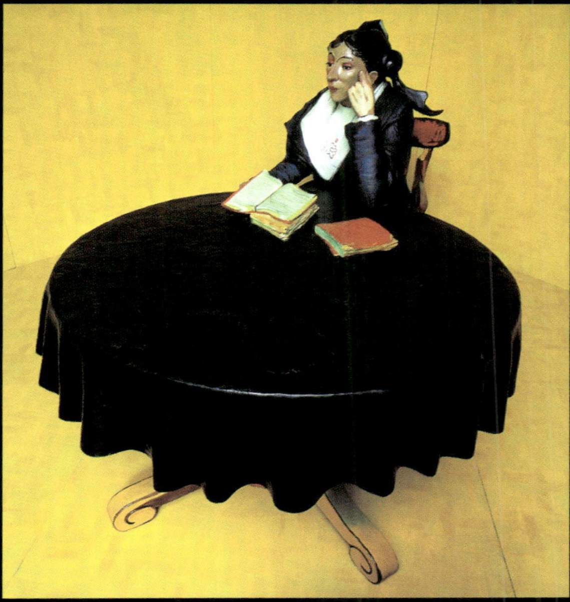

BEYOND THE FRAME

IMPRESSIONISM REVISITED

THE SCULPTURES OF J. SEWARD JOHNSON, JR.

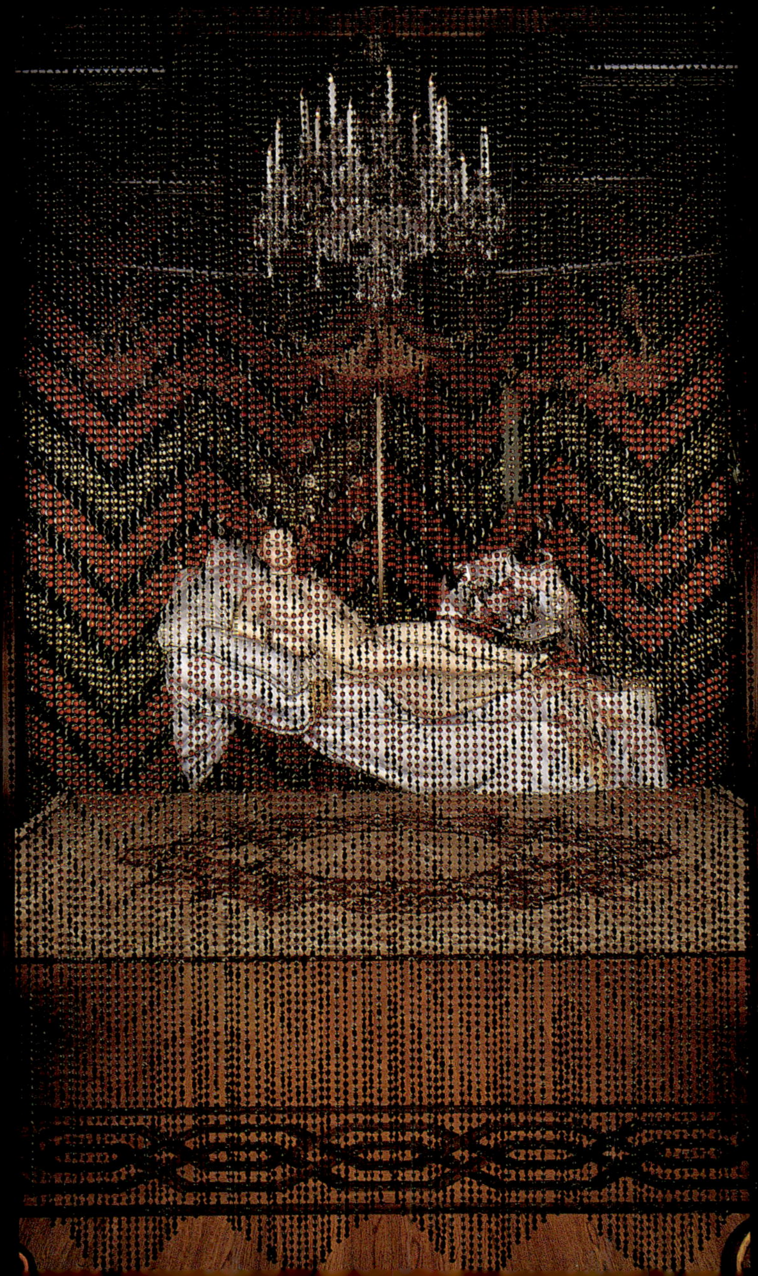

BEYOND THE FRAME

IMPRESSIONISM REVISITED

THE SCULPTURES OF J. SEWARD JOHNSON, JR.

FOREWORD BY DAVID C. LEVY
ESSAY BY PETRA TEN-DOESSCHATE CHU
CONVERSATION WITH RED GROOMS

In Association with the Corcoran Gallery of Art

Bulfinch Press
AOL Time Warner Book Group
Boston • New York • London

First Edition

ISBN 0-8212-2878-1

Library of Congress Control Number 2003103056

Bulfinch Press is a division of AOL Time Warner Book Group.

Produced by Grayson Publishing, Washington, DC
Book design by James Pittman

PRINTED IN CHINA

Foreword

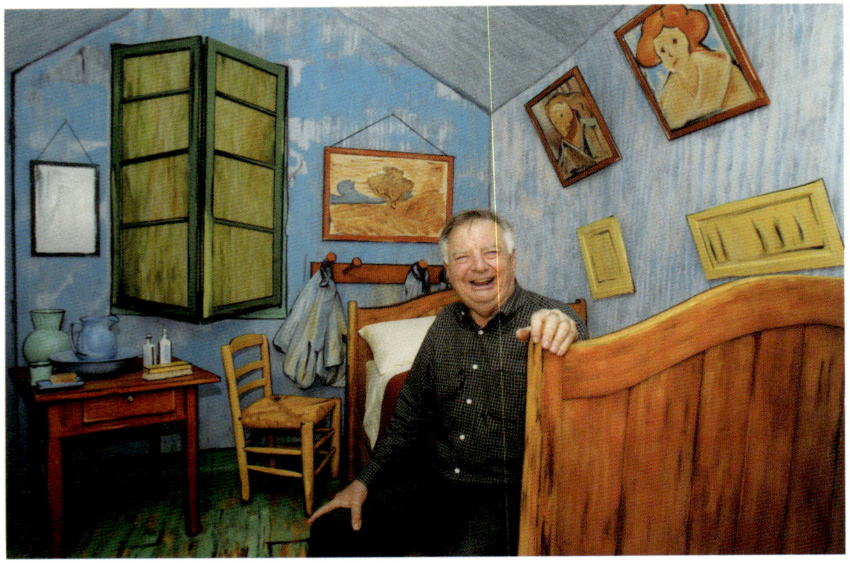

J. Seward Johnson, Jr. in his installation of ***Welcome Home,*** **after Vincent van Gogh's** ***The Bedroom.***

If you were to ask most Americans about the work of J. Seward Johnson, Jr., they would probably answer "J. Seward Who?" But if you asked instead what they thought of the inventive "double-take" street sculptures that so often intrigued and beguiled them in countless public settings across the country, they would almost surely say "Oh yes, of course—*that* guy!" Because Johnson's work is actually recognized by more Americans than that of any other living sculptor—they just don't know it.

There is a message in this phenomenon that reveals a good deal about this enigmatic artist. Scion of one of America's most prominent families and raised to take his place in business among other members of the Johnson & Johnson dynasty, he chose instead to become a sculptor, pioneering advanced foundry techniques while producing work that sought its audience among a broad segment of the public rather than the more rarified atmosphere of the art world. A possibly inadvertent outcome has been the virtual anonymity of the artist himself, along with a distancing of his work from the mainstream of the art establishment. One purpose of the current exhibition, therefore, is to bring both the man and his art more fully into the contemporary critical dialogue. We participated in a similar exercise a few years ago with another artist of broad public appeal and limited art-world recognition—Norman Rockwell. Today, many museum exhibitions and scholarly publications later, Rockwell's place is secure. We look to a similar outcome in the current instance.

When, years ago, I first became aware of Johnson's work I was intrigued by its cleverness and its humor. It was always something of an adventure to come upon a Johnson sculpture in the streetscape, initially sensed as an inchoate *presence* that seemed alive and real but sent out subliminal and disturbing signals that something was amiss. Upon coming closer, the reason (that the piece was clearly inanimate and purposefully unrealistic) would reveal itself. This was particularly true in the early monochromatic sculpture.

The eeriness of this visual ambiguity was, and to some degree remains, a key element in Johnson's work. It is a perceptual illusion that he has now brought to a high level of perfection. But it is also necessary to look deeper and to see the tongue-in-cheek humor—steeped in a celebration of the ordinary along with an existential fascination with the small absurdities of life—to recognize the degree of quirky irreverence in this artist who, at first blush, gives the illusion of being the most conventional of the conventional. Johnson has now moved away from the imagery of his early street sculpture days. His current, fully polychromed figures, which are the subject of this exhibition and book, would have been hard to predict from that work. To be sure, his new work continues to radiate his pervasive *joie de vivre* (a defining aspect of his personality) but it is also an expression of his regard for his predecessors. Respectful though it may be, Johnson's irrepressible and irreverent sense of humor is ever present. This playfulness is yet another quality that defines these appropriated images as imaginative artistic statements in their own right. He not only pokes occasional fun at their Impressionist prototypes, he invites us to laugh at him and at ourselves as well. The result is a body of work that balances the serious against the lighthearted, while providing a compelling and accessible introduction to great masterpieces of art for young and old alike—an entirely new way of seeing and (literally) feeling our artistic heritage.

Johnson's translation of two-dimensional imagery to three-dimensional sculpture is clearly a new twist on the notion of appropriation. So, for example, in his *Confrontational Vulnerability*, based on Manet's *Olympia*, we start with Titian appropriating Giorgione, Manet appropriating Titian, and, finally Johnson creating a walk-in (!) appropriation of Manet. Still another dimension is evident in the fact that each piece is, in essence, a work of installation art. Johnson not only applies the most advanced foundry techniques to the casting of his sculpture but he creates complex tableaux in which the sculpture is often set in digitally produced and optically adjusted dioramas, stage-set rooms, or entirely man-made outdoor environments. These innovations represent yet another layer of perception, using advanced imaging capabilities and an extraordinary vocabulary of three-dimensional craft.

It is revealing that Johnson is viewed by many working sculptors as a hero (note the interview with Red Grooms in this book). Some would say he is a sculptor's sculptor. In addition, his technical mastery and straightforward approach are particularly refreshing in a cultural scene that has found in his "conservatism" a convenient excuse to apply its own brand of reverse class snobbery to this artist. Born to wealth and privilege, Johnson defies the stereotype of the former middle-class kid, now living at the poverty line on New York's Lower East Side while hanging rocks and road kill on string to express man's inhumanity to man. Though often transparently sophomoric, the contemporary art establishment often hails such behavior as the expression of a "fresh, edgy and daring new voice."

Finally, readers should know that Johnson is one of America's great citizens of the arts. He single-handedly created Grounds for Sculpture, an extraordinary 15-acre sculpture park on the old New Jersey State Fair Grounds between Princeton and Trenton. Along with its lovingly renovated and restored Art Deco buildings, Grounds contains some 200 sculptures, including work by almost every modern American master, from George Segal and Beverly Pepper to Ronald Bladen, John Henry, Mark di Suvero, and Kiki Smith. By itself it would be sufficient evidence of Johnson's public-spirited commitment to the future of sculpture. When coupled with his creation of the Johnson Atelier, a state-of-the art foundry and stone-cutting facility where the work of many contemporary sculptors is cast or fabricated by master craftsmen and by apprentices who come there to train from every corner of the globe, or, again, with his important philanthropic commitment to the International Sculpture Center, his contribution to the art of our time is astonishing.

It is our hope that this exhibition will bring about a deeper understanding of this artist. We know that large and diverse audiences will share Johnson's joy and exuberance as they explore this fulsome representation of his work, and it pleases us to be able to make this experience possible.

DAVID C. LEVY
President and Director, Corcoran Gallery of Art

The Reality of Illusion, The Illusion of Reality

Petra ten-Doesschate Chu

EXPLORATION

"We want them to enter into the painting."

—J. Seward Johnson, Jr., speaking about his work, Hamilton, New Jersey, December 13, 2002

In one sequence of Akira Kurosawa's classic movie, *Dreams* (1990), a young Japanese art student (presumably a stand-in for young Kurosawa himself) visits an exhibition of the works of Vincent van Gogh. Having admired several of the artist's paintings, including *The Bedroom* (Amsterdam, Van Gogh Museum), he is drawn to *The Langlois Bridge with Women Washing* (Otterlo, Rijksmuseum Kröller-Müller), a painting of a drawbridge over a French canal with, in the foreground, a group of women washing clothes. As he stands transfixed, engaged in intense observation, our student suddenly feels himself transported into the painting. Instead of looking at a flat paint surface, he is standing on the bank of the Arles-Bouc canal, feeling the warmth of the summer sun, smelling the fresh grass, and hearing the splashing of the water and the chattering and singing of the laundresses. Realizing that this is his chance to meet the artist and pose the questions that will help unlock the mystery of his work, he asks the women where he can find "Monsieur van Gogh." After crossing the bridge, he embarks on a magic walk that leads him past the motifs of several of the artist's paintings (such as his signature haystacks and the *Tarascon Diligence*), to the Master himself (played by Martin Scorsese), bandages and all. But instead of enlightening the student on the significance and the magic of his paintings, van Gogh crossly rebuffs him and sends him on his way. Like Alice in Wonderland, the art student suddenly becomes dwarfed and enters into the maze of lines and hatchings of one of van Gogh's pen and ink drawings, before making his way through the jungle of giant brushstrokes of one of the artist's paintings. He finally regains his former size and reenters reality as he ends up in a wheat field, just at the moment when a group of crows takes off in flight.

What makes the sequence, called "Crows," so compelling is that it allows viewers to enter "into" van Gogh's paintings, giving them an opportunity to explore both the historic reality on which they were based—as in the beginning of the sequence, where the art student walks into a re-creation of the scene represented in *The Langlois Bridge with Women Washing*. It also helps viewers understand the way in which those images of reality were constructed—as in the scenes where the student literally gets caught in the brushstrokes of van Gogh's paintings.

Like Kurosawa's *Dreams*, though in an entirely different way, J. Seward Johnson, Jr.'s sculptural tableaux invite the viewer to walk into paintings by van Gogh as well as other nineteenth-century artists such as Manet, Monet, and Renoir. A series of life-size, three-dimensional reproductions, or should one say, reinterpretations of Impressionist and Post-Impressionist paintings, Johnson's works welcome viewers into the pictorial space to interact with the figures and the objects represented in them. The sensation is at once more and less powerful than the viewing of Kurosawa's film. In "Crows," seeing the filmmaker's youthful alter ego traverse van Gogh's passionate brushwork is an intense experience, but it is a vicarious one. Entering Johnson's reimaginings of Impressionist paintings is direct, more tangible (quite literally, because one is invited to touch the works), but it lacks the spellbinding, even haunting quality of Kurosawa's work. Instead, it provokes a mixture of amazement and amusement.[1]

Both Johnson's works and Kurosawa's "Crows" allow the viewer to enter into the prohibited zone that lies "behind" the picture plane. To enter that zone, even in one's imagination, seems to offer a guarantee of a better understanding of the painting. At the Dulwich Picture Gallery, children are invited to "trace a path in the air with ... [their] finger" indicating how they might walk into a landscape by Jacob van Ruisdael (without, of course, touching the painting!).[2] This activity, apparently, is designed to help them gain a more vivid "insight" into the work of the seventeenth-century Dutch master. In the Musée des Beaux-Arts de Montréal, docents are advised to ask visitors what they would hear, feel, and smell if they were able to take a walk inside the painting.[3] This suggests that someone looking at a painting would be able to better grasp its meaning if they could experience it with all their senses: touch, hearing, smell. At the Children's Museum of Manhattan, educators tried to give children precisely those sensations. For their exhibition "Art

Inside Out," they asked artist Elizabeth Murray to create a three-dimensional version of her painting *Plan 9*, a vibrantly colored abstract-surrealist still life. The three-dimensional version allowed children not merely to "enter into" the painting but also to interact with it, by rearranging the objects in their own way. It even let them, momentarily, become integral parts of the work—moments eagerly recorded in adoring parents' photo shoots.[4]

In the fifteenth century, artists like Masaccio and Paolo Uccello developed this pictorial strategy precisely to create for the viewers the illusion that they were looking *through* (Latin: *perspicere*) rather than *at* the picture plane, as they had in medieval paintings.[5] The Renaissance architect and theorist Leon Battista Alberti wanted paintings to be like windows through which the viewer would see a landscape or a scene from history.[6] But linear perspective had its limitations. Just as a window prevents us from seeing a scene from different directions and from entering into or interacting with it, so the Renaissance painting welcomes our gaze but prohibits our physical entrance. From the Renaissance onwards, artists worked steadily at overcoming those limitations and enhancing the illusion that bodily entrance into their paintings *might* be possible. In the seventeenth century, Dutch artists like Samuel van Hoogstraten constructed peepshow boxes that, through a careful manipulation of linear perspective and the real, though limited space of the box, and by a combination of real and painted light, made viewers believe that they were looking through a keyhole into the interior of a house. If only they could find the key, they'd be able to enter. Around the same time, in Italy, painters like Giovanni Battista Gaulli and Andrea del Pozzo created ceiling paintings in Roman churches that suggested to the viewer an unbroken continuum between the human space of the church and the heavens that their paintings portrayed. To do so, they had their paintings "overlap" their frames by means of painted stucco figures that formed the transition between the real and painted space. Here too, the possibility of bodily entrance into the painting was made conditional—in this case, on a tall enough ladder.

Naturally, neither van Hoogstraten's peepshow boxes nor Gaulli and del Pozzo's tour-de-force ceiling paintings allowed the viewer to enter physically into their paintings. That entrance, be it limited, was finally made possible in the nineteenth century, in two quite different ways. First, there was the panorama—an enormous painting, usually mounted in the round and meant to be seen from the center. The panorama made it possible for the viewer to turn around and see a 360-degree view of a landscape or an historic scene, rather than the partial, cropped views that were presented in traditional paintings. Moreover, to heighten the illusion of reality, most panoramas included a "transitional" area between the viewer and the painting that was a three-dimensional extension "in real time" of the virtual reality of the two-dimensional painting. Viewers of the movie *Vincent and Theo* may remember the sequence in which the two brothers visit the famous *Panorama of Scheveningen* (The Hague, The Netherlands), painted by the Dutch painter Hendrik Willem Mesdag. Apparently oblivious to (or perhaps disdainful of?) the artifice of the setting, Vincent jumps over the railing of the viewing platform to relieve himself in the "dunes," a sand-covered sloping area, punctuated by pieces of driftwood and tufts of artificial grass, that forms the transition between viewer and painting. The panorama, as the movie suggests, allows a limited entrance into the work though further penetration is barred as the viewer reaches the canvas.

J. Seward Johnson, Jr.'s sculptural tableaux invite the viewer to walk into paintings—by van Gogh as well as other nineteenth-century artists such as Manet, Monet, and Renoir.

A second mode of entrance into paintings introduced in the nineteenth century was the *tableau vivant* or living picture. Unlike panoramas, tableaux vivants were not produced by artists, but were the works of groups of pantomime actors, usually amateurs, who took on various poses to imitate well-known works of art or enact dramatic scenes from history or literature.[7] The tableau vivant offered entrance into the painting in two ways. The actors, who "embodied" the painted figures, became, in a sense, one with the painting. For the viewers, these living pictures were, as the author of one tableau vivant manual stated, "the realization [in the literal sense of 'making real'] of a picture on canvas," or a way to "assimilate the real with the ideal."[8]

Johnson's sculptural tableaux have something in common with many of the works discussed above. Like tableaux vivants, they are three-dimensional "realizations" of well-known paintings—paintings, incidentally, that were executed precisely at the time when linear perspective as a pictorial device first became questioned. But while tableaux vivants are composed of living people, Johnson's works are made up of sculpted figures and objects that are

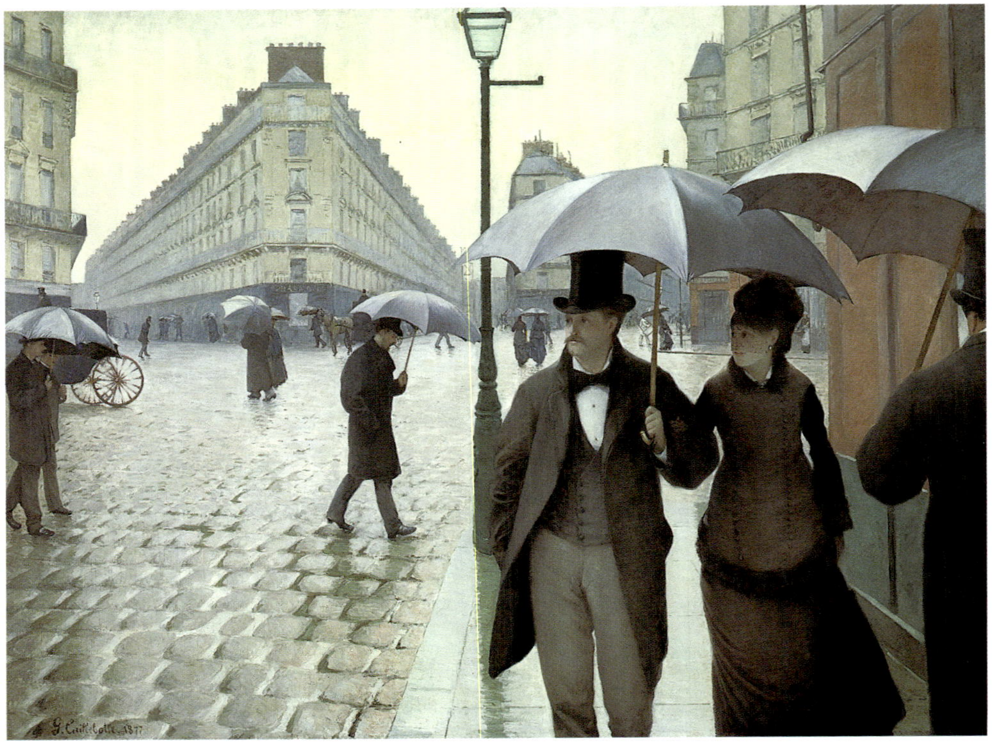

***Paris Street; Rainy Day*, by Gustave Caillebotte**
The Art Institute of Chicago

Who would not want to have a snapshot of oneself, sitting on van Gogh's bed, stroking Olympia's leg, or putting an arm around the shoulder of Manet's little fifer in *Follow Me*?

***Garden at Sainte-Adresse*, by Claude Monet**
The Metropolitan Museum of Art, New York

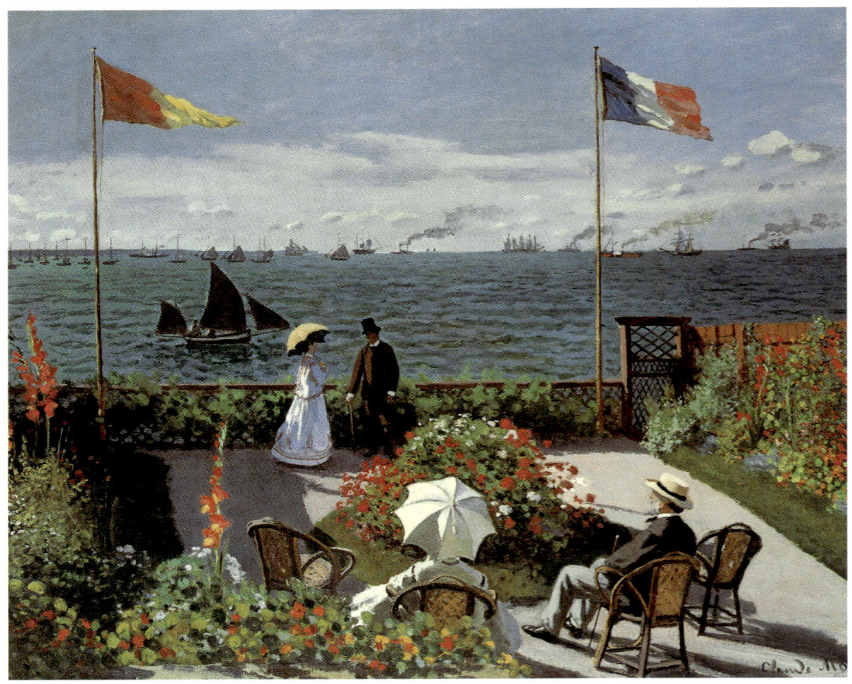

painted to resemble the figures in the paintings they "re-present." (It is important to stress that Johnson's works do not attempt to re-create the original situations on which the Impressionist paintings were based, but that they are three-dimensional variants on the paintings.) Unlike the tableaux vivants, which allowed physical access to the viewer in principle but not in practice (as they were acted out on a stage), Johnson's works allow the viewer to enter; although, as in the panorama, that entrance may be limited. In many of the works shown in the Corcoran exhibition, such as *La Promenade* (p. 72), based on Gustave Caillebotte's *Paris Street; Rainy Day* and, especially, in *If It Were Time*, based on Monet's *Garden at Sainte-Adresse*, the figures are placed in front of an elaborate painted backdrop that limits the extent to which the viewer can explore the picture space.[9] These backdrops, which are curved like panorama paintings, replace the flat landscape backgrounds of the original pictures on which Johnson's works are based. Their perspective has been adjusted so that the viewer sees the backgrounds as he would see them in the painting. The works are meant to be seen from a "sweet spot," where the viewer experiences an effect that is as close as possible to that of the original painting.

Johnson's works, then, are both highly illusionist, combining paintings with sculpture, like the ceiling paintings by Gaulli and del Pozzo (which, incidentally, also were meant to be seen from a "sweet spot"[10]) and "real," as they allow the viewer to enter into the work and walk around the figures, touch them, and—in a limited and one-sided way—interact with them. This reality is especially powerful in the interior scenes—those that do not need a painted landscape background—such as *Confrontational Vulnerability* (p. 30), based on Manet's *Olympia* and *Welcome Home*, (p. 92), based on van Gogh's *The Bedroom*. Here the artist has recreated the complete spatial environment, including even that part of it that is invisible to the viewer—the part of the room on "our side" of the canvas. Thus the viewer is able not only to walk into the painting but, once in, to turn around and to look out.

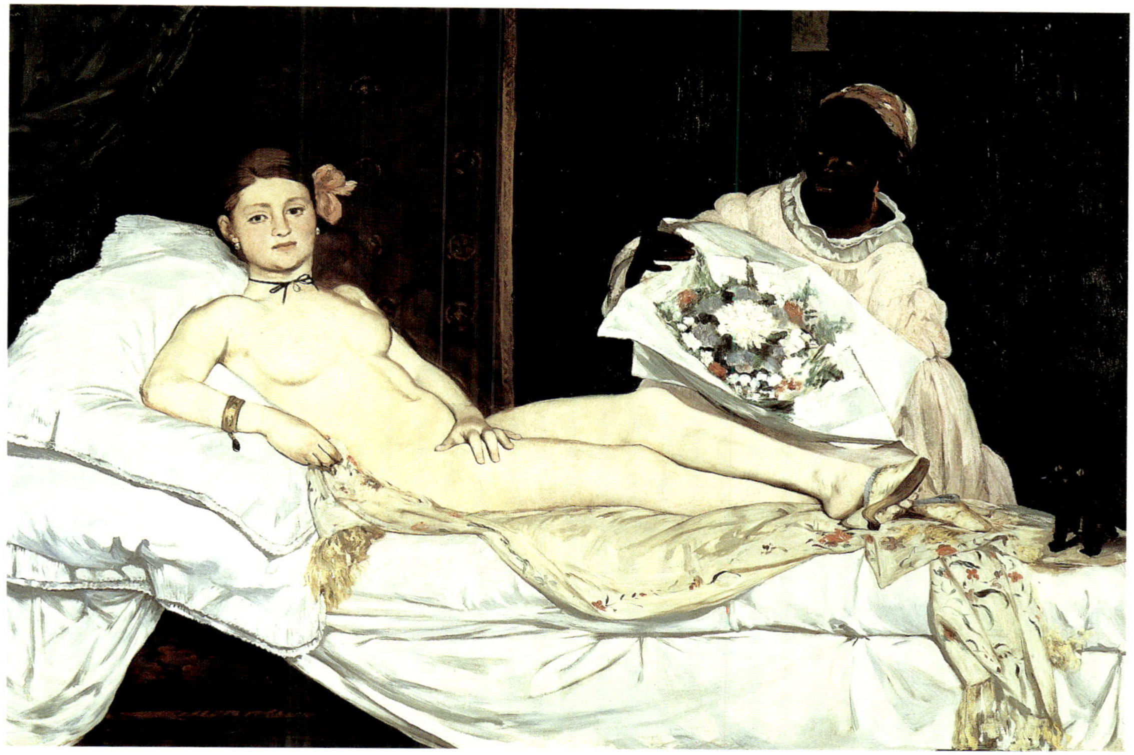

***Olympia*, by Edouard Manet**
Musée d'Orsay, Paris

What is Olympia looking at? What would van Gogh see if he were lying in his bed? Here, of course, an artist can use his/her imagination—as did Peter Clements in his playful *The Other End*, a computer-generated view of either side of van Gogh's bedroom. For Johnson too, this is the area where "he has his fun"; it is, as he says, "his side." [11] In *Confrontational Vulnerability* he has added some imitation Louis XV chairs, where, presumably, the visitors entering the room through the beaded curtain can take a seat as well as a table with a stereoscope, which offers a three-dimensional (!) view of "dirty pictures."

***The Bedroom*, by Vincent van Gogh**
The Art Institute of Chicago

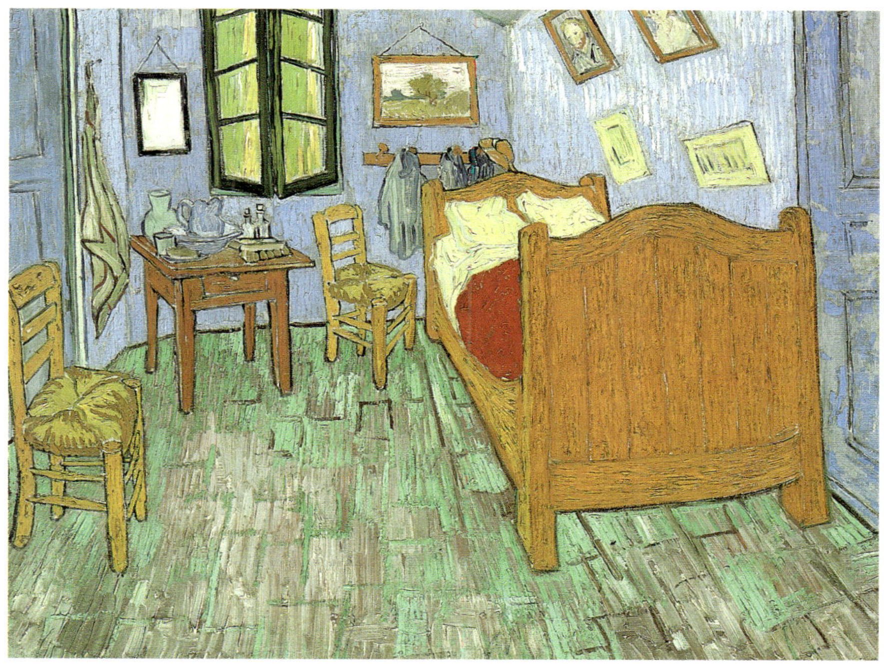

Does the sensation of being "in" the picture, particularly in such works as *Confrontational Vulnerability* and *Welcome Home*, indeed intensify the viewer's engagement with the pictures on which they are based? There is no doubt that to have touched Olympia's cast-off slipper or to have manipulated the objects on Vincent's table (much like the children in "Art Inside Out") does give the viewer an altered relationship to the original picture, a sense of familiarity, a feeling that one "was there" and affected the artwork. No wonder that Johnson's works induce endless photo-ops. Who would not want to have a snapshot of oneself, sitting on van Gogh's bed, stroking Olympia's leg, or putting an arm around the shoulder of Manet's little fifer in *Follow Me* (p. 40)? As for myself, attached as I am to a picture of my mother sitting next to the old man in Johnson's *If It Were Time*, I'll never be

Appropriation in art is done for a variety of reasons—personal, political, artistic. Pablo Picasso, one of the first artists to appropriate on a large scale, appears to have engaged in it as a way of artistic emulation.

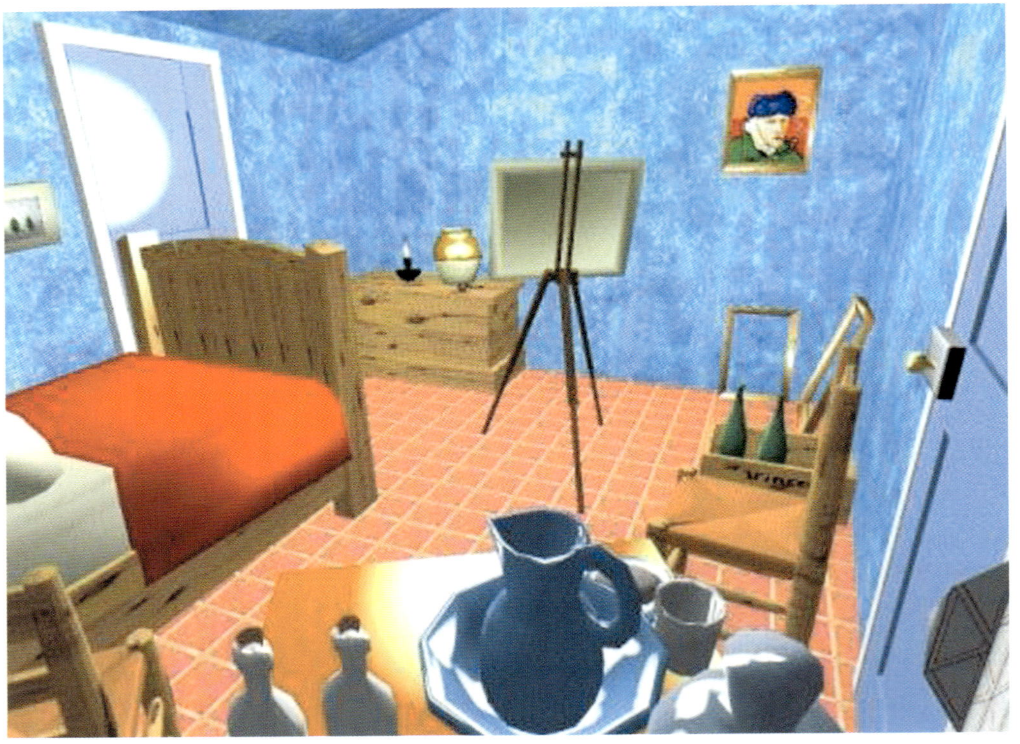

***Van Gogh's Bedroom: The Other End*, by Peter Clements**

Lidy ten Doesschate-Ameling seated by *If It Were Time* by J. Seward Johnson, Jr. at Grounds for Sculpture, Hamilton, New Jersey

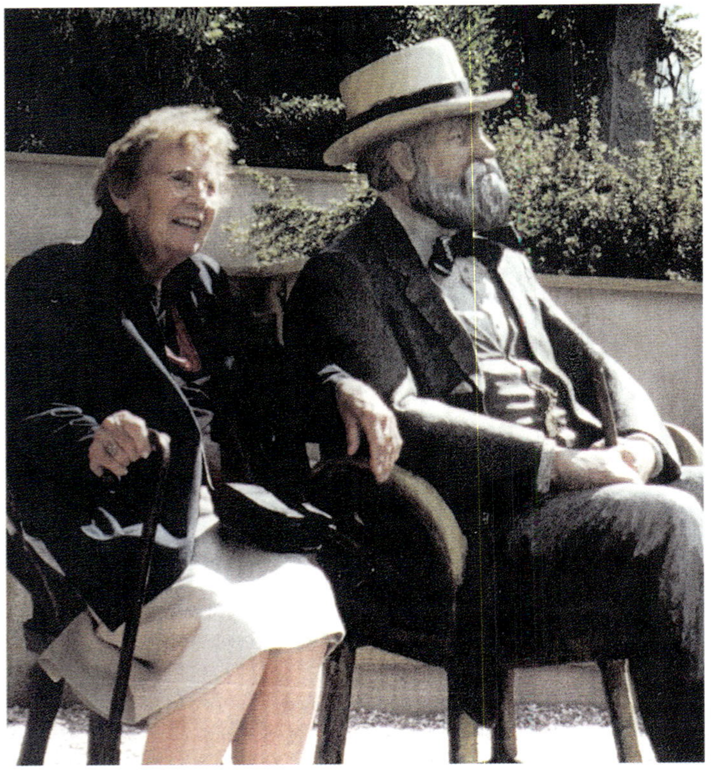

able to look at Monet's *Garden at Sainte-Adresse* (p. 10) without thinking of her. Is that a good thing? For my mother, yes. But what about "Art?" Johnson welcomes the kind of personal bonding with Impressionist paintings that his works bring about: "I find it so moving to watch people interact with these sculptures. That is one thing that these pieces do—they invite an intimacy with the paintings that the paintings themselves don't allow simply due to the limitation of scale, depth, and access."[12] Purists might object that such a sentimental attachment to a painting distorts one's aesthetic response. No one can deny, however, that Johnson's sculptures cause us to see the paintings on which they are based in a new and different way. To paraphrase Marcel Duchamp, Johnson does create new thoughts for existing objects.[13] And if these objects happen to be works of art that, due to their endless reproduction on Hallmark cards, chocolate tins, and umbrellas, make it nearly impossible to have any thoughts about at all, this is no simple feat!

"I am playing with icons."
—J. Seward Johnson, Jr., *The Times of Trenton*, July 22, 2002

How do we define Johnson's works? In his book *Solid Impressions*, Johnson refers to them as "translation[s] from two dimensions to three, "as "retelling[s]," as "bronze sculpture[s] based upon [Impressionist paintings]" and as "re-imagined iconic images."[14] Others have referred to them as "reconfigur[ations of] classic Impressionist paintings ... into modified, sculptural scenes"[15] or as "painted bronze castings of famous Impressionist paintings."[16]

Looking at Johnson's work in a larger art-critical context, they are perhaps most aptly classified as "appropriations." Appropriation has been defined by Jonathan Fineberg as an artistic phenomenon in which "artists of the late [nineteen-]seventies increasingly looked to ready-made images or ideas as the data of personal experience as well as the raw material of one's own expressive work."[17] Fineberg sees the origins of appropriation in early twentieth-century collage as well as in Pop Art, which—and here he quotes John Carlin—"replaced the mimetic basis of realism ... with a purely semiotic one." To Carlin, in effect, Pop Art was not just a phenomenon of the 1960s but it became the dominant form of realism in the late twentieth and, we might add, early twenty-first century. For the realist artists of this period, according to Carlin, "The primary reference is no longer nature but culture—the fabricated system of signs that has taken the place of things in our consciousness."[18]

How is this twentieth-century appropriation different from the "borrowing" of motifs, poses, attitudes that we see in earlier art? Manet, as everyone knows, "borrowed" the theme and composition of *Olympia* (p. 11) from Titian's *Venus* and "used" the poses of the three river gods in Marcantonio Raimondi's print after Raphael of the *Judgment of Paris* for the figures in his *Déjeuner sur l'herbe* (p.14). How is this unlike Johnson's "appropriation" of Manet's work in his *Déjeuner Déjà Vu* (p. 60)? To draw a parallel with "colonialism" and "imperialism" may make the difference clearer. The on-line dictionary *Hyperdic* defines colonialism as "... the use of the weaker country's resources to strengthen and enrich the stronger country" and imperialism as "any instance of aggressive extension of authority [over another country]."[19] By analogy, "borrowing" may be called a form of artistic colonialism, "appropriation" an instance of imperialism. But just as the line between colonialism and imperialism is a fine one, so too is the line between borrowing and appropriation. Johnson certainly seems to feel that way.

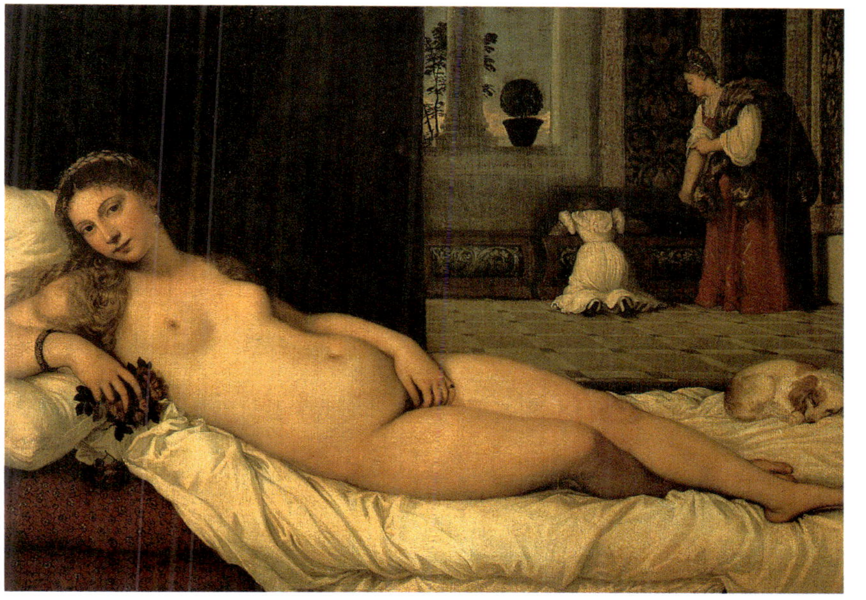

***Venus of Urbino*, by Titian**
Uffizi Gallery, Florence

***Judgment of Paris*, by Marcantonio Raimondi**
Louvre, Paris

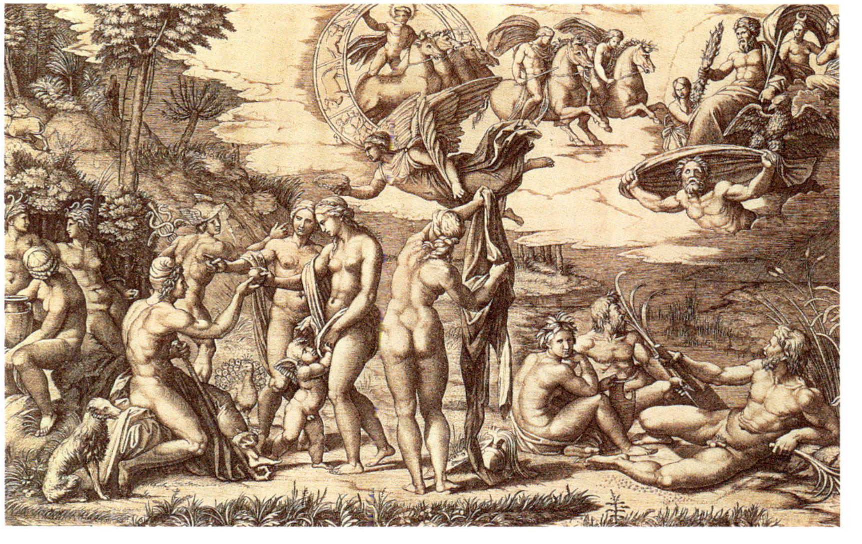

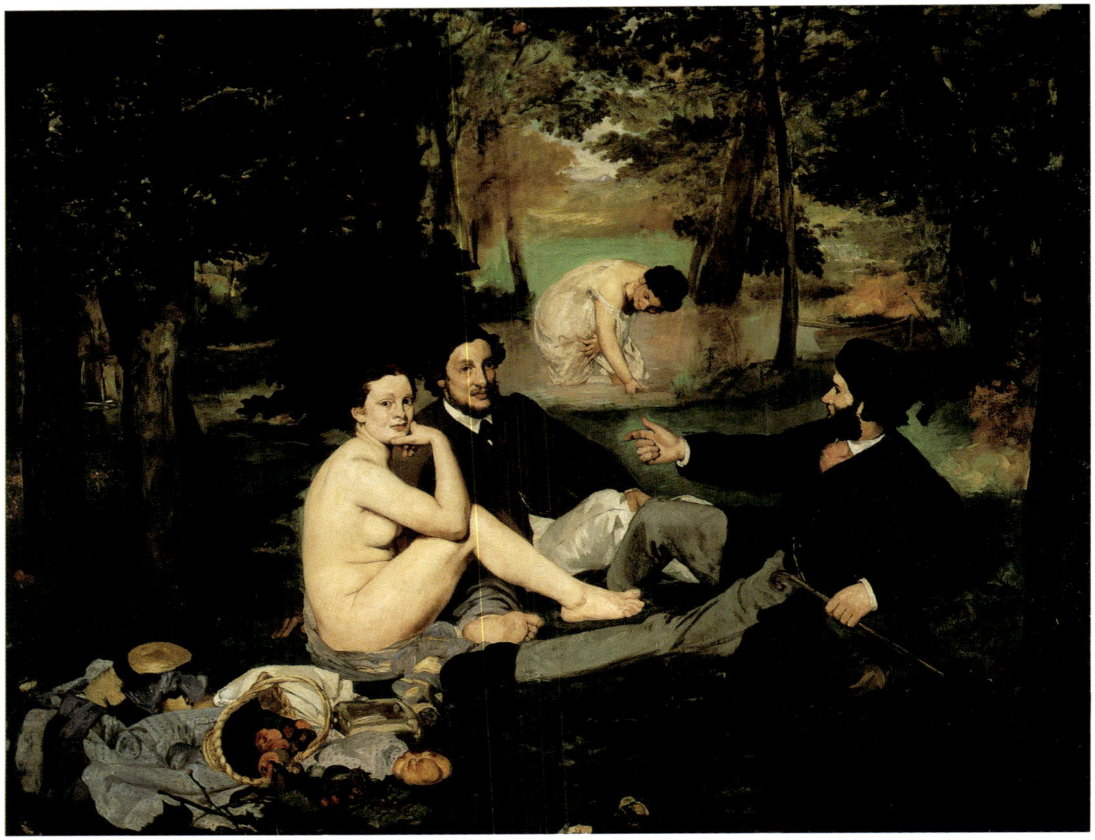

***Le Déjeuner sur l'herbe*, by Edouard Manet**
Musée d'Orsay, Paris

In his *Déjeuner Déjà Vu*, he has inserted a book on the grass behind the three figures in which Raimondi's print is reproduced. The implication seems to be that Manet's figures strike the poses of Raimondi's river gods, as if they were actors in a tableau vivant version of this well-known composition.

Appropriation in art is done for a variety of reasons—personal, political, artistic. Pablo Picasso, one of the first artists to appropriate on a large scale, appears to have engaged in it as a way of artistic emulation. His biographer John Richardson once put Picasso's approach into a rhetorical question when he wrote, "Why did he lock horns with one great painter after another? Was it a trial of strength like arm wrestling? Was it out of admiration or mockery, irony or homage, Oedipal rivalry or Spanish chauvinism?"[20] Looking at the artist's interpretation of Manet's *Déjeuner sur l'herbe*—one of a group of about thirty variations on the nineteenth-century artist's composition painted in the course of 1961-62—we see, indeed, a work that seems to be the product of struggle—one in which Picasso tried to measure himself against the great founder of modernism by making an assault on his signature work.[21]

While Picasso's appropriations seem motivated by an Oedipal battle against the father figure of modern painting, appropriation may also serve the opposite purpose—a gesture of love and appreciation for the accomplishments of the older artist. Larry Rivers' *Homage to van Gogh* shows one of the Dutch artist's self-portraits seen against the background of his *Bedroom*. Judging by the title, the painting is a way to honor the older artist rather than to "arm wrestle" him, even though Rivers confessed he always had "mixed feelings about the works of van Gogh." And, he added, "This work of mine on van Gogh has not done away with them. But I have lived a long time with mixed feelings about my own work."[22] Perhaps Rivers identified with van Gogh, who, like himself, experienced anxiety and insecurity about his work.

***Luncheon on the Grass (after Manet)*, by Pablo Picasso**
Musée Picasso, Paris

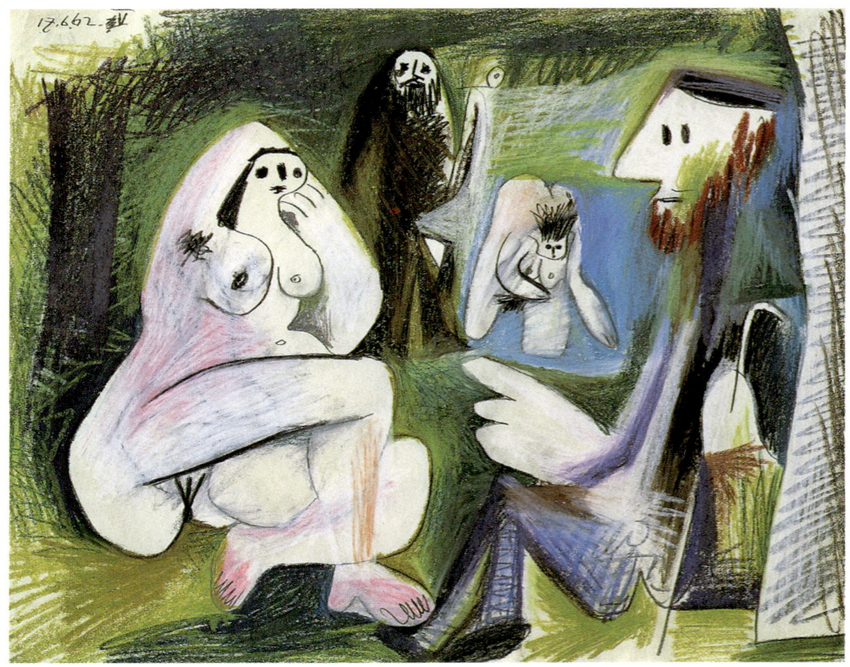

Rivers did not always use the appropriative strategy for the purpose of homage. His *I Like Olympia in Blackface* is a satirical statement appropriate to the sociopolitical climate of the late 1960s and early 1970s when this work was created. In Rivers' work, a caricature reproduction of Manet's *Olympia* recedes behind a reformulation of the painting in its opposite colors—Olympia black, the maid (and the cat) white, reversing the stereotype roles of European and African as master and slave.[23] While Rivers appropriated Manet's *Olympia* to make a statement on race, July Rrap took possession of the painting to boost the feminist cause. Her *Untitled* (after Manet's *Olympia)* and *Fleshed Out*, a print and a sculpture that are meant to be seen together, is a wry comment on a culture of pinups and centerfolds, in which women are presented as nothing but appetizing chunks of flesh.

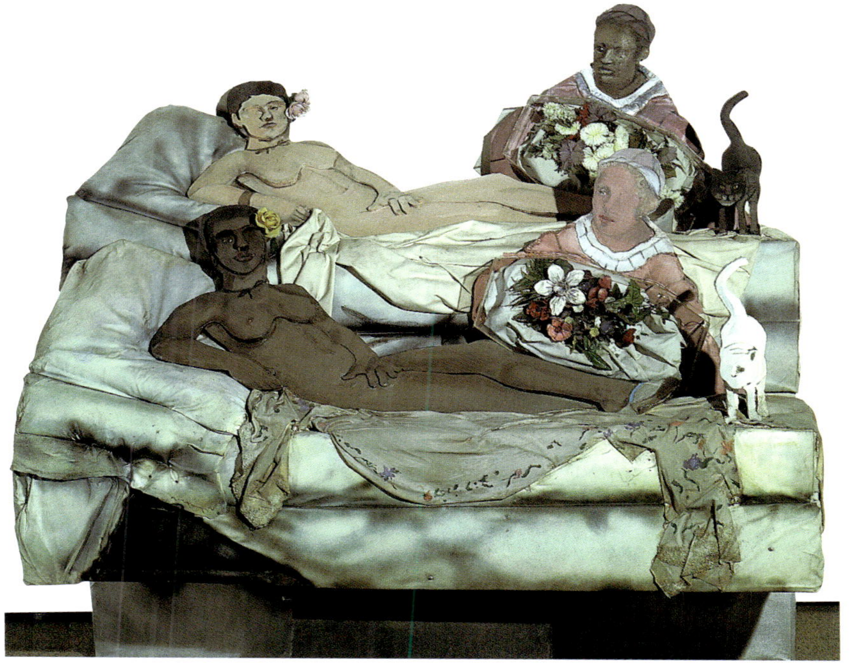

***I Like Olympia in Blackface*, by Larry Rivers**
Musée National d'Art Moderne, Centre Georges Pompidou, Paris

While appropriation has served competitive, reverential, as well as political purposes, many contemporary artists who use appropriation seem to be interested in exploring "the possibility of expressing oneself using the ready-made expressions of someone else."[24] The fact that most of them turn to iconic artistic images is explained only in part by the fact that, in order to have an effect on the viewer, the images they appropriate need to be easily recognized. More importantly, appropriation is often used to give new meaning to works whose iconic, mass-culture status have caused them to lose what Walter Benjamin called their "aura," i.e., their unique presence in time and space.[25]

Both Roy Lichtenstein and Jean Michel Basquiat appear to want to become what Richard Prince has called "the author of [another] artist's work" by imposing their artistic styles and cultural identities on works of the past.[26] Roy Lichtenstein's *Bedroom at Arles* is a remaking of van Gogh's highly individualized, expressive, and emotionally charged painting in what he himself called his "unartistic style, as artificial as possible."[27] In his painting, van Gogh's impassioned brushwork has been replaced by Lichtenstein's impersonal benday dots that simulate mechanical printing. In Basquiat's *Arroz con Pollo* (p. 16) the artist has imposed both his graffiti style of painting and his Afro-Caribbean cultural heritage on the painting of the Dutch artist. Instead of the Calvinist simplicity, chastity, and stillness of Van Gogh's *Bedroom*, *Arroz con Pollo* is noisy, rife with sex, and full of the rich odor of fried chicken. While van Gogh's painting is done largely in primary colors—yellow, red, blue—Basquiat added a great deal of purple and green, particularly in the unruly figures that have invaded van Gogh's quiet bedroom. If there is a political agenda here, it is a post-colonial one: Basquiat's figures have literally invaded van Gogh's bedroom for a one-night stand, in an aggressive extension of authority that calls to mind the Dutch Imperial role in the Caribbean.[28]

***Bedroom at Arles*, by Roy Lichtenstein**
Robert and Jane Meyerhoff

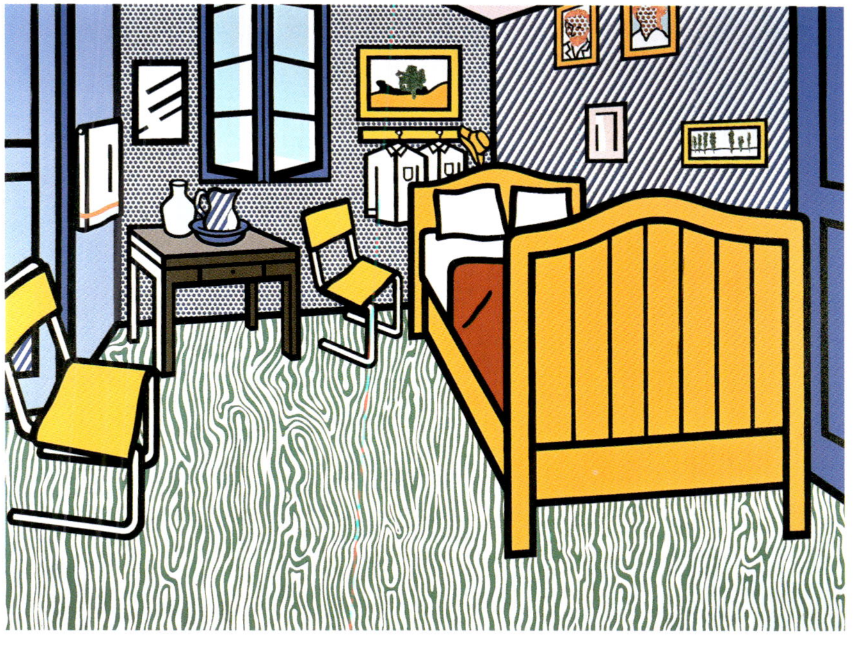

Johnson's enterprise seems inspired by populist motifs. His works allow a public, cowed by the "star" status of artistic masterpieces (reflected in the outlandish estimates of their monetary worth), to become intimate, even familiar with them.

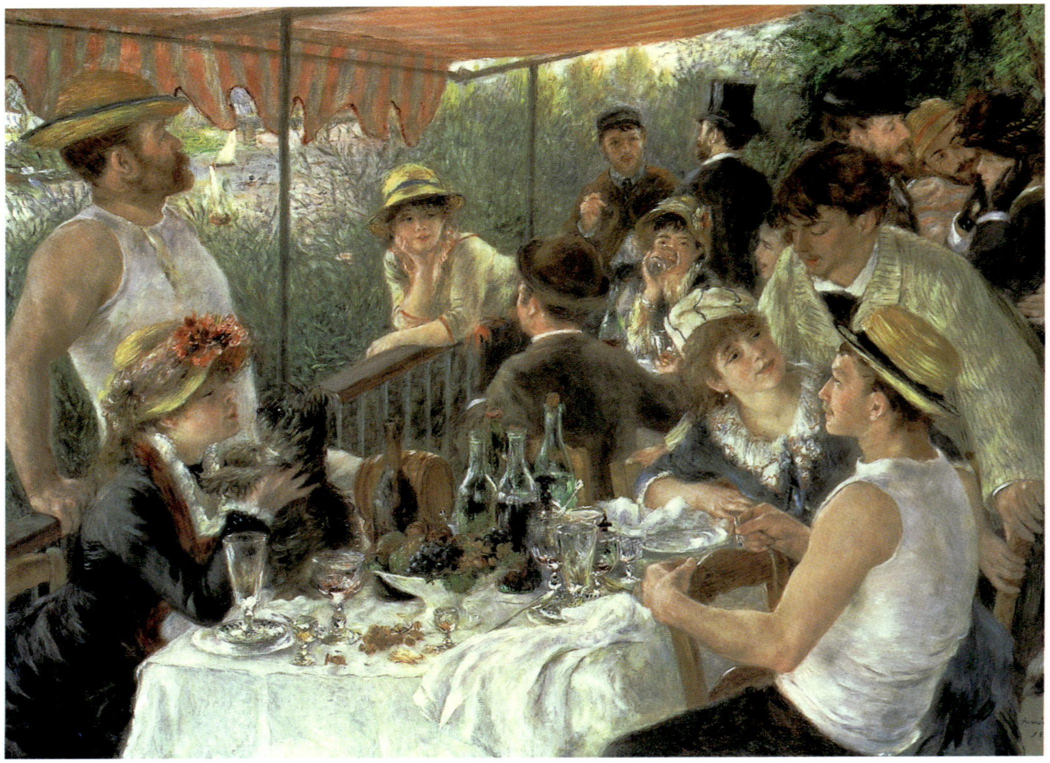

***Luncheon of the Boating Party*, by Pierre-Auguste Renoir**
The Phillips Collection, Washington, D.C.

***Arroz con Pollo*, by Jean Michel Basquiat**
Tony Shafrazi Gallery, New York

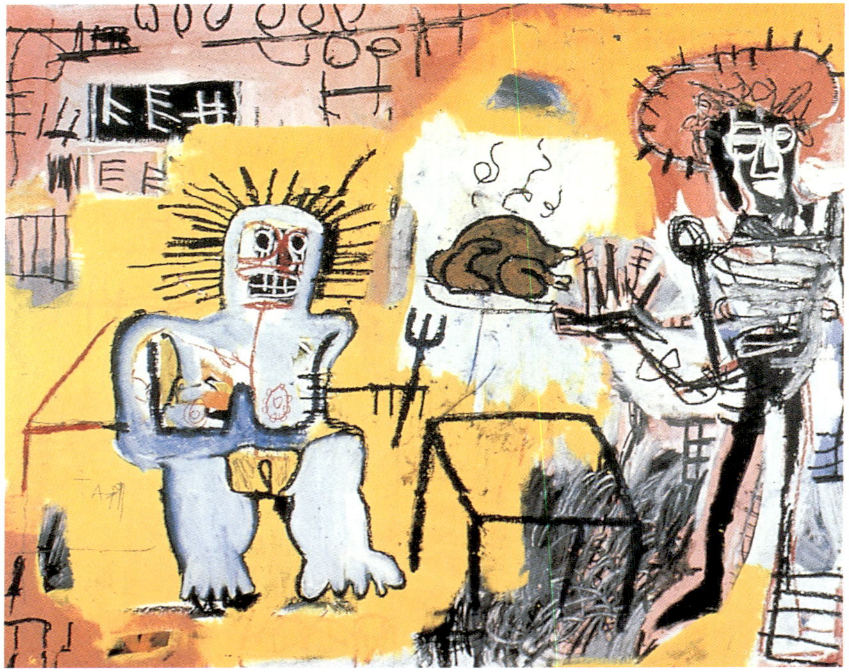

Turning to Johnson, the artist himself has referred to his appropriative strategy as "playing with icons." "I've given these iconic works a third dimension, and yet that makes them seem more real than the original."[29] Johnson's enterprise seems inspired by populist motifs. His works allow a public, cowed by the "star" status of artistic masterpieces (reflected in the outlandish estimates of their monetary worth), to become intimate, even familiar with them. "It is central to Mr. Johnson's mission," one critic writes, "to empower the untrained viewer." And he quotes Johnson as saying, "Most people who like my work are timid about their own sense of art. I love to draw it out of them, because they have strong inner feelings. They've been intimidated by the art world." [30]

The sense of intimacy and familiarity with artistic masterpieces that Johnson attempts to bring about is achieved not merely by giving these paintings three dimensions. It also has to do with size (the figures in Johnson's work are all "our size") and with the artist's addition, in almost all of his works, of "familiarizing" elements. In *If It Were Time*, for example, the old man (whose back is turned to us in Monet's painting) has closed his left eye (on his sister's side) and opened the other to peek at the couple by the railing. In *Eye of the Beholder* Johnson has ever so slightly altered the demeanor and expression of the young man to express his interpretation of the painting as a "man slobbering over a school teacher."[31] And in *Were You Invited?* he has added some twenty-first-century party crashers to the luncheon in Renoir's *Luncheon of the Boating Party*, including himself and friends and fellow sculptors Red Grooms, Bill Barrett, and Andrew Pitynski. Gallery owner Phillip Bruno, dressed in nineteenth-century top hat and paletot is chasing the insolent foursome away.[32] The introduction of these psychological and/or anecdotal elements invites viewers to make up a story, further empowering them in their roles as interpreters.

In an important essay titled "L'Institution de l'anomie" (1987) Pierre Bourdieu suggested that one of the great innovations of Manet was his "institutionalization" of anomie, by which he meant the sense of uncertainty, even alienation, viewers feel when looking at the artist's paintings. That sense appears to come from the refusal of Manet's paintings to be "read" in a conventional way. "Que signifie cette peinture?" or "what does that picture mean," wrote H. Escoffier after seeing Manet's *Olympia* at the 1865 Salon, no doubt expressing the view of most of his own as well as Johnson's contemporaries.[33] Johnson's works provide an answer to this question, whether it is asked of Manet's *Olympia* or other paintings by the artist and his Impressionist followers. He has made Manet eminently "readable," to use Bourdieu's term, like a caricature by Honoré Daumier or an illustration by Norman Rockwell—two artists Johnson professes to admire.[34]

The late George Segal, a fellow New Jersey sculptor, once told Johnson that the problem with his early street sculptures was that they were "just there—" that they were lacking that artistic element that expressed how his figures were feeling.[35] Johnson then and there decided that what was needed was not necessarily more by way of gesture or facial expression in his figures but the possibility for more interaction between viewer and sculpture—to put "the viewer to work interpreting," as he said. The current series may be seen as his way to send viewers on the road to interpreting Impressionist and Post-Impressionist paintings, by encouraging both physical and psychological interaction with the figures in the paintings. The ultimate goal is communication for, as Johnson says, "As long as the communication is complete, then the piece is a success."[36]

HYPERREALITY

"Here you have stepped into another reality."
—J. Seward Johnson, Jr., *Solid Impressions*

In his essay *Travels in Hyperreality*, first published in English in 1986, Umberto Eco argues that there is an "America of furious hyperreality."[37] This America, he writes, is not the country of Frank Lloyd Wright and Jackson Pollock; nor is it, according to Eco, the America of Pop Art, Mickey Mouse, or Hollywood movies. It is another, "more secret America," that is "snubbed by the European visitor as well as the American intellectual" but that is the "preserve of the average family, the tourist, the politician."[38]

In *Travels in Hyperreality*, Eco sets out to explore this "secret America," during a virtual tour that takes him from the dioramas of New Amsterdam in the Museum of the City of New York to the Madonna Inn in San Luis Obispo, with its "theme rooms"—prehistoric, Hawaiian, etc. It's amazing how many of Eco's destinations turn out to be based on works of art. Between San Francisco and Los Angeles, he claims to have seen seven wax versions of Leonardo's *Last Supper*, all displayed next to a poor reproduction of the painting to set off the superiority of the wax version over the "original."[39] Eco also describes in detail his visit to the Palace of Living Art in Buena Vista, California, where he admires wax copies of, among others, Rembrandt's *Aristotle Contemplating the Bust of Homer* (New York, The Metropolitan Museum of Art), Jean-Auguste-Dominique Ingres' *Grande Odalisque* (Paris, Musée du Louvre), Jan van Eyck's *Portrait of Arnolfini and his Bride* (London, National Gallery), and what Eco refers to as the "acme of the Palace," van Gogh's *Bedroom* (p. 18). The installation startles and fascinates him because the room is not empty but includes the artist himself.

> Poor Vincent is sitting, with his electroshock look, on one of the chairs he painted elsewhere, against the background of a rumpled bed as he actually painted it, and with some little van Goghs on the walls. But the striking thing is the face of the great lunatic: in wax, naturally, but meant to render faithfully the rapid, tormented brushstrokes of the artist, and thus the face seems devoured by some disgusting eczema, the beard is palpably moth-eaten, and the skin is flaking, with scurvy, herpes zoster, mycosis.[40]

The Palace of Living Art closed its doors in 1982.[41] Also gone are the dioramas from the Museum of the City of New York, which were "retired" in 1991.[42] But

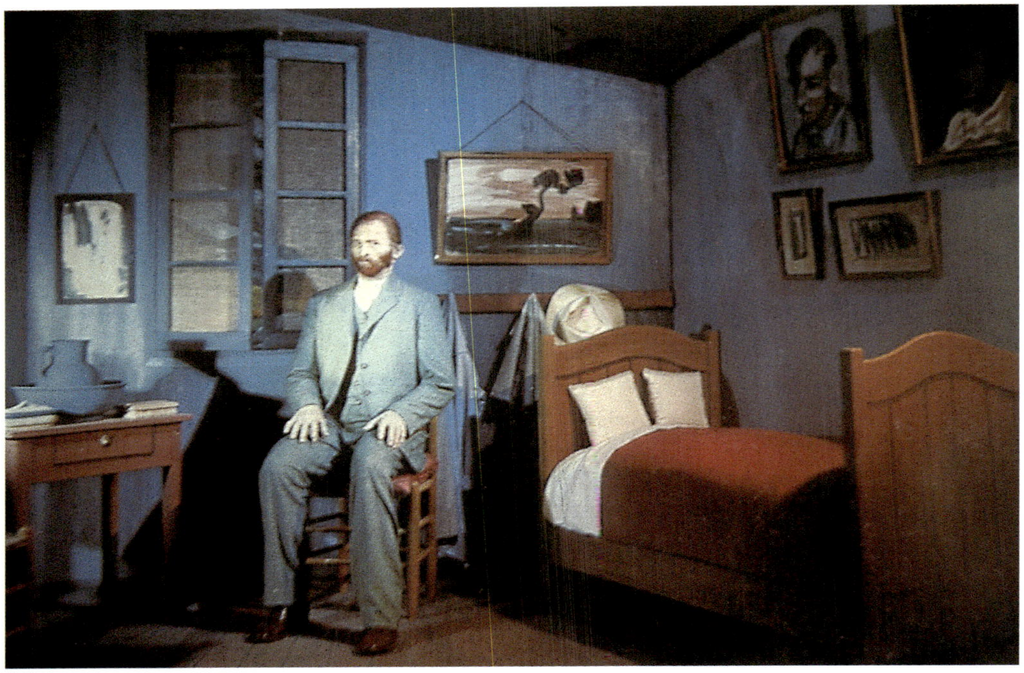

Van Gogh's Bedroom
Wax Museum, Fisherman's Wharf, San Francisco, California, formerly in the collection of the Palace of Living Art, Buena Vista, California

These sculptures are a logical outcome of his earlier works—life-size painted bronze sculptures reproducing ordinary Americans in ordinary American situations

while they have gone, new adventures in hyperreality have cropped up. In the Artist's Inn and Cottage in South Pasadena, California, visitors can stay overnight in the Van Gogh Room. Designed, according to the hotel's web page, "to replicate... *Van Gogh's Bedroom*," this room "has a double bed, desk and faces north. The private bath has a shower, antique sink, and is painted with van Gogh's sunflowers."[43] On the other side of the country, Norman Rockwell's village of Stockbridge, Massachusetts, organizes the "Annual Stockbridge Main Street at Christmas" festival, during which, according to the town's website, "Main Street, little changed from the time it was painted by Norman Rockwell [in his famous painting, *Stockbridge Main Street at Christmas*] is closed off to vehicle traffic." Antique cars are parked as they were in Rockwell's painting, and visitors are invited to "walk into the painting." Meanwhile, in the Southern part of the country, Bob Jones University in Greenville, South Carolina, has produced, since 1998, its Living Gallery—amazing tableaux vivants that re-create "great masterworks of religious art," including paintings, sculptures, and stained glass windows.[44] The reality of these performances, which combine elaborate stage sets with expert lighting, costuming, and grooming, is just short of unbelievable.

After *The Storm on the Sea of Galilee*, by Rembrandt
Living Gallery, Bob Jones University, Greenville, South Carolina

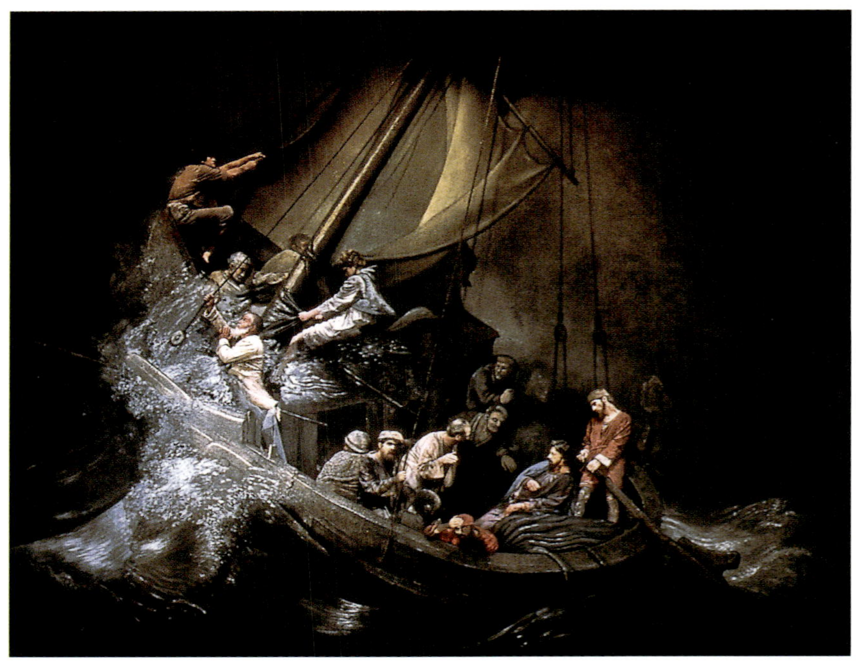

Johnson's tableaux draw their inspiration from and owe their success to the popular sensibility that gives rise to such phenomena as the Artists' Inn and the Living Gallery. These sculptures are a logical outcome of his earlier works—life-size painted bronze sculptures reproducing ordinary Americans in ordinary American situations: a man hailing a taxi (*Taxi*, New York City, Chemical Bank Headquarters), a street cleaner sweeping up after the weekend (*Aftermath*, Dallas, Trammel and Crow Company, or a child by a stop sign, waiting to cross (*Waiting to Cross*, Washington, D.C., on loan to the Capital Children's Museum), etc.[45] In an interview conducted in the mid 1980s, Johnson accepted hyperrealism and ultra-realism as "fair" labels for his "street work," and classed himself in a "group" that included "Duane Hanson and maybe one or two others."[46] Johnson realized that the effect of his street works was the result of what he called a "double-take" response:

> People will rush by one of my works in a public place and be fooled into thinking, "That's a real person." Then they try to come up with reasons or excuses for why they were mistaken. They make up stories or little fictions to explain their initial surprise. They start talking to themselves; they look around to see if anyone caught them being startled. Or they pinch the sculpture on the nose to pretend they knew all along it was made of bronze.[47]

The unease and discomfort with his street sculptures that Johnson describes may be diagnosed as what Sigmund Freud has called a sense of *Unheimlichkeit* (literally, un-home-like-ness) or the uncanny. In his essay, "The Uncanny," Freud cites as the originator of this concept the psychiatrist Alfred Jentsch, who wrote that feelings of the uncanny may be aroused by "doubts whether an apparently animate being is really alive; or conversely, whether a lifeless object might not be in fact animate." Freud goes on to tell us that Jentsch has related the notion of "uncanny" to "the impression made by waxwork figures, ingeniously constructed dolls and automata."[48]

Johnson's street sculptures "unfamiliarize" the familiar, hence the double take, hence the discomfort. Johnson has tried to erase this sense of unease by encouraging interaction with his works and by injecting them with a dose of humor.

> What I am trying to do is to draw attention to the simple pleasures, to show how much fun life is. That's why there are so many humorous details in my work—people with their faces stuffed with food, guys scratching their backs and heads, kids leaving their shoes behind, a girl reading a love letter from one boy with another boy's name written on her ID bracelet. I think that's what people like most about my work. And I like it, too.[49]

Johnson's turn to the three-dimensional representations of works of art may be seen as another strategy to avoid the sense of the uncanny his street works produce. No one who comes upon his Impressionist-inspired pieces can mistake them for the "real thing," for the simple reason that the "real thing," i.e., the painting, is less rather than more real than Johnson's sculptures. As opposed to his street sculptures, this series familiarizes the unfamiliar, they make the viewer feel at home (Freud might have said, *sich heimish fühlen*) in a place that at first seemed foreign to them.

ART, KITSCH, OR VIEWERS' DELIGHT

"How can we tell you all the pleasures you've given us here?"
—Visitor to Grounds for Sculpture[50]

Kitsch is a word often in the air where Johnson's sculptures are found. "His painted bronze castings of famous Impressionist paintings are among the oddest, kitchiest things in today's art world—which is saying a lot," writes John Zeaman, staff writer of the *Bergen Record* in Johnson's home state of New Jersey. The well-known art critic Robert Hughes would agree. Writing about Johnson's street sculptures, he wrote, "Johnson's work is chocolate-box rubbish. It has no imaginative component that I can see and apparently appeals to dull corporate minds like his own—the sort of people who run American motels and malls."[51] Johnson himself shows little concern with the Art-with-a-capital-A status of his art. With reference to his street sculptures, he once said "...the beauty of hyperrealism [is that it] doesn't try to be grand. It purposely doesn't frame itself or stare down at you from a pedestal. Realism never proclaims itself as art. Realism practically tries to say, "This is not art."[52] But that does not mean that he is ready to accept the term "kitsch" as an appropriate label for his art. Speaking about his sculptures of children, he once said that he made it a point not to idealize them for he did not want to make "Hummel figurines" or other such "kitsch art."[53]

Johnson creates an art for the common man. He is leery of the "so-called art expert" because he feels art is chosen "viscerally and not intellectually." Art, and especially public sculpture, to him should please the people "who will be

When it comes to Johnson, the lines often seem blurred. His career, his creative process, and his work all seem to be a function of our postmodern culture, which calls into question traditional definitions and roles of the artist as well as of the art work itself.

looking at it all day."[54] According to Richard Lacayo, cultural critic of *Time Magazine*, Johnson's art is a response to "a growing desire by ordinary people to see representational art. They are beginning to dictate the market, and that gets everyone's attention. Plus, Johnson's work is a welcome relief from what is called plunk art, mediocre abstract sculpture plopped down in public plazas."[55] Johnson himself has this to say about the matter: "I feel the *art* community in America has begun to acknowledge its audience better. Perhaps I've been more aware of it than some of my colleagues.[56]

Artist or public entertainer? Missionary or entrepreneur? Producer of art or of kitsch? When it comes to Johnson, the lines often seem blurred. His career, his creative process, and his work all seem to be a function of our postmodern culture, which calls into question traditional definitions and roles of the artist as well as of the art work itself. As an artist, Johnson seems eons removed from the hallowed notion, dear to the modernists, of the artist as creative genius. Terms like "avant-garde" and "originality" are not applicable to him. Irony, self-doubt, the agony of the creative process—the traits and trials that we associate with the very modernists whose works he reproduces—are alien to him. Johnson "enjoys" his work.[57] He is devoid of self-doubt: One of his favorite activities is "to anonymously loiter around his public sculptures and make negative remarks" to fellow viewers of the art to see what the real response to his work is! He loves to get into the position of having the stranger unwittingly defend the sculpture to this "hostile" art critic.[58]

Unlike a Manet or van Gogh, Johnson is no lone creator. Like other postmodern artists, such as Andy Warhol or Jeff Koons, he has an army of assistants who help in the production of his works. Two large factory buildings in Hamilton, New Jersey, are used for this purpose. One is the Johnson Atelier, where his figures are cast in bronze or other lighter metals;[59] the other is devoted to the creation of the environments of his sculptural tableaux. Here his assistants use sophisticated computer programs to aid them in painting the backdrops of the sculptures or to reproduce the furniture in *The Bedroom*—distortions and all.[60] Or they spend countless hours painting bottles carefully selected for shape and size for *Were You Invited?*, to reproduce exactly Renoir's colors and highlights. The aim of it all is to produce a perfect copy. For Johnson is a perfectionist.[61] He prides himself on the "attention to detail" in his work.[62] Johnson may be called an "art production manager." The artist himself prefers to be seen as "more of a director" and his works as "almost theater."[63]

As for the point of his work, it lacks the loftiness of purpose of traditional art—to rouse religious experience, to glorify the ruler, or to "ennoble" the viewer and make him or her a better person. Nor is it art for art's sake, like most Modernist art. Indeed, Johnson would probably not agree with Oscar Wilde's famous definition of a work of art as: ... "the unique result of a unique temperament." And he would certainly scoff at Wilde's elucidation of this definition: "Its beauty comes from the fact that the author is what he is. It has nothing to do with the fact that other people want what they want. Indeed, the moment that an artist takes notice of what other people want, and tries to supply the demand, he ceases to be an artist, and becomes a dull or an amusing craftsman, an honest or dishonest tradesman. He has no further claim to be considered as an artist."[64]

I would venture that Johnson would rather be seen as Wilde's "amusing craftsman" and "honest or dishonest tradesman" (perhaps not the latter!) than as his self-absorbed, self-possessed "author." Johnson calls himself "a serious artist who is not serious."[65] He wants, as he has said, to "keep his customers content," and "to keep them comfortable while getting a little culture."[66] In this sense, Johnson sees his role as an artist much as did Henri Matisse, who wanted to create art "which might be for every mental worker, be he businessman or writer, like an appeasing influence, like a mental soother, something like a good armchair in which to rest from physical fatigue."[67] Writing about his most important creation, the sculpture park Grounds for Sculpture, Johnson once wrote: "I want it to be a place that causes people to be creative. And I love the fact that people come here, sometimes in pain or loss, and find it a balm. They're moved here, but they laugh too."[68]

NOTES

Many thanks go to my researcher and editor Hsiao-Yun Chu, without whose help I could not have written this essay. I am grateful as well to Laura Coyle, Dario Gamboni, and Aaron H. De Groft, for information and advice.

1. Cf. John Zeaman, "Where Eccentric Meets Essential: Adventures in Sculpture," *Bergen Record*, July 7, 2002, p. 36: "It's about ... scratching your head with disbelief as you find yourself in the middle of Renoir's "The Luncheon of the Boating Party."
2. See AFA Education, *Rembrandt to Gainsborough: Masterpieces from England's Dulwich Picture Gallery* http://www.afaweb.org/education/dulwich_brochure.asp (accessed March 11, 2003).
3. See Musée des Beaux-Arts de Montréal, "Activités pour tous" <http://www.mbam.qc.ca/education/fr-conseils.html> (accessed March 11, 2003).
4. See "Art Inside Out," *Museum News*, (September/October 2002), p. 17.
5. This, of course, is only partially true. Medieval painters had already used other means to suggest three-dimensionality, such as overlapping, foreshortening, and various forms of pseudo-perspective. See G. ten Doesschate, *Perspective* (Nieuwkoop: B. de Graaf, 1964), pl. 10-118.
6. Ibid., p. 123.
7. On the early history of the *tableau vivant*, see Kirsten Holmstrom, *Monodrama, Attitudes, Tableaux Vivants: Studies on Some Trends in Theatrical Fashion*, 1770-1815 (Stockholm: Almqvist and Wiksell, 1967). Though its origins are found in Europe, the *tableau vivant* became especially popular in the United States. See Jack W. McCullough, *Living Pictures on the New York Stage* (New York: Columbia University Press, 1986). See also the interesting article by Mary Chapman, "'Living Pictures': Women and *Tableaux Vivants* in Nineteenth-Century American Fiction and Culture," *Wide Angle* 18.3 (1996), pp. 22–52.
8. Cited in Chapman 1996, p. 24.
9. This is true for the versions of Johnson's work that are in the Corcoran exhibition, but not for those that may be seen in Grounds of Sculpture, the sculpture garden created by Johnson in Hamilton, New Jersey. There, for example, *If It Were Time* is staged in a landscape setting with a real garden and real water in the background (be it not the English Channel but a small lake).
10. In Sant' Ignazio di Loyola in Rome, del Pozzo's ceiling painting of the *Apotheosis of Saint Ignatius* is meant to be seen from a marble slab on the floor, put there for that express purpose.
11. Speaking about his work, in Hamilton, New Jersey (12/13/2002).
12. See J. Seward Johnson, Jr., *Solid Impressions* (Hamilton, New Jersey: The Sculpture Foundation, 2002), p. 4.
13. In his famous defense of R. Mutt, the fictional creator of Duchamp's *Fountain*, the artist wrote, "Whether Mr. Mutt with his own hands made the fountain or not has no importance. He CHOSE it. He took an ordinary article of life, placed it so that its useful significance disappeared under new title and point of view—created a new thought for that object." Marcel Duchamp, *The Blind Man*, (May 1917)
14. Johnson 2002, pp. 35, 44, 60, and 67.
15. Ibid.
16. John Zeaman 2002.
17. Jonathan Fineberg, *Art Since 1945: Strategies of Being* (Englewood Cliffs: Prentice Hall, 2000), 467.
18. Cited ibid. from Carlin's exhibition brochure *Pop Apocalypse* (New York: Gracie Mansion Gallery, 1988), unpaginated.
19. See http://www.hyperdic.net/dic (accessed March 12, 2003), s.v. "colonialism" and "imperialism."
20. Cited in Cohen, "A Contemporary Touch" *RA Magazine* (Summer 2000).
21. On Picasso's interpretations of Manet's *Déjeuner*, see Susan Grace Galassi, *Picasso's Variations on the Masters: Confrontations with the Past* (New York: Abrams, 1996), ch. 7.
22. Vincent van Gogh Foundation, "Selection of some works realized in homage to Vincent van Gogh." (accessed March 12, 2003) <http://www.fondationvangogh-arles.org/anglais/GALERIE/Img0032.htm.>
23. On Rivers' and other artists' appropriations of Manet's *Olympia*, see Theodore Reff, *Olympia* (New York: Viking, 1977), ch. I ("Critical and Artistic Responses").
24. Fineberg 2000, 467.
25. See Walter Benjamin, "The Work of Art in the Age of Mechanical Reproduction," in: *Illuminations: Essays and Reflections*, ed., Hannah Arendt, (New York: Schocken Books, 1969), pp. 217-252.
26. Cited in Fineberg 2000, p. 468.
27. Cited in Carol Strickland, "Roy Lichtenstein: Keen Observer of Life's Little Ironies" *Christian Science Monitor*, (October 3, 1997).
28. Since Basquiat's father came from Haiti and his mother from Puerto Rico, he must have been aware of the crucial role of the Dutch in the colonization of the West Indies. He may have known, for example, that in 1515, the Dutch had exported the entire native Indian population of Curacao to Hispaniola, the island that would later become Haiti and the Dominican Republic. As a person of African descent, he must also have known of the important part played by the Dutch in the slave trade, particularly in the seventeenth and eighteenth centuries.
29. Schlegel 2002.
30. Cited in J.D. Reed, "Seward's Follies," *The New York Times*, (June 30, 2002), Section 14 NJ, p. 1.
31. Speaking about his work, in Hamilton, New Jersey (12/13/2002).
32. See Johnson 2002, 46-51.
33. Escoffier's words are cited in T. J. Clark, *The Painter of Modern Life: Paris in the Art of Manet and his Followers* (Princeton: Princeton University Press, 1984), p. 92.
34. *Celebrating the Familiar: The Sculpture of J. Seward Johnson, Jr* (New York: Alfred van der Marck, 1987), pp. 34-35.
35. Ibid., p. 30.
36. Ibid.
37. Umberto Eco, *Travels in Hyperreality* (Orlando, Florida: Harcourt Brace Jovanovich, 1986), p. 7
38. Ibid., pp. 6-7.
39. Ibid., pp. 16-18.
40. Ibid., p. 20.
41. *Van Gogh's Bedroom* was transferred to San Fransisco's Wax Museum at Fisherman's Wharf, where it can still be seen today.
42. According to the museum's website: < http://www.mcny.org> (accessed March 13, 2003)
43. See < http://www.artistsinns.com/rooms_rates.htm> (accessed March 13, 2003).
44. All information is based on the Living Gallery's newsletter, "Behind the Scenes" (March 2002).
45. Reproductions of these and other works may be found in *Celebrating the Familiar* 1987.
46. *Celebrating the Familiar* 1987, 25.
47. Ibid., p. 25.
48. Sigmund Freud, "The Uncanny," in *The Standard Edition of the Complete Psychological Works of Sigmund Freud*, ed. & trs. James Strachey, vol. XVII (London: Hogarth, 1953), pp. 219-252.
49. *Celebrating the Familiar* 1987, p. 25.
50. Cited in Schlegel 2002.
51. Reed 2002, p. 1.
52. *Celebrating the Familiar*, p. 25. Compare these words with those by George Segal, who told the Associated Press in a 1985 interview: "I wanted something solid, something I could walk into and walk around and be a part of. But I also want this marriage between the physical and the state of mind."
53. *Celebrating the Familiar* 1987, p. 53
54. Ibid., p. 27.
55. Cited in Reed 2002. See also Allen Freeman (*Architecture*, July 1983): "[Johnson's sculptures] represent the most accessible of public art."
56. *Celebrating the Familiar* 1987, p. 39.
57. Speaking about his work, in Hamilton, New Jersey (12/13/2002).
58. See FAQ section on Johnson's home page at http://www.sewardjohnson.com (accessed March 14, 2003).
59. While Johnson's *Solid Impressions in Grounds for Sculpture* are all made of bronze, many of the figures in the Corcoran exhibition are cast of lighter materials.
60. On the making of Johnson's work, see the essay by Jan Rothchild in this catalogue.
61. Cf. Reed 2002.
62. *Celebrating the Familiar*, p. 25.
63. Speaking about his work, in Hamilton, New Jersey (12/13/2002).
64. Oscar Wilde, "The Soul of Man under Socialism" in: *The Works of Oscar Wilde* (London: Spring Books, 1963), p. 924.
65. Speaking about his work, in Hamilton, New Jersey (12/13/2002).
66. Speaking about his work, in Hamilton, New Jersey (12/13/2002).
67. Cited in Herschell B. Chipp, *Theories of Modern Art: A Source Book by Artists and Critics* (Berkeley/Los Angeles: University of California Press, 1968), p. 135.
68. Cited in Schlegel 2002.

Red Grooms on J. Seward Johnson, Jr.

Conversation with Jacquelyn Days Serwer, January 2003

Opening Gala for *Were You Invited?*, by J. Seward Johnson, Jr. (detail)

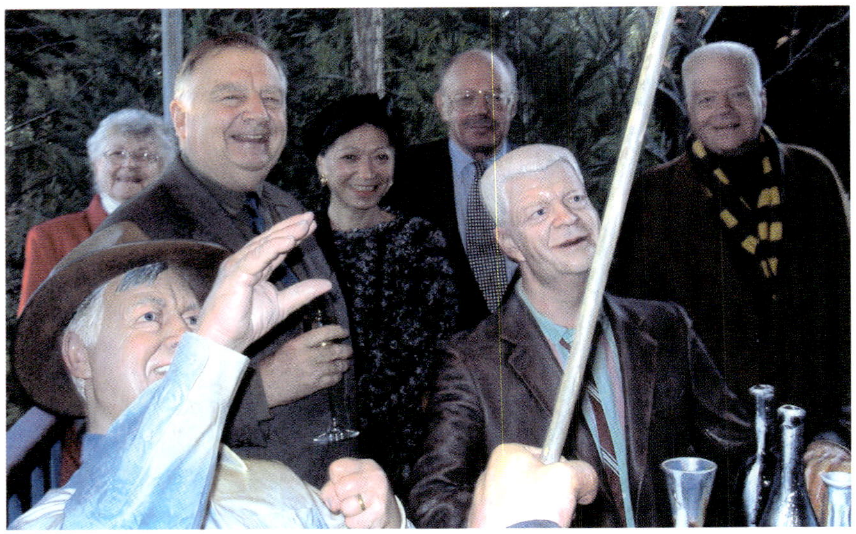

ABOUT RED GROOMS

Red Grooms (b.1937) is a painter, sculptor, printmaker, filmmaker, and performance artist. For more than three decades his bold, irreverent, and original approach to artmaking has given him a high profile as a populist in the rarified world of contemporary art. He has always embraced a provocative and exaggerated treatment of his subject matter as a way of engaging with popular culture while disarming his audience into engaging with him. One of his most memorable creations consisted of a sprawling, three-dimensional walk-through rendition of New York City entitled *Ruckus Manhattan* (1975–76). This colorful, witty interpretation of America's great metropolis established a new sculptural printmaking genre that Grooms continues to explore today.

In the early 1980s Grooms enjoyed a residency at Grounds for Sculpture, the sculpture park and atelier in Hamilton, New Jersey, founded by J. Seward Johnson, Jr. This experience brought Grooms into contact with Johnson's earlier work. Later, in 2000, when Grounds for Sculpture hosted Grooms' sculpture retrospective, he came to know both Johnson's current work and Johnson himself. The two artists have much in common. Both see art as a means of exploring the past, which includes reinterpreting the work of some of history's most celebrated artists. They also aim to make their art amusing and accessible to art lovers of all persuasions.

SERWER: Please tell me about your familiarity with Seward and Grounds for Sculpture.

GROOMS: I did a bronze casting at the Johnson Atelier in 1984, which I think was my first piece there. I knew of Seward's work before that, but they had a very high-ceilinged room with shelves that were filled with casts of his sculptures. It seemed like an enormous amount. And, it struck me right then that, in the future, he would be discovered in a different sort of way. That he would seem like a civilization almost unto himself. You know, to this day, they've kept all the molds from when I saw them nearly 20 years ago.

SERWER: Yes, it's interesting to imagine that the idea for the present pieces, and the components they might require, were taking shape that long ago.

GROOMS: Now getting more to the tableaux, I did not actually meet Seward until I had a show at Grounds for Sculpture in 2000. Seward invited us to Rats [the restaurant at Grounds for Sculpture] and then took us to his studio where his piece *Were You Invited?* was sitting in clay. I've got to say it's probably the most exciting work I've ever seen in an artist's studio. His studio is a good size, but it's still like a regular studio. And so, in that compressed space, the vitality of the piece was outstanding. Seward really had a kind of renaissance with these pieces. It becomes just superb, like *Designated*

Coachmen, which is based on the two stagecoaches from a Vincent van Gogh painting. There aren't even any figures. I find that piece intriguing, almost mysterious. It suggests somehow that the narrative is not yet complete, that the main action is still to take place. It becomes theatrical and transforming.

SERWER: Can you tell me what your reaction was when you saw his first piece, after Manet's *Déjeuner sur l'herbe*, or, as Seward calls it, *Déjeuner Déjà Vu*, at Grounds for Sculpture?

GROOMS: Well, I realize one of the great things about his work is the use of the landscape itself. It's marvelous. And then there's this terrific Pirandello-like quality about the light. For instance, in the photograph, it's fall, so the beautiful colored leaves are on the ground. It will go through the whole seasonal cycle, so there's a natural evolution of the piece. The landscape changes our perception of the work of art as the seasons evolve. This is genius, you know, because it's so natural, but also unassuming.

SERWER: And, in a sense, very subtle, because you would only realize the seasonal changes by seeing the piece more than once and at different times of the year.

GROOMS: I would think so, yes. Actually that occurred to me when I looked at the photograph. You realize, "Hey, this is fall." When there's snow on the ground, it is hilarious. Especially because it plays up the nudity. But, very gently.

SERWER: I, myself, was very struck the first time I saw *Déjeuner* at the garden because I felt such a sense of shock walking through there—in a way that one doesn't feel as a twenty-first-century person looking at the original painting. My response must be similar to that of Manet's contemporaries when they first caught a glimpse of the painting. I think it's important that Johnson is able to create a comparable sensation for today's audiences.

GROOMS: Right. In fact, when I first saw the works in the garden, I thought, "Wow, this is going to be really popular." Then it occurred to me that people don't like high art. But, I think the way Seward's done it, if they're going to like high art, here is their opportunity. It evokes the original works, but makes them more accessible by inviting the viewer to experience them physically, as well as visually. I see it as a great populist thing, except for the fact that you do need to have a little bit of a reference point to really have fun with it.

SERWER: That's quite true. At the Corcoran, I hope that many more people will be introduced to Seward's work and the physical experience it offers.

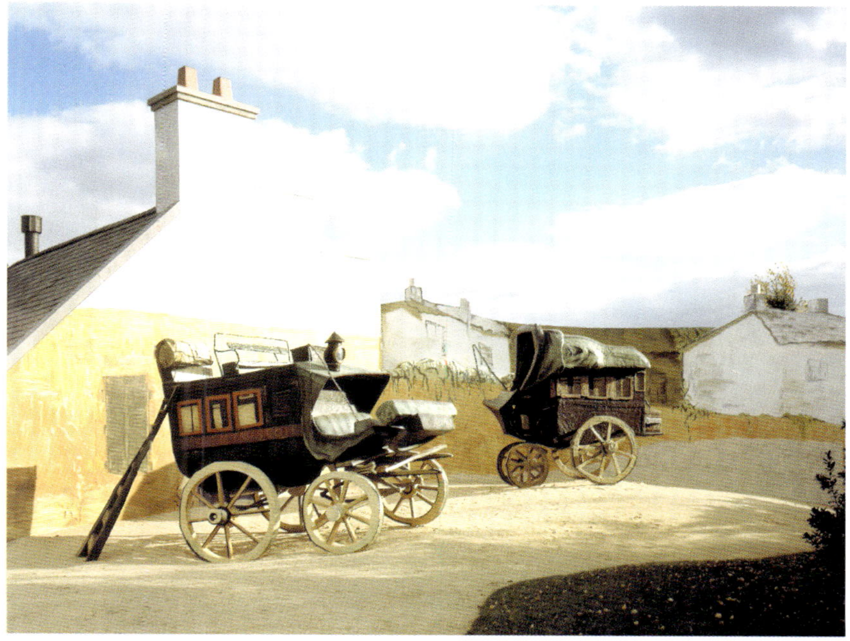

***Designated Coachmen*, by J. Seward Johnson, Jr.**

***Ruckus Manhattan*, by Red Grooms (Installation at Grand Central Station)**
Marlborough Gallery, New York

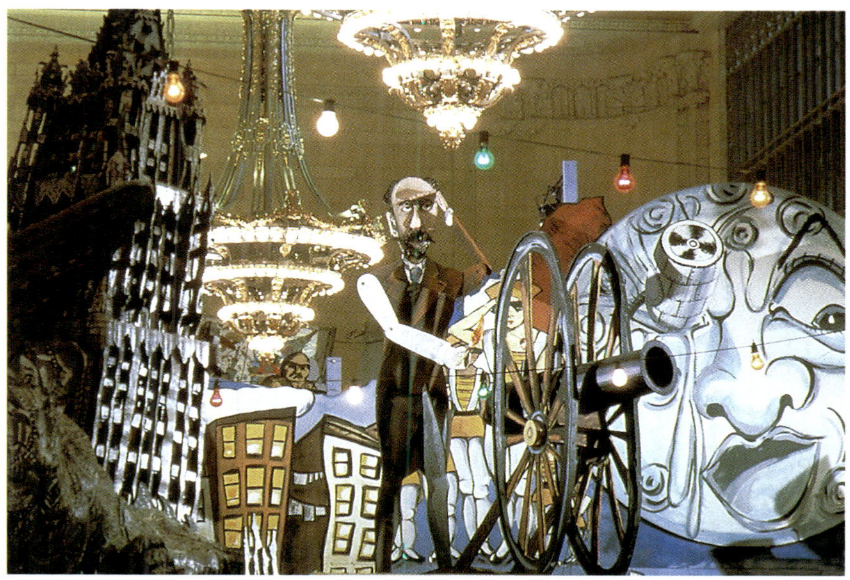

In effect, he really has invented a new way of working with a team, like an industrialist, but he's applied it to art in a way that no other artist I can think of has been able to do.

***Déjeuner Déjà Vu,* by J. Seward Johnson, Jr. (detail)**

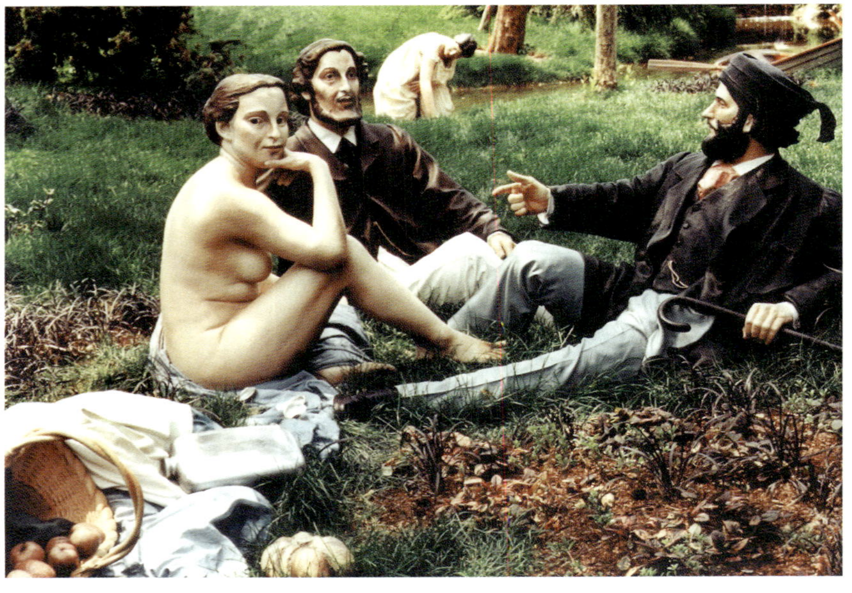

But, of course, the encounter you have with a work of art depends to some extent on what you bring to it.

GROOMS: Yes, I think people will always have a variety of responses.

SERWER: How do you see Seward's approach to sculpture? As works in the round derived from iconic two-dimensional images, or do you think he has established a new genre, much in the way that you created a new genre of three-dimensional prints?

GROOMS: Well, I think it is new. And, actually, my reaction should have been one of jealousy because, with his new art form, Seward really supplemented my efforts in bringing humor into art. It's just something you can't be jealous of because it has such goodness about it. There is great generosity to the work and I realize that all artists, no matter what their means, if they're good, use them to the fullest. Seward is unusual because he has a lot of means. In effect, he really has invented a new way of working with a team, like an industrialist, but he's applied it to art in a way that no other artist I can think of has been able to do. It's worth remembering that there is a long tradition of this, if you think about the big studios of the past. Even an artist like Michelangelo had many artists working for him. Or Rubens, who had many assistants collaborating in his studio. The history of art offers many precedents for this kind of cooperation. It was kind of like an industrial process. Something I really rather like, or have liked at different periods. I have realized that I can't live on that scale, except for relatively short periods of time, because I miss the privacy. Personally, I just couldn't sustain the teamwork.

SERWER: Yes. I understand you like to work on your own.

GROOMS: The latest thing I've seen is the big dance couple that Seward has named *A Turn of the Century*. That piece really blew me away because of its scale and grace. Another thing that Seward's doing is just using every technology at hand right now.

SERWER: Yes. I think we're all fascinated by his use of computer technology to create the backdrops for the pieces because, of course, here at the Corcoran they won't be outdoors. When the figures are removed from their background there are empty spaces. Those spaces are filled in by adapting visual material derived from the original canvas. Then the completed image is adjusted to fit the backdrop's self-contained curved shape. I think the backdrops really add to the illusion and the theatricality of these pieces. They will actually evoke the original paintings, and it's fascinating to see how cleverly this has been done. The technology he's used will be a revelation to visitors and will probably be of interest to other artists as well.

GROOMS: It will be yet another surprise.

SERWER: I'm fascinated by artists who are driven to get into the minds of earlier artists. Of course all artists look back to the history of art. But I think in your case, and in Seward's case, you seem to have found a way of getting into the psyches of these earlier artists in order to come up with your own interpretation of their work, one which tells us something about their thought process that we wouldn't ordinarily know.

GROOMS: Well, it's sort of a complicated thing to figure out. I realized from an early age that I was a fan of artists. At first, it was the great illustrators of the late 1940s and early 1950s. I would actually cut out their works from magazines. When I was introduced to fine art, I did the same. And so aside from being an artist myself, I had this kind of fan-dom. And, I think, when you are an artist you like to work with the materials and things you admire in other artists. One of the reasons you do it is for the tactile or manual, but also for the thought process. And so, there are the two things: the fan that sees it from the outside just like anybody else, and the person who works in the same media, always looking and needing a subject as all artists do.

SERWER: So, you look at a picture of an artist you admire and you begin to work with that image until you create a connection?

GROOMS: Yes, it stands in as a kind of subject matter. Something that already has a mythology that you can sink your teeth into. This is in lieu of not having, say, the religious mythology that artists used to have.

SERWER: That's a great insight. These older artists become almost your artistic gods who offer an example, and a mode of operation that is helpful in coming to your own creations.

GROOMS: It is a strange and complicated situation. Actually, this has been an interesting period where many artists have used other artists as subject matter. Seward is one of our foremost, if not the foremost, at this point. But, you know, many others have done it. Larry Rivers did it very well, I think. I've always thought the most of Larry and was highly influenced by him.

SERWER: Yes, I can imagine that. Rivers also admired you and did a wonderful portrait of you in his *Art and the Artist* series. As I looked through your material, I noted that, like Rivers, both you and Seward have interacted with artists from the past, but each in your own way.

GROOMS: An artist needs a subject somehow. You're sitting there ready to go, you've got a studio and you've got the materials and everything. What are you actually going to do?

SERWER: You describe an artist's dilemma that I don't think art historians often think about. Those of us who aren't artists assume artists have no trouble coming up with subjects.

GROOMS: You need one that really captures your imagination. One that you feel has some kind of truth. But Seward has a very smooth flow between one work and the next. Although I'm sure he ruminates on which one to do next.

SERWER: There are certainly many, many works from that era that he could have chosen and he's made a very careful selection. He must also think a lot about the new titles he gives to them. *Confrontational Vulnerability* for *Olympia* is one of my favorites. The titles provide a clue to what he's thinking and why he finds particular pictures intriguing and worthy of presenting in a way that can incorporate his own commentary on the original.

GROOMS: Right. Well, you mentioned *Were You Invited?*, after Renoir's *The Luncheon of the Boating Party*. And I thought that, really, his thinking was not so much about what Renoir was thinking, but more about the difference between Americans and the French. My wife is French, so I'm sort of aware that there is a strong difference.

SERWER: Meaning that the French are more formal?

GROOMS: Yes. They're very precise. Their formalities and the way that they organize their lives are different from the more casual approach of Americans. Seward felt sort of left out of the picture and we, the four of us [the four American sculptors including Johnson, Grooms, Bill Barrett, and Andrew Pitynski] are intruding. The other members of the party are about to throw us out. So, there's a feeling of rejection as Americans, more than anything else. Of course I've always loved French culture, but it's difficult. You can't just roll in there and become one of them. The French have their rules and they have their requirements and Seward is thinking about how hard it is to be a part of the French tradition. In fact he's asserting that. In a way, it's a more aggressive idea than you find in some of the other pieces. He has decided that he and his fellow American sculptors are entitled to be at the party, so to speak, and the man in the top hat, dealer Philip Bruno, provides the transition. But, it also extends the drama, like what would happen if we did barge in like that? It would be a kind of brawl or something. There is that tension in the piece. It's actually a stray, wild extension added to the original drama in the painting.

Abstract art was a lot of fun, but I didn't know what the heck I was doing. I didn't know when it was finished because I only looked at them stylistically. I didn't know the process, only results.

Sunday in the Park with George
Kennedy Center, Washington, D.C.

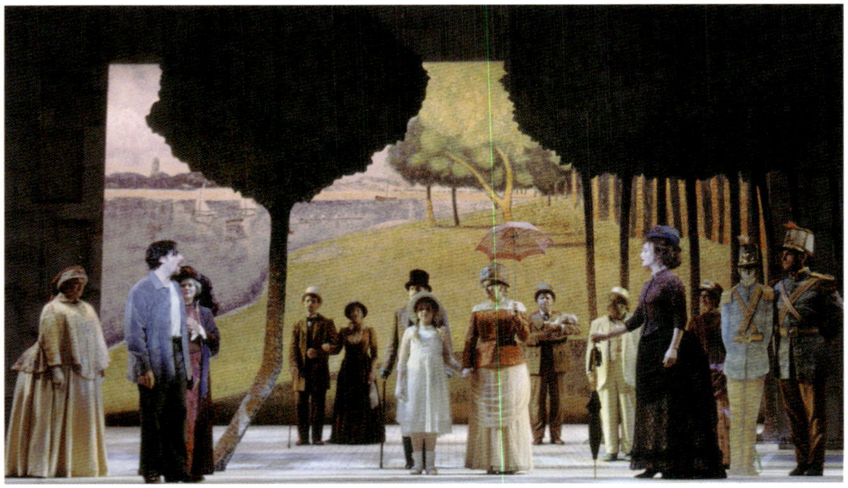

SERWER: That's an important observation. I have seen the piece in the studio and outside the restaurant and it seemed very benign. But now that you draw my attention to the potential conflict, I can see an edginess about it that adds to the effect. People will respond to that.

GROOMS: This is true but, again, he does it in such a nice way, really, that they possibly might not get it. And he doesn't necessarily want you to get it completely.

SERWER: This is Seward's way of adding something to these pieces that brings in the contemporary viewer.

GROOMS: Well again, I think it's the Pirandello approach, where Seward just delights in giving us his insight into life. That's what he did in the very beginning with the street pieces, where he so brilliantly used the cityscape. But there's something about the fantasy of these new tableaux that not only startles but charms the viewer. The color helps. And, although Seward's assistants came into my studio and measured me, the figures are slightly larger than life. At least they give that impression. It is intriguing, the way he plays with scale. I've also thought a lot recently about the piece at the World Trade Center. It became such an icon for the World Trade Center disaster. And, again, the phenomenon we spoke about earlier in relation to the seasons— that in the park the sculpture changes with its environment.

SERWER: Tell me about your attachment to representation in your work, despite the fact that you belong to a generation that was largely concerned with abstract art.

GROOMS: I'm not really part of a second generation of abstract expressionists. I'm kind of like the third generation. My generation included Bob Thompson, even Larry Rivers. Figurative as well as abstract artists. Larry was a source of inspiration for me because I tried to do abstractions. Abstract art was a lot of fun, but I didn't know what the heck I was doing. I didn't know when it was finished because I only looked at them stylistically. I didn't know the process, only results. It's like getting the answer to a math problem but not knowing how to get there. So, I guess my natural fit is figuration. I was brought up with this generation where you didn't have to have a program about your work. That would have been kind of academic.

SERWER: I think artists like yourself and certainly Rivers, too, never wanted to be put into a box. Clearly you've done what has come naturally, which is your particular form of representation. And, in a certain sense, that's what Seward has come to as well. He's found his niche and an approach that suits his idea of representation and narrative.

GROOMS: That's the way it played out. Yes.

SERWER: That brings me to a question about the theater. What do you think of the image from Stephen Sondheim's *Sunday in the Park with George* (p. 26)?

GROOMS: It's a very good connection and I happened to see the production. They did a terrific job with the scenic effects of getting the painting into the play. It actually influenced me when I did my *Sunday Afternoon in the Park [La Grande Jatte II]*. I did my wife in the piece. She's at the bank of the river where the boy's got his feet in the water. I've got her very large. It's her back. She has a very nice hairdo in it. And, I did it in this pseudo-photographic style.

SERWER: Fascinating. I'm wondering whether one of the intriguing aspects of Seward's work is that it brings together theater, visual art, and sculpture in an original way that blurs the boundries?

GROOMS: Yes. It links these things, and when you start to get works that intersect in this way, it seems very evocative of our time. There is a real contemporary feel to it. At the same time, there are so many traditional components to it, yet he's managed to create something that feels new. It not only relates to theater but to performance art and to an open-ended narrative that is found in a lot of contemporary art. I was mad about theater when I was a child, and later as well. One of the most important things was that the space and people on the stage were just so magical. They represented a different world and I wanted to be part of the illusion. I would imagine that the theater also played a role in Seward's imagination because one of the things he's done with the sculpture garden pieces is to bring theater outside. He invented this new approach using real space to create his stage. Brilliantly, actually, and even spookily.

SERWER: Yes, at Grounds for Sculpture the pieces are not readily viewable as you walk along. You have to discover them and, as a result, the illusion is even more dramatic. We hope to re-create some of that feeling of discovery in our installation at the Corcoran.

GROOMS: That's going to be great.

SERWER: What do you think about literary parallels, like the passage from Vladimir Nabokov's autobiography (p. 29)?

GROOMS: Oh, the Nabokov quote is great. And, being in the picture is the same thing as being on the stage. With Seward, we all get to live out that fantasy ourselves.

I would imagine that the theater also played a role in Seward's imagination because one of the things he's done with the sculpture garden pieces is to bring theater outside.

***La Grande Jatte II*, by Red Grooms**
Collection of Lysiane Grooms

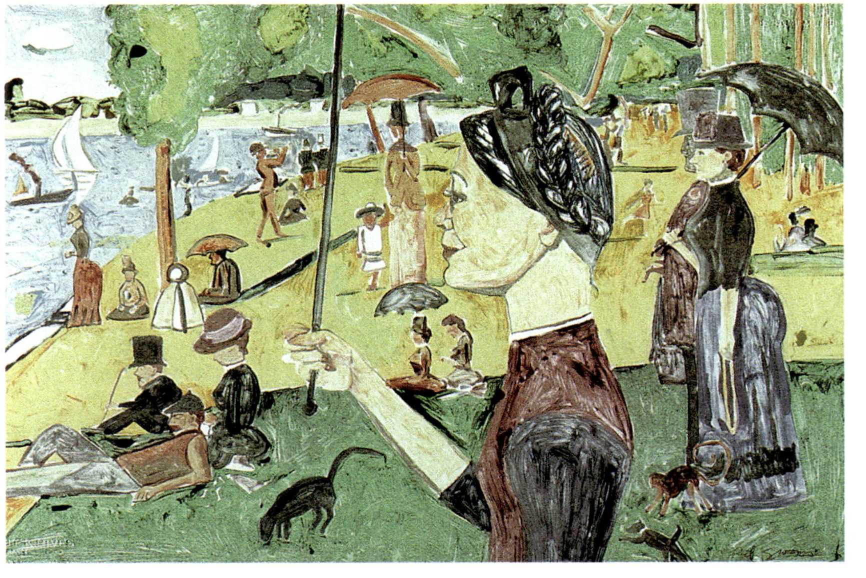

It's really a question of how much you can let yourself go. For example, the piece inspired by a Renior painting called *Dance at Bougival*. It's so clearly a Renoir, but it becomes a contemporary piece of sculpture by its form, scale, and technique.

SERWER: You talked a little bit about collaborations earlier, and you said that you have enjoyed those experiences when you did your happenings and movies, and that you find it necessary to work with a team sometimes and, other times, alone.

GROOMS: It takes so much energy and imagination to work with a lot of people. Seward works with a team. He's very generous to work that way. It brings something special to the work that so many people have contributed a kind of creative and spiritual underpinning to it. He must be a good director. But it's definitely his ambition and vision that's driving the project.

SERWER: I wanted to ask you about humor, too. It seems to me that your works are full of whimsy and fun. Nobody can look at one of your works without smiling. In Seward's work humor is also very important.

GROOMS: Yes, with Seward, there is always that element of surprise. No matter how serious the original subject, you're likely to discover a joke you wouldn't have enjoyed otherwise—like the Samurai hiding under the kimono in Seward's version of Monet's *La Japonaise*, which he calls *Oriental Fan*.

SERWER: We've been mulling over the idea of how critics have received Seward, and we were reminded of the fact that a lot of these nineteenth-century artists who produced the new work in their own time were not, themselves, so well received. And so I wonder if you see parallels there, especially concerning the claim some make that the works are not original. How do you think Seward has made these pieces his own?

GROOMS: That's really interesting and I think he's certainly done it, but it is almost cutting edge in itself, you know, his appropriations have been so complete. He's found out something about the original paintings that he incorporates to make the pieces his own. He touches on something that's a contemporary topic. It's really a question of how much you can let yourself go. For example, the piece inspired by a Renior painting called *Dance at Bougival*. It's so clearly a Renoir, but it becomes a contemporary piece of sculpture by its form, scale, and technique. Even the abstraction of certain things, like the way that he used the woman's skirt to become the base transforms it. It's not like a conventional base. It's just a terrific sculptural solution for a giant figure composition.

SERWER: That is a very helpful description of the dynamic in which Seward's work is inspired by another work, yet has its own character and presence that make it distinctive from the original.

GROOMS: It's not really a thinking thing. It just hits you in the face if you see it. You have a real visual reaction to it. It's not an intellectual concept.

SERWER: Well, one last question. I love the idea that both you and Seward find it very important that your art should appeal to ordinary people. And, unlike a lot of other artists, neither of you is obsessed with the critics and collectors. You share a mission to create art that is immediately appealing to people, art that doesn't necessarily require some sort of intellectual preparation to be understood.

GROOMS: Right. Could it be that we both have some sort of aspiration to be showmen? Showmen need large numbers of people to be successful. Therefore, it's not really a conscious decision to appeal to the ordinary citizen. You'd be happy to have the most elite types there as well as the person on the street. An audience is what you want.

In an English fairy tale my mother had once read to me, a small boy stepped out of his bed into a picture and rode his hobbyhorse along a painted path between silent trees. While I knelt on my pillow in a mist of drowsiness and talc powdered well-being, half sitting on my calves and rapidly going through my prayer, I imagined the motion of climbing into the picture above my bed and plunging into that enchanted beechwood—which I did visit in due time.

—Vladimir Nabokov, *Speak, Memory*

Confrontational Vulnerability

J. Seward Johnson, Jr.

after

Olympia 1863

Edouard Manet

Musée d'Orsay, Paris

> "*Olympia*; that wan, wasted courtesan, showing to the public, for the first time, the nontraditional, unconventional nude .... Rarely has any modern work been more applauded by so few, or more deeply damned by the many, than was that of this innovator."

— Stephen Mallarmé

> "Manet's distinctly modern 'Old Master' is a sophisticated mixture of ambiguity, tease, and homage, and these are the reasons why the painting continues to challenge and confound."

—Alan Krell

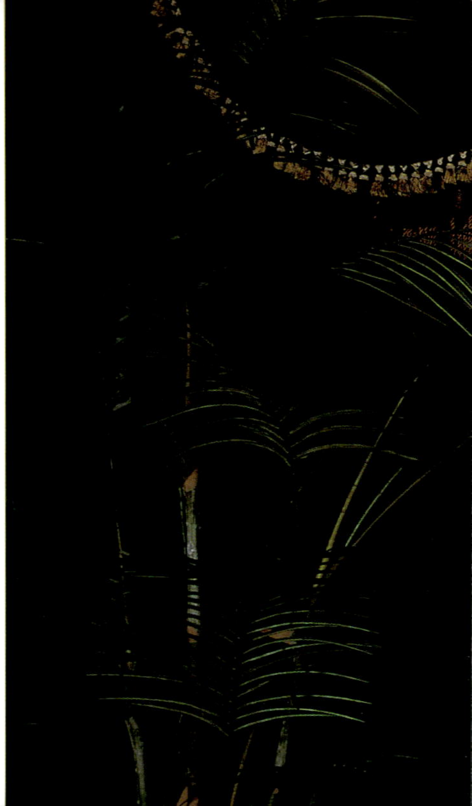

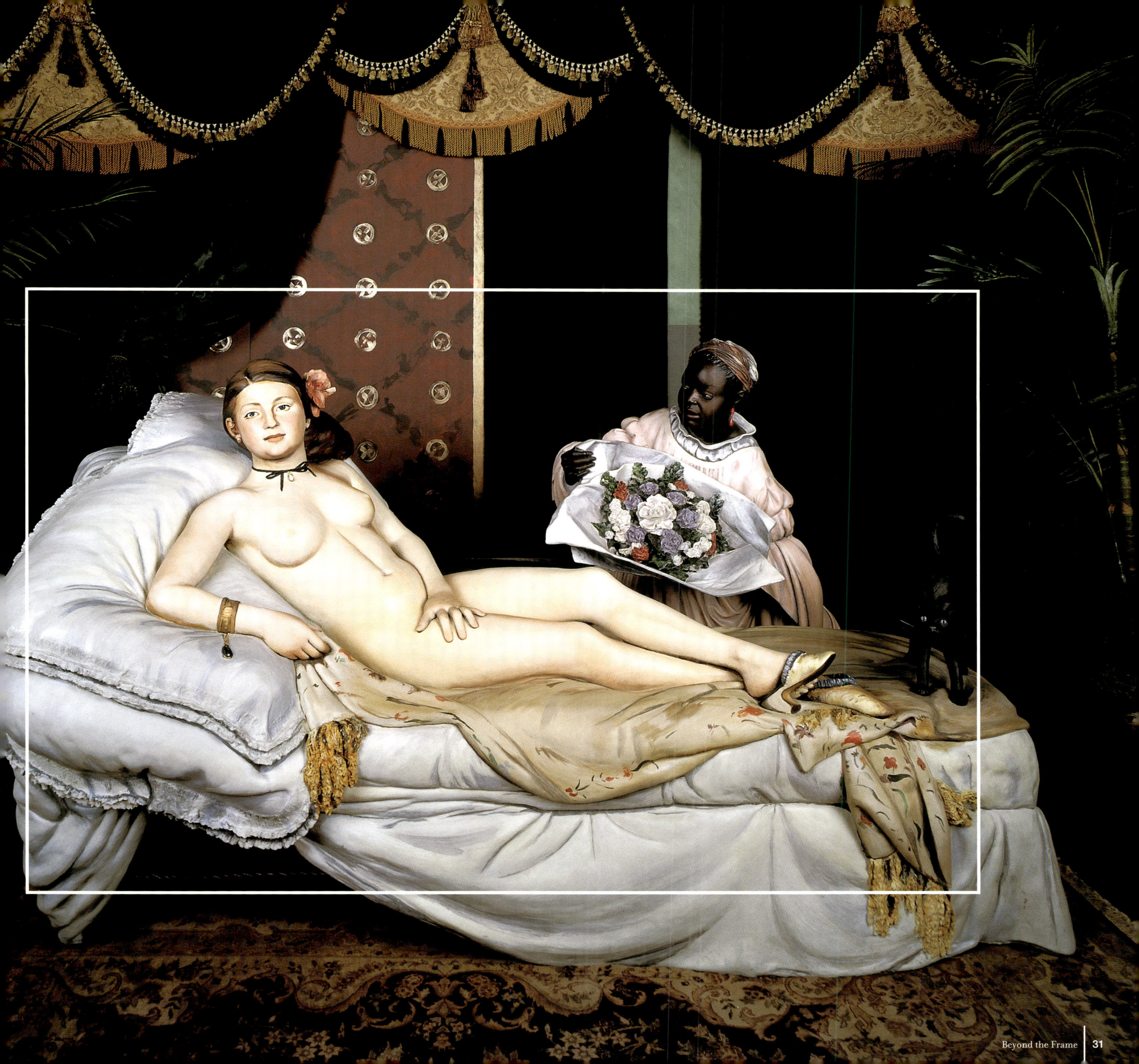

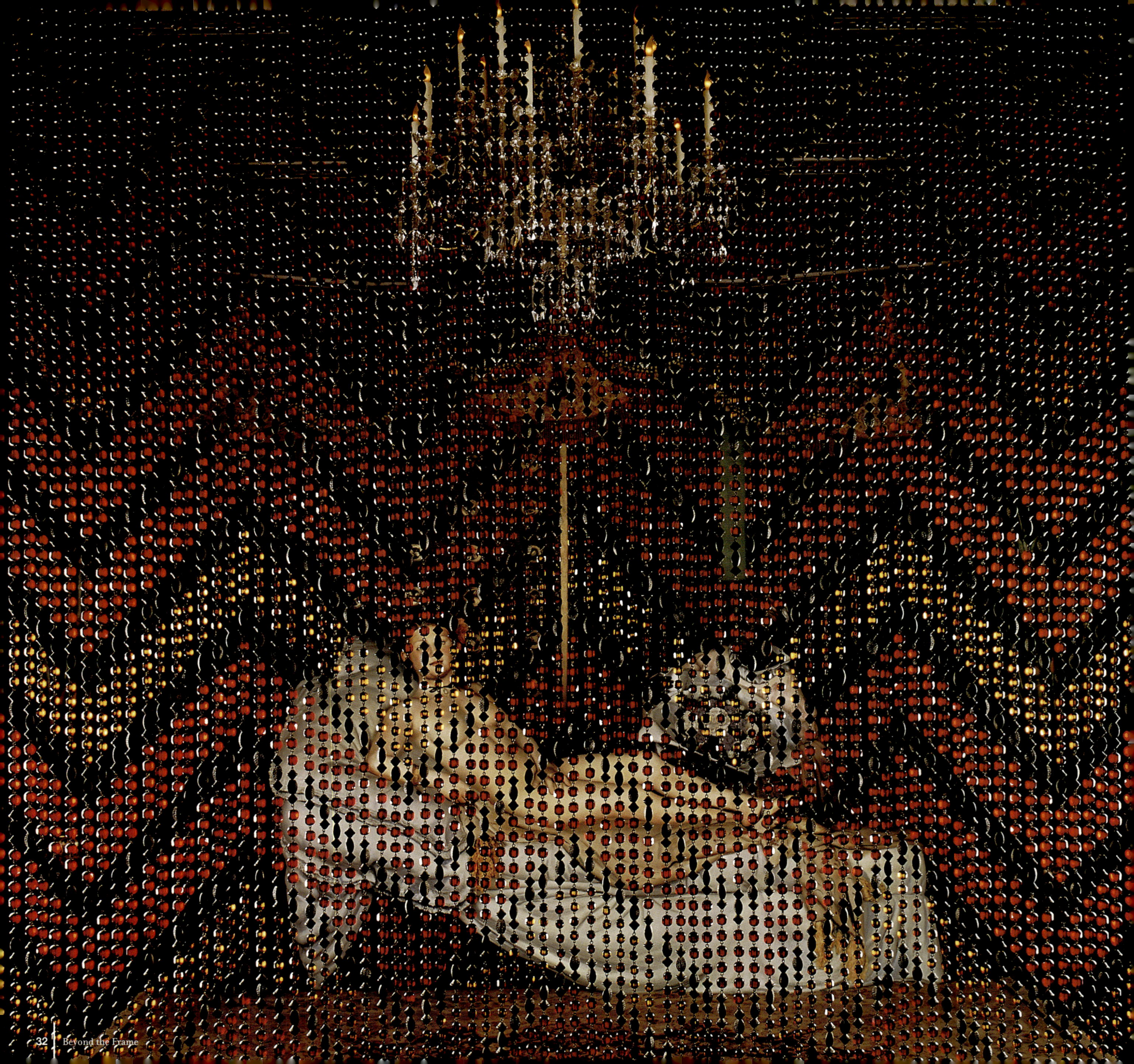

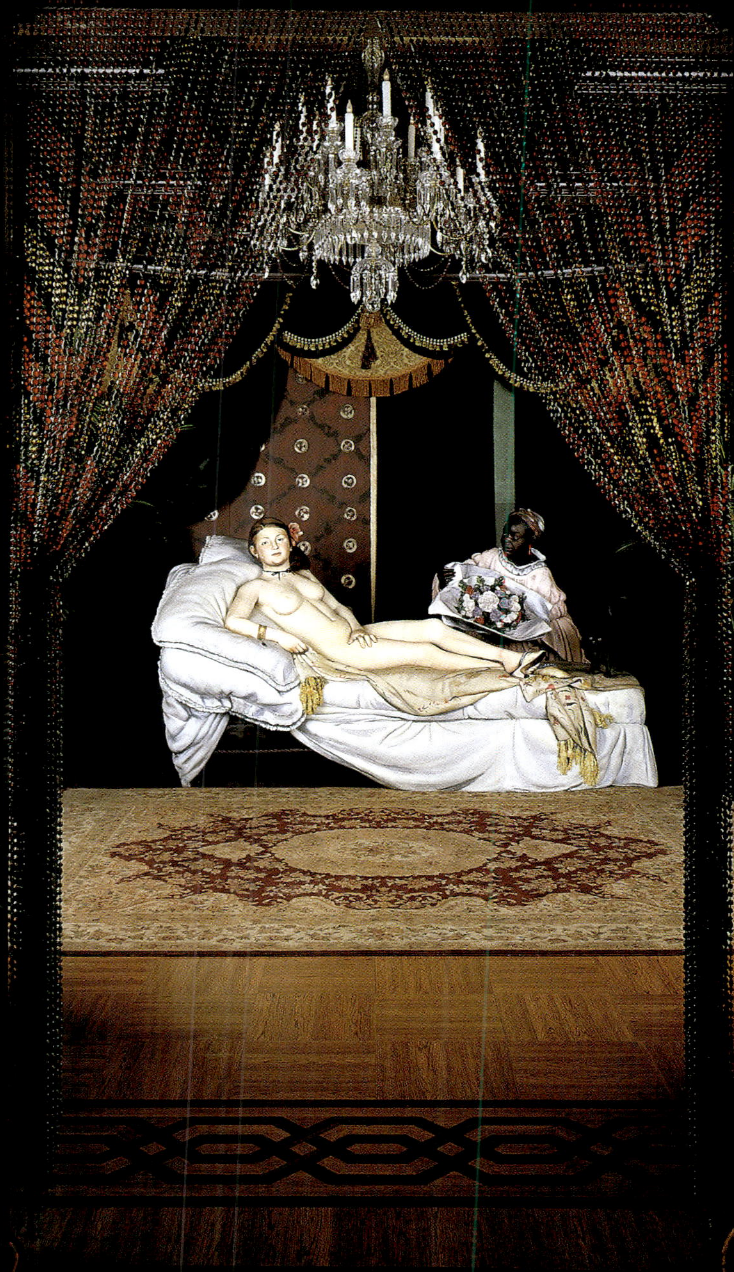

We enter Olympia's splendid boudoir through a pair of glittering bead curtains. Her graceful maid presents her lady a brilliant bouquet, no doubt from an admirer. And at Olympia's daintily clad feet her malevolent black cat, back arched, eyes us with suspicion.
—J. Seward Johnson, Jr.

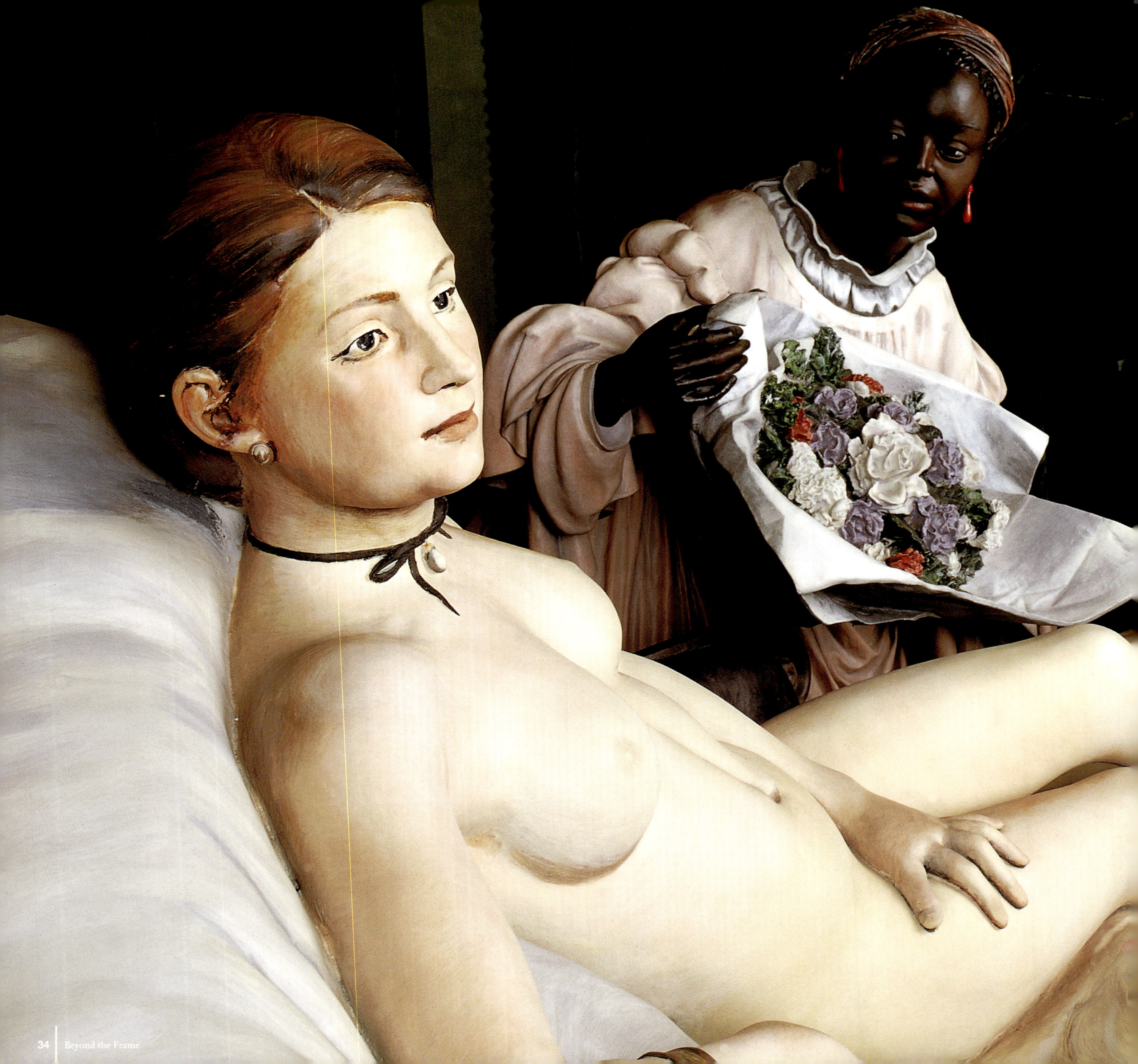

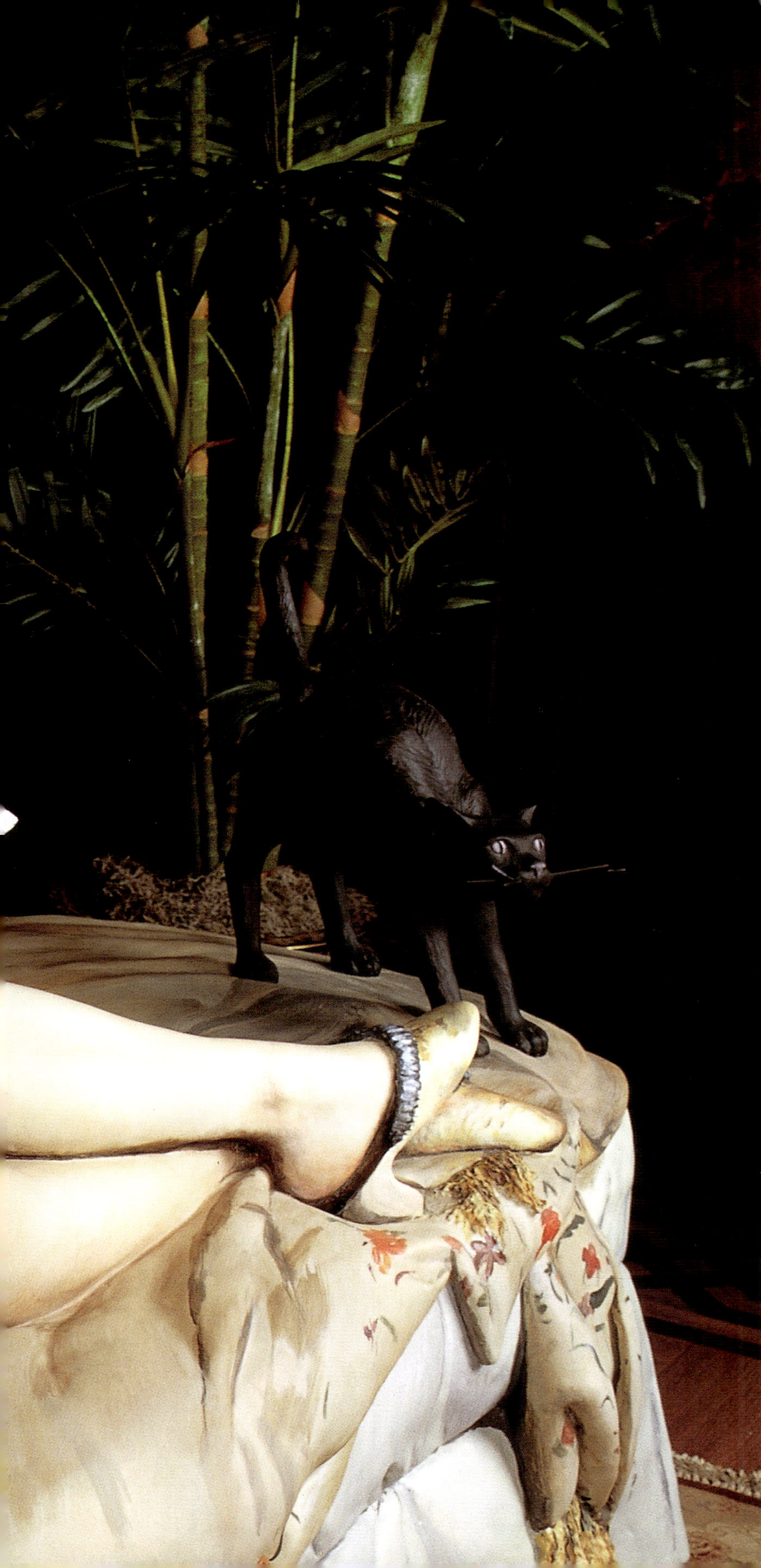

> "Olympia's black choker and fashionable slipper make it clear that she is not a mythical being, but a mercenary love goddess of the nineteenth century."

—Petra ten-Doesschate Chu

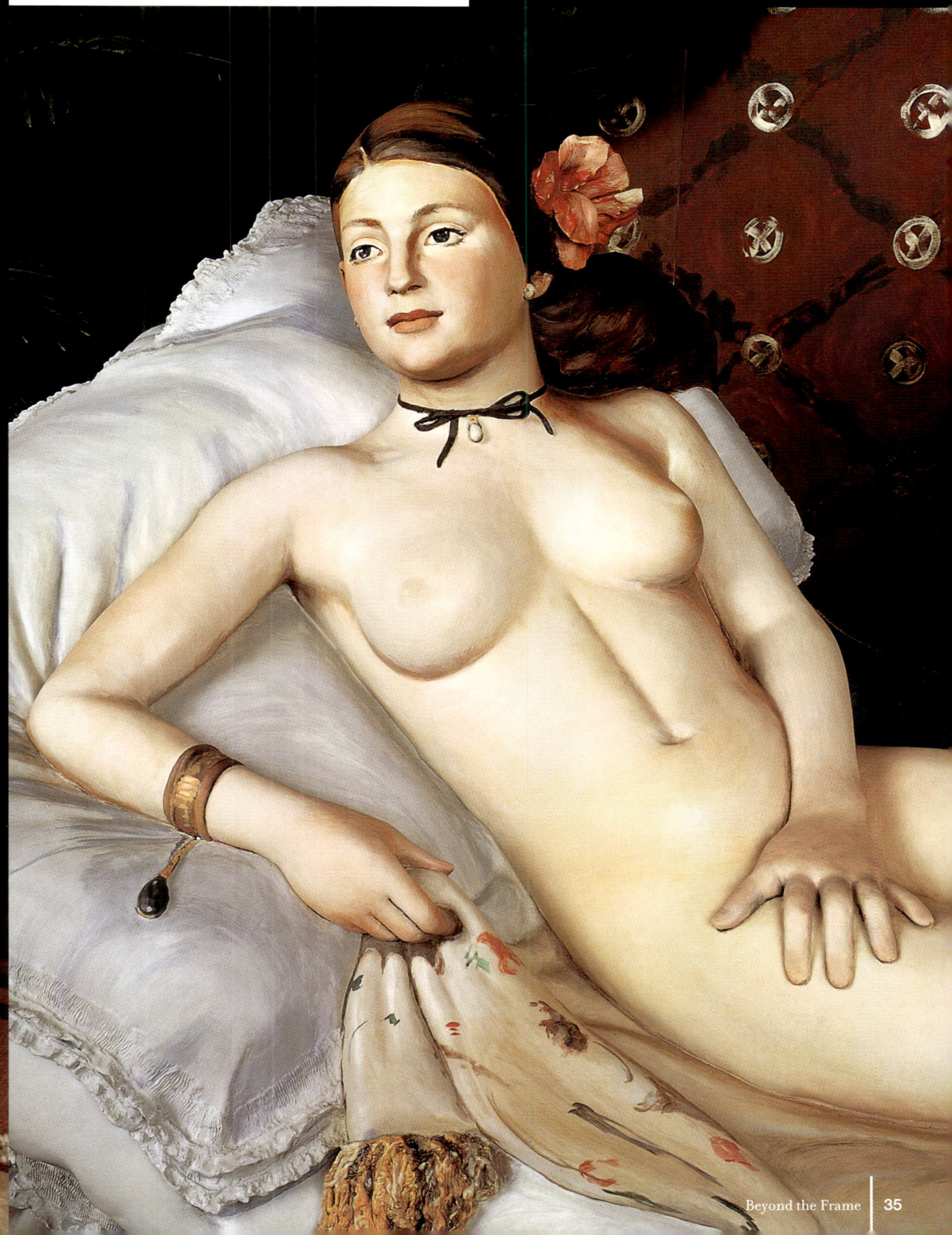

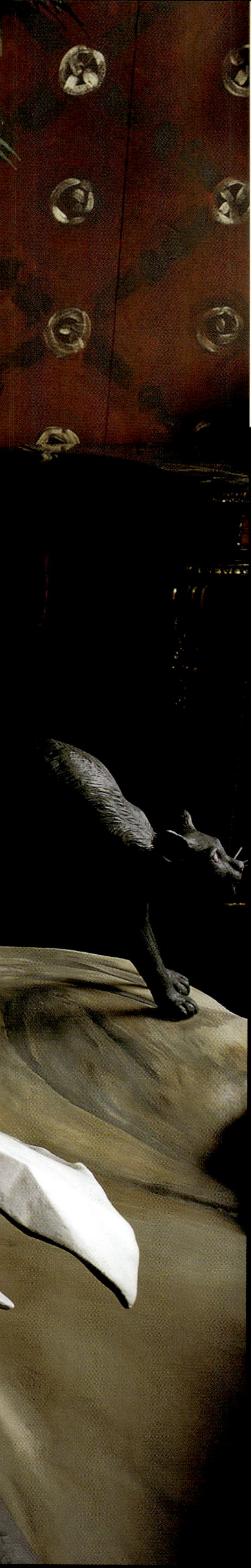

> "I myself worry very little about what could have been said on art. But if I had to give an opinion, I would formulate one in this way: everything that has the soul of humanity, everything that has the soul of contemporaneity is interesting. Everything that is deprived of it is worthless."

—Edouard Manet

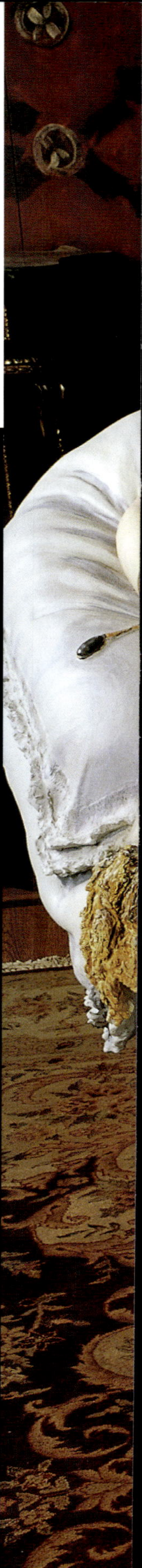

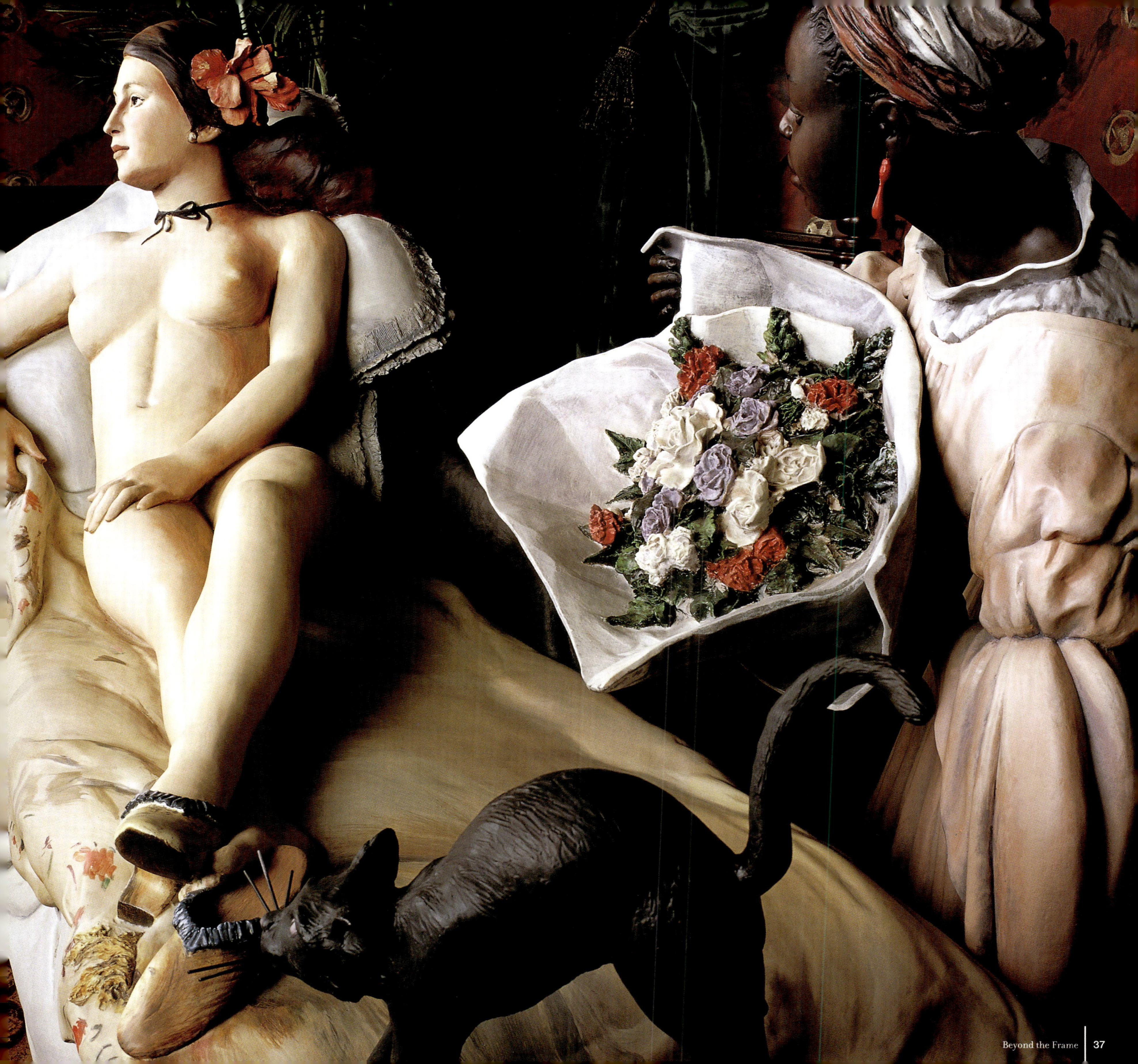

Oriental Fan

J. Seward Johnson, Jr.

after

La Japonaise (Camille Monet in Japanese Costume) 1876

Claude Monet

Museum of Fine Arts, Boston

> "*La Japonaise* was Monet's only venture into a popular genre subject. He was in desperate financial straits, and he probably conceived *La Japonaise* as a potboiler, an illusionistic tour-de-force in a flamboyant style that would be successful with the public. It did in fact sell quickly and at quite a high price."

—Virginia Spate

> "*La Japonaise* is not a Japanese woman, but a Parisienne dressed as a Japanese. It's my first wife who posed."

—Claude Monet

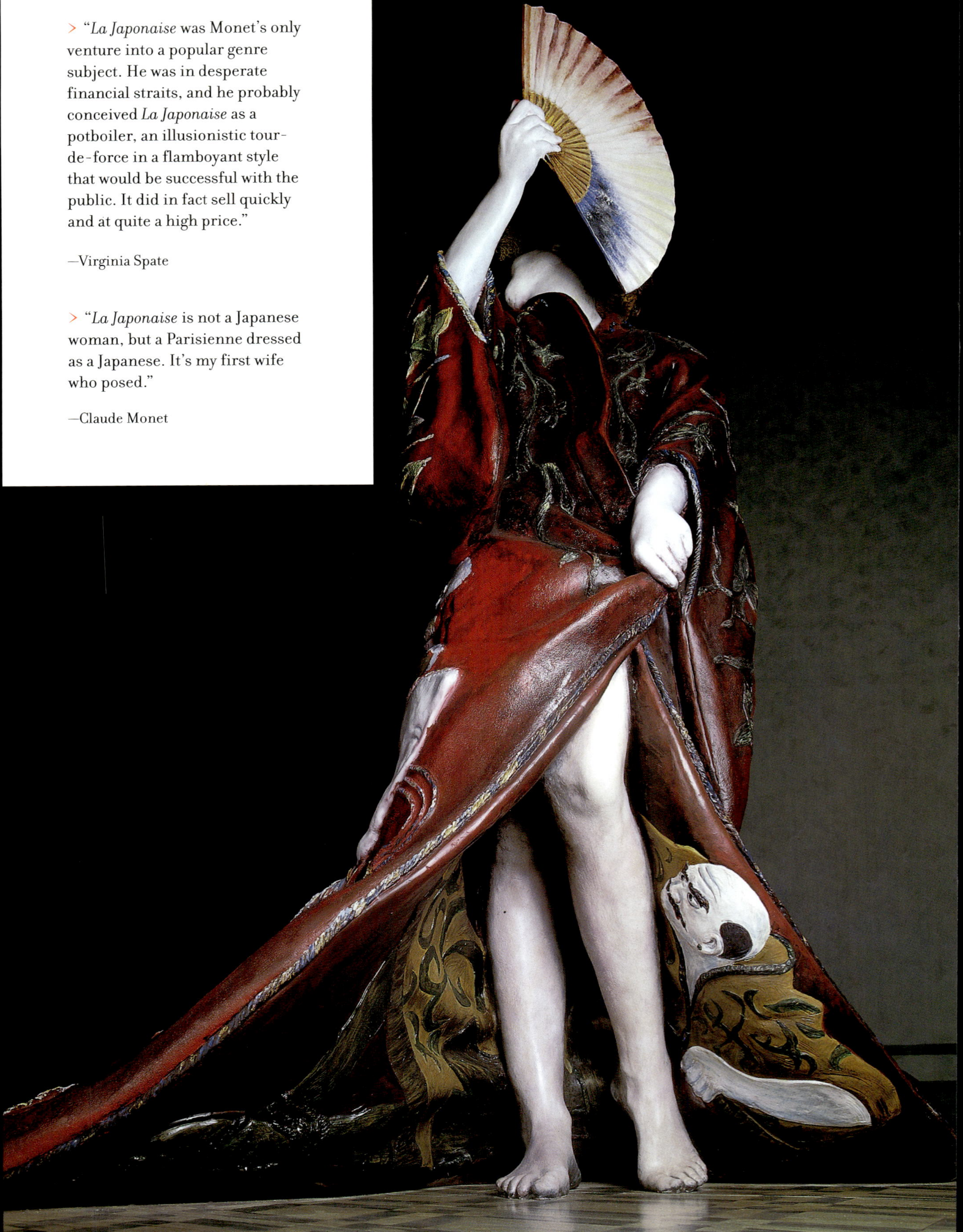

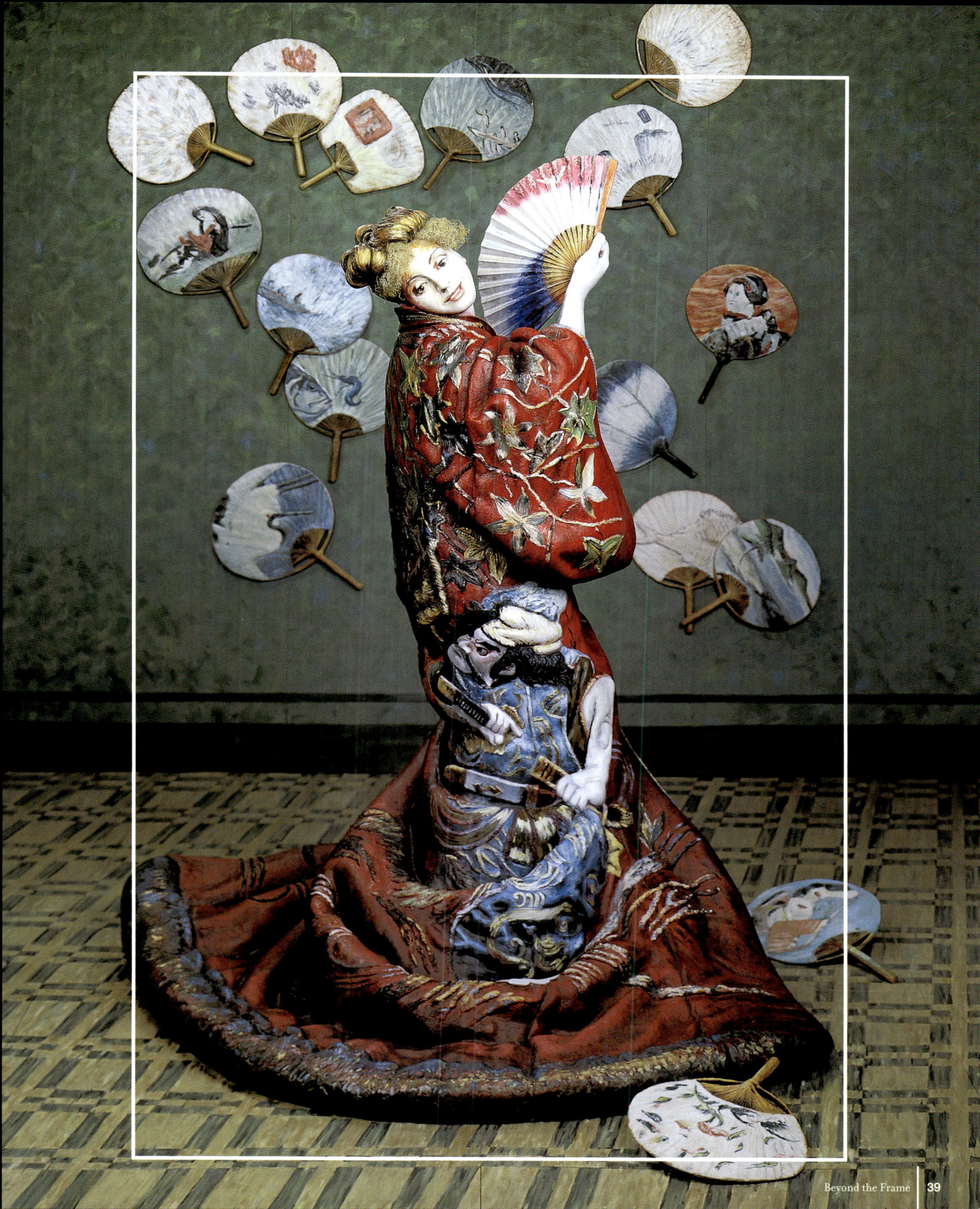

Monet was having fun with this one, so I did too! The Samarai looking up her dress is for the discoverer.

—J. Seward Johnson, Jr.

> "[Manet] lends an unforgettable grace, both bizarre and naïve, to this gamin disguised as a warrior, planted on his feet in oversized shoes and white spats."

—Paul Jamot

> "Manet made no attempt to suggest perspective; only the short shadows behind the boy's heels indicate a source of light and depth."

—Beth Archer Brombert

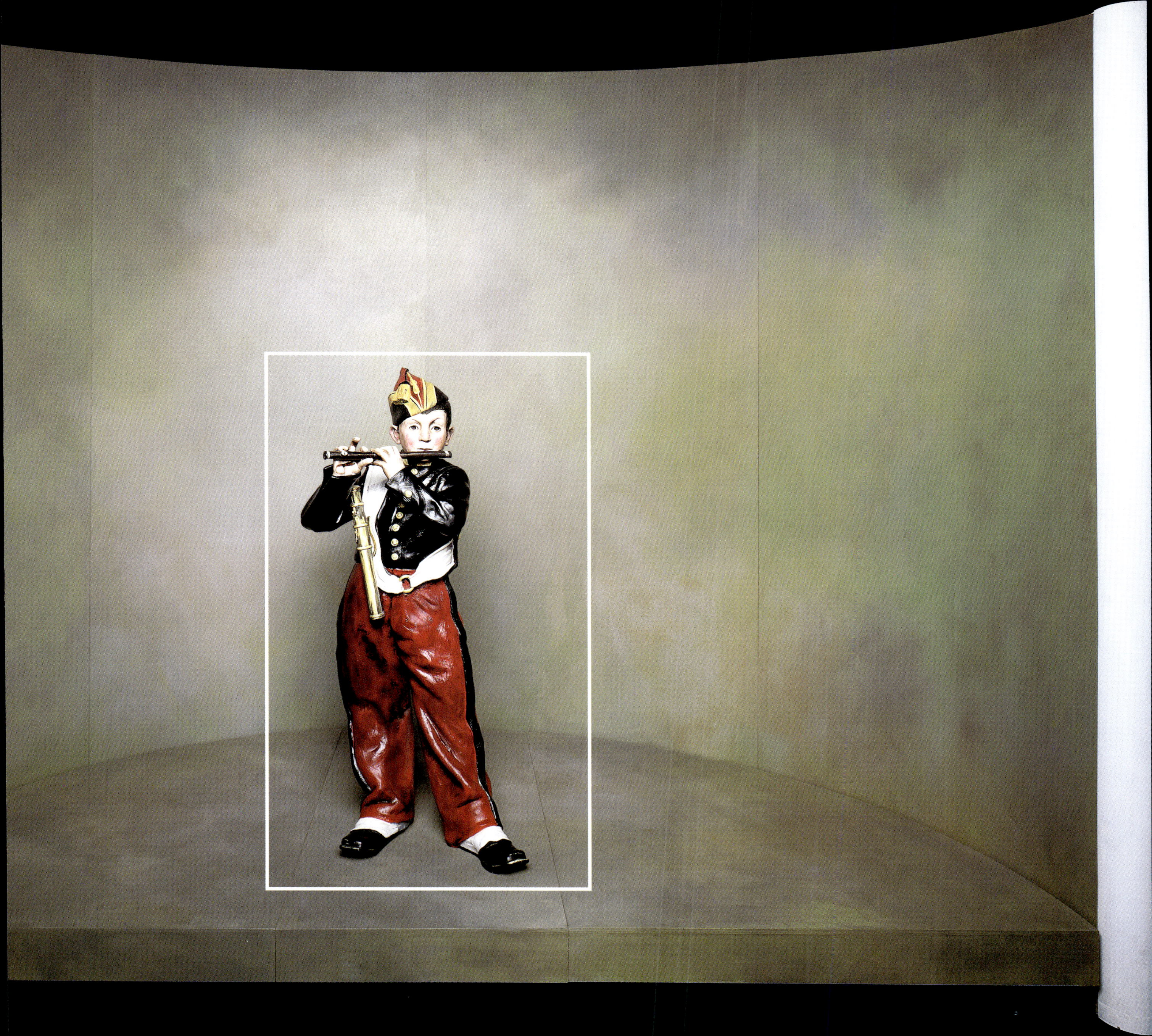

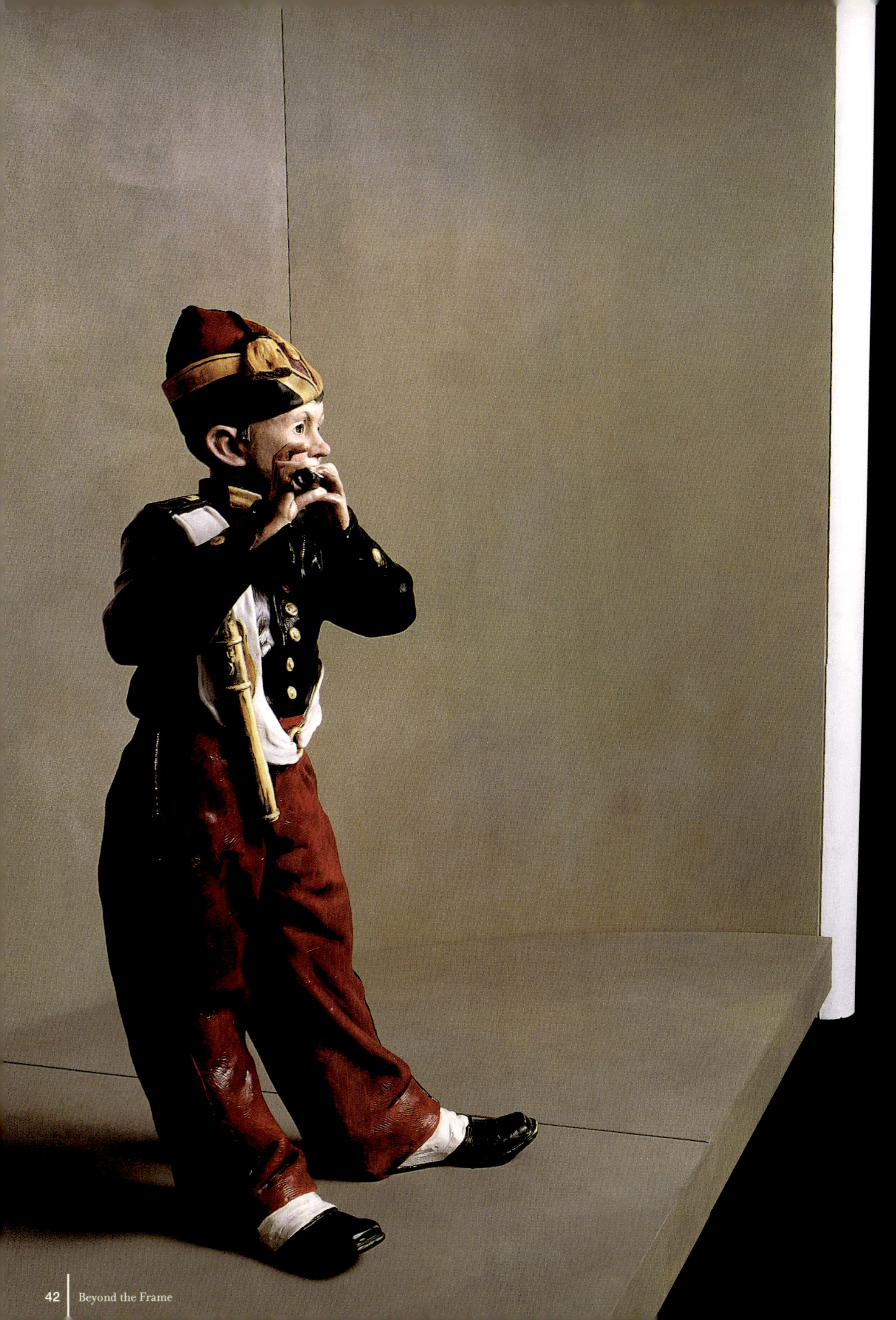

> "The artist [Manet], confronting any subject whatever, allows himself to be guided by his eyes, which perceive the subject in terms of broad tints that need to control each other. A head placed against a wall is but a more or less white spot against a more or less gray background, and the clothing next to the face becomes, for example, a more or less blue spot next to the more or less white spot. From this comes a great simplicity almost completely without details, an assembly of exact and delicate spots that at a short distance produce painting of striking relief."

— Emile Zola

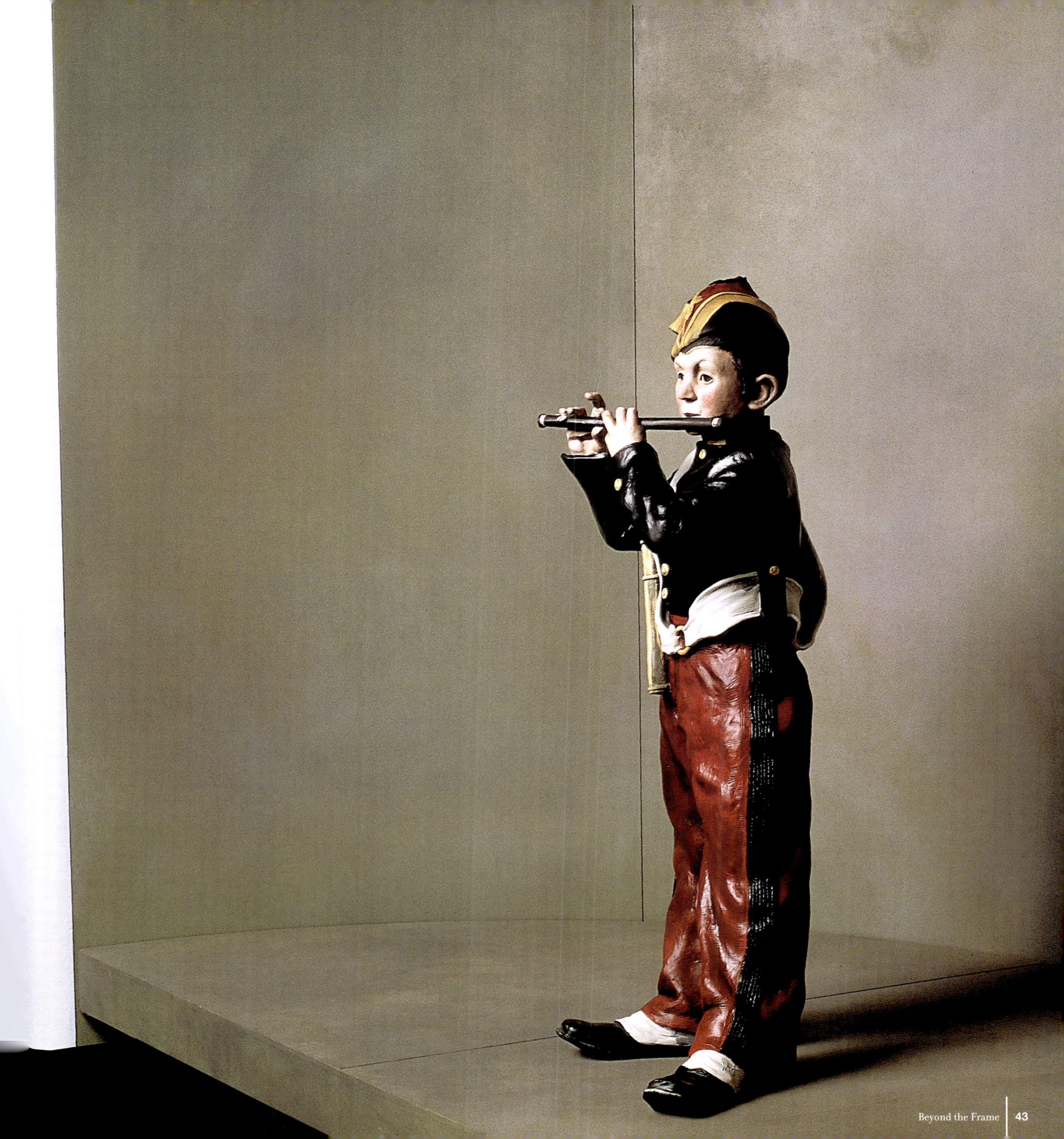

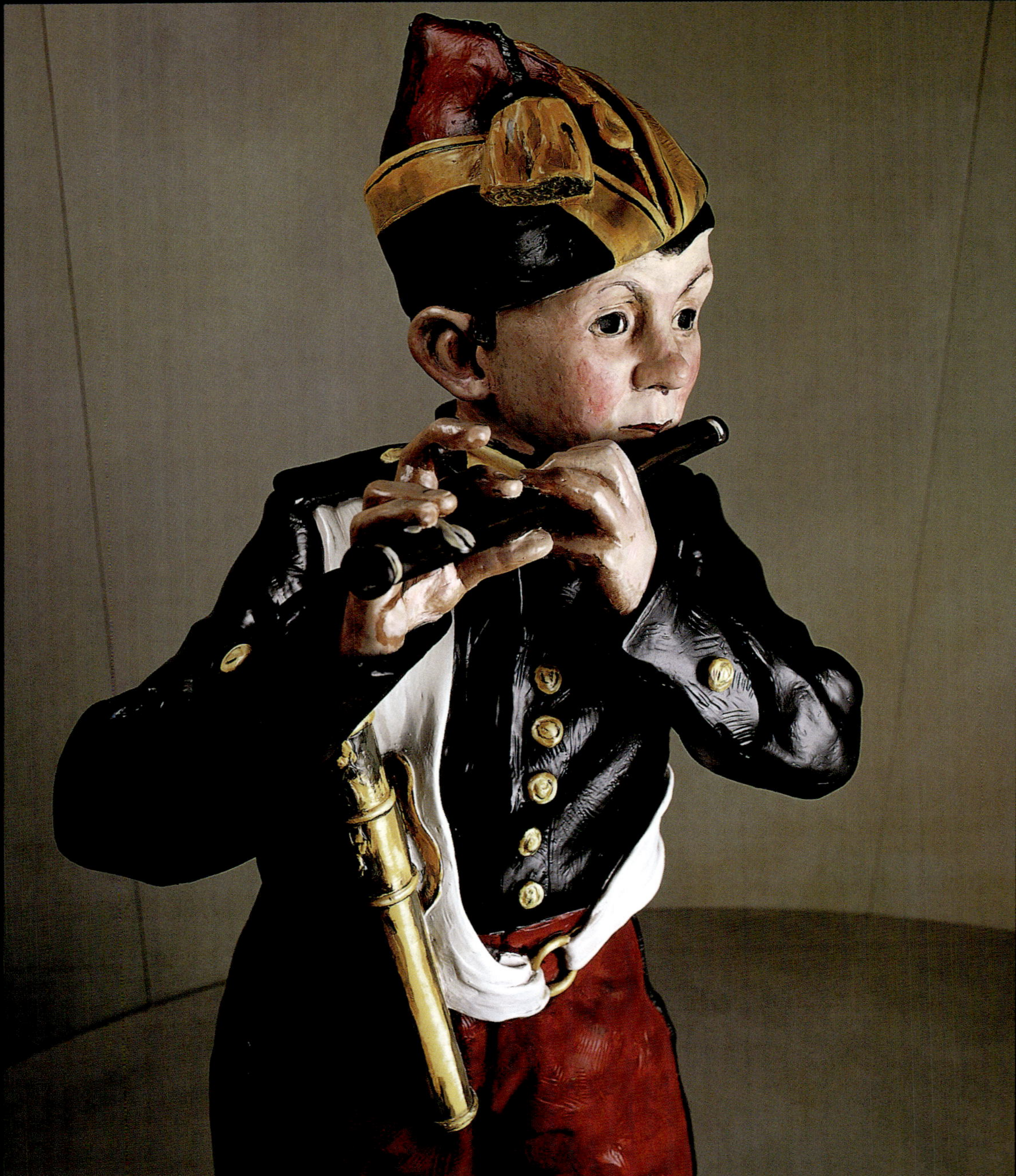

> "Manet's talent lies in exactness and simplicity, and I was thinking in particular of the impression this canvas had made upon me."

—Emile Zola

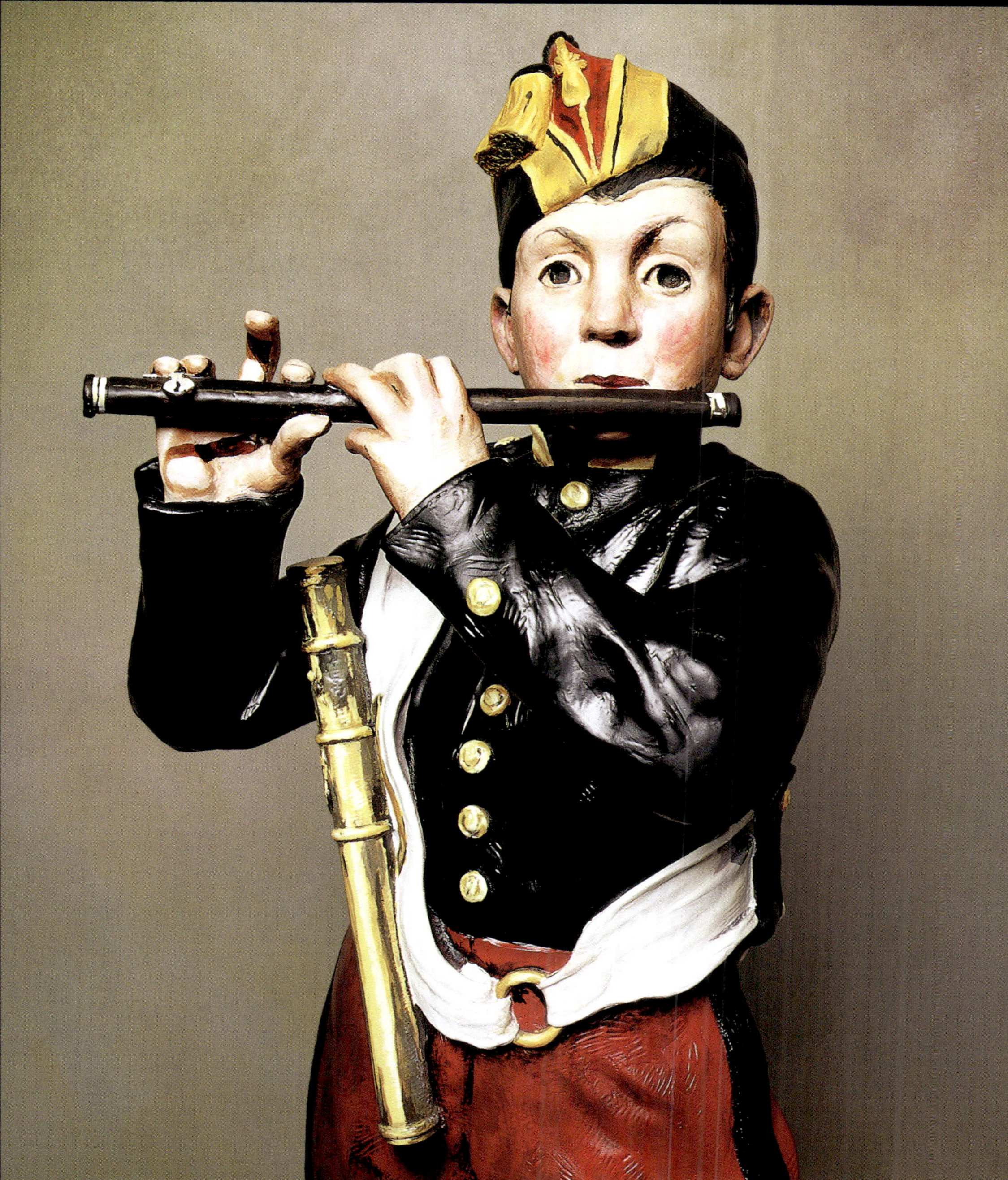

> "Zola saw *The Fifer*, another work rejected by the Salon, as exemplifying Manet's artistic qualities: simplicity and perceptiveness, accuracy and energy, daring and truthfulness—superior qualities that he was sure would one day ensure the painter a well-deserved place in the Louvre."

—Hajo Düchting

Landlady

J. Seward Johnson, Jr.

after

L' Arlésienne: Madame Joseph-Michel Ginoux 1888

Vincent van Gogh

Metropolitan Museum of Art, New York

> "Then I have an Arlésienne at last, a figure ... slashed on in an hour, background pale citron, the face gray, the clothes black, black, black, with perfectly raw Prussian blue. She is leaning on a green table and seated in an armchair of orange wood."

—Vincent van Gogh

> "The image has, through the books, connotations of modernity in which Mme Ginoux is given emblematic status as an ideal, literate modern woman."

—Lauren Soth

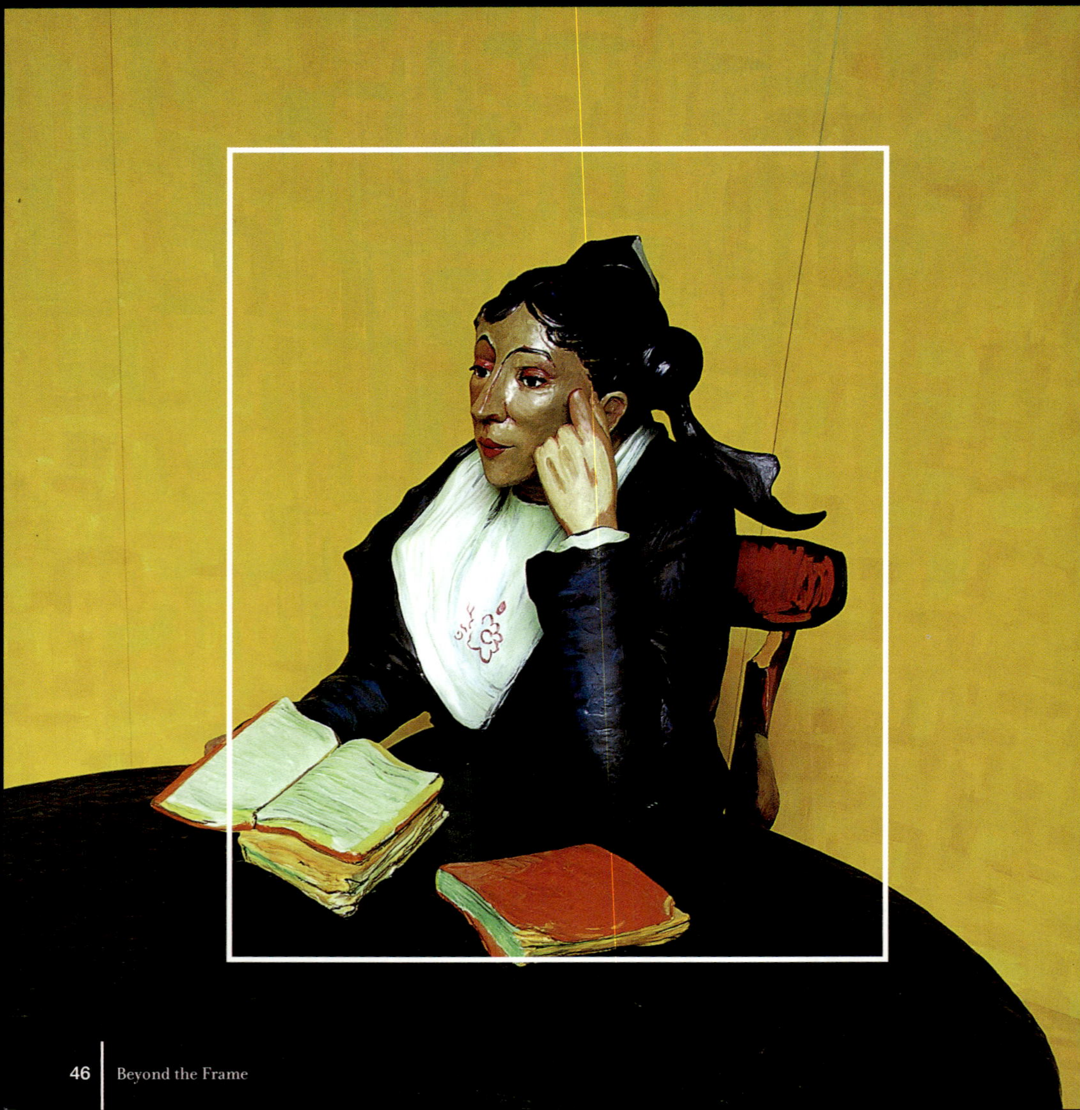

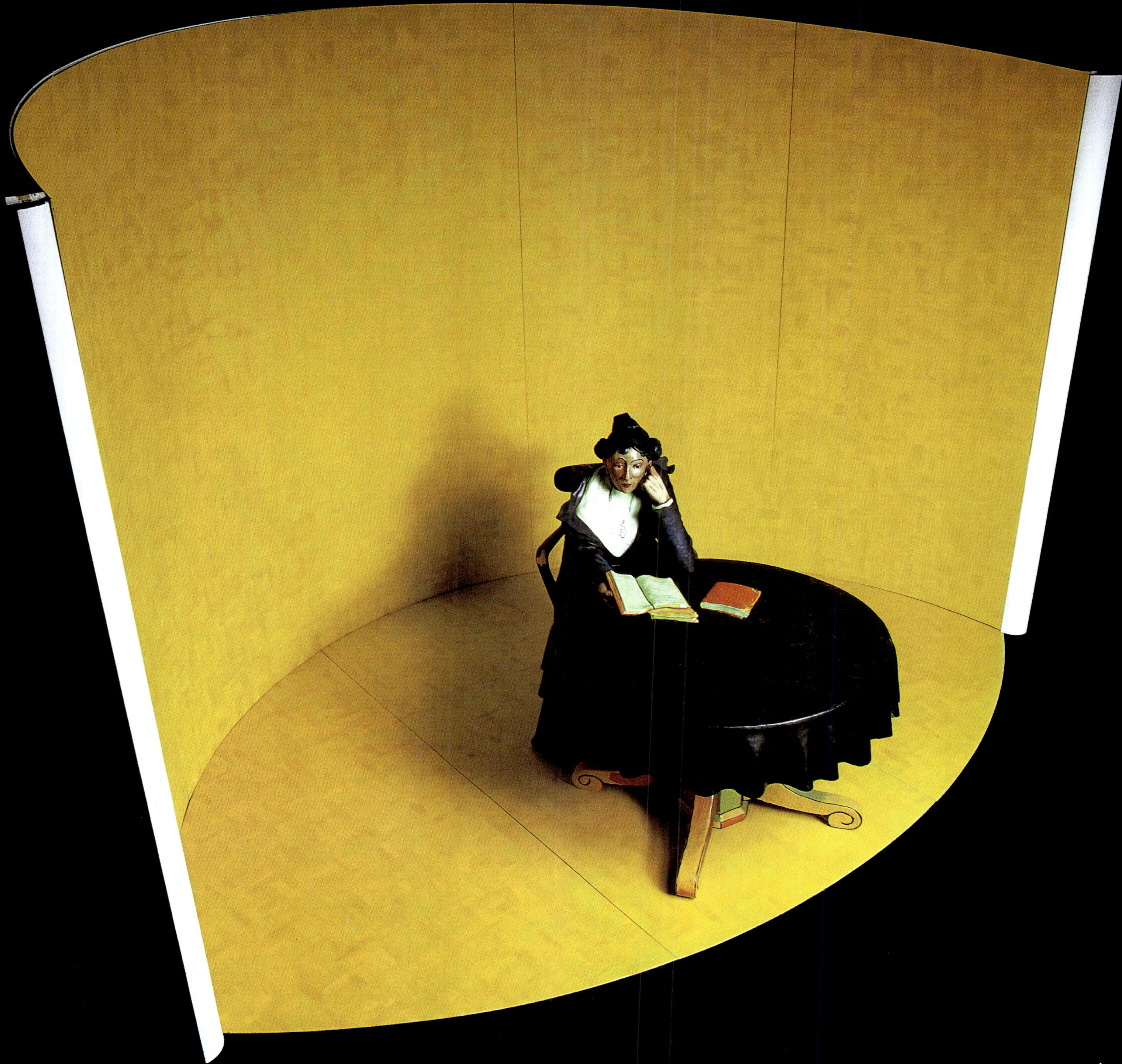

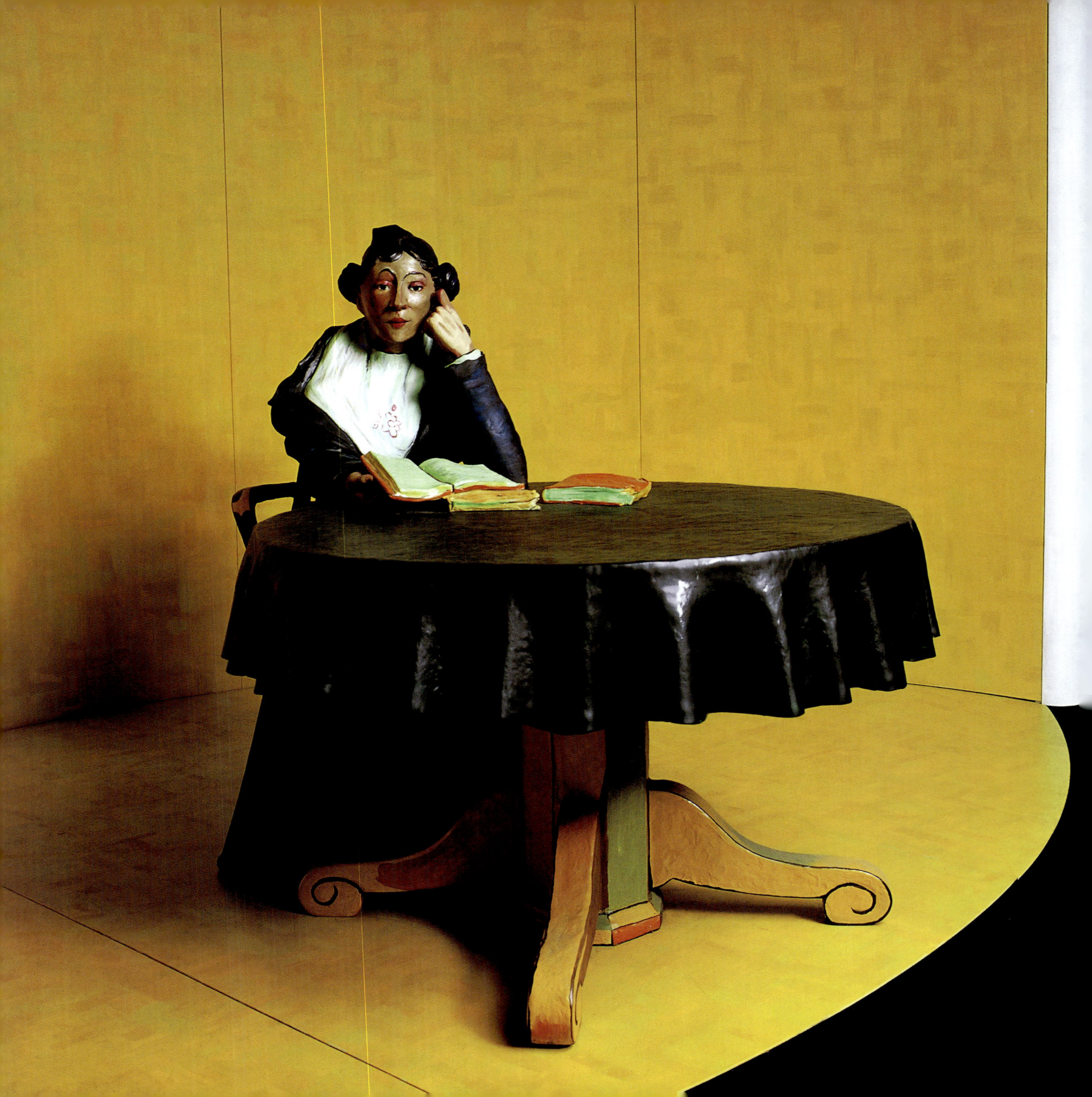

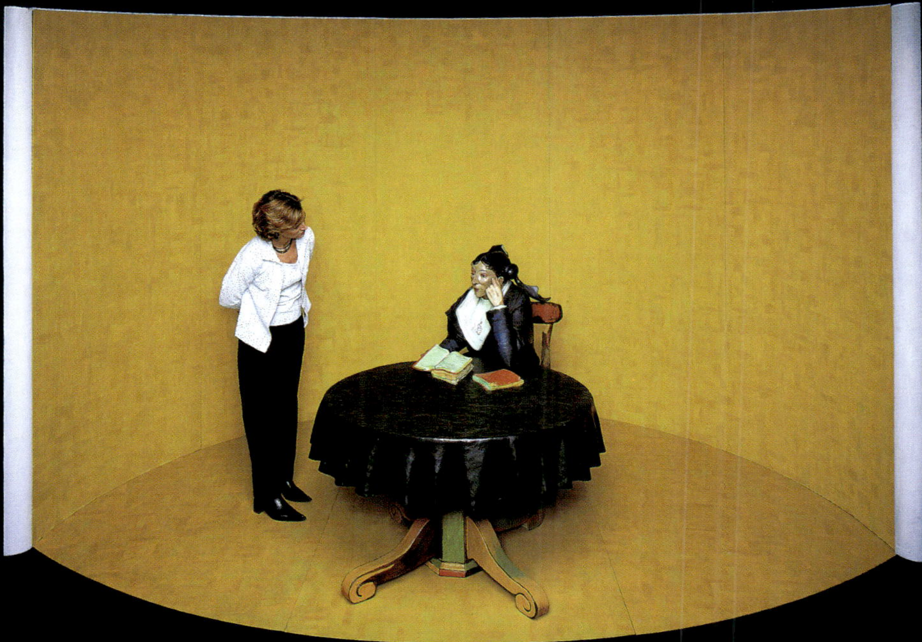

This is what I had to do against impossible perspective. If you look at the painting, the book is floating in the air! So in the sculpture we had to raise the table cloth under it. Henry James said that it is the artist's job to tell a story that is going to hang together, and sometimes he has to stretch certain things to do it.

—J. Seward Johnson, Jr.

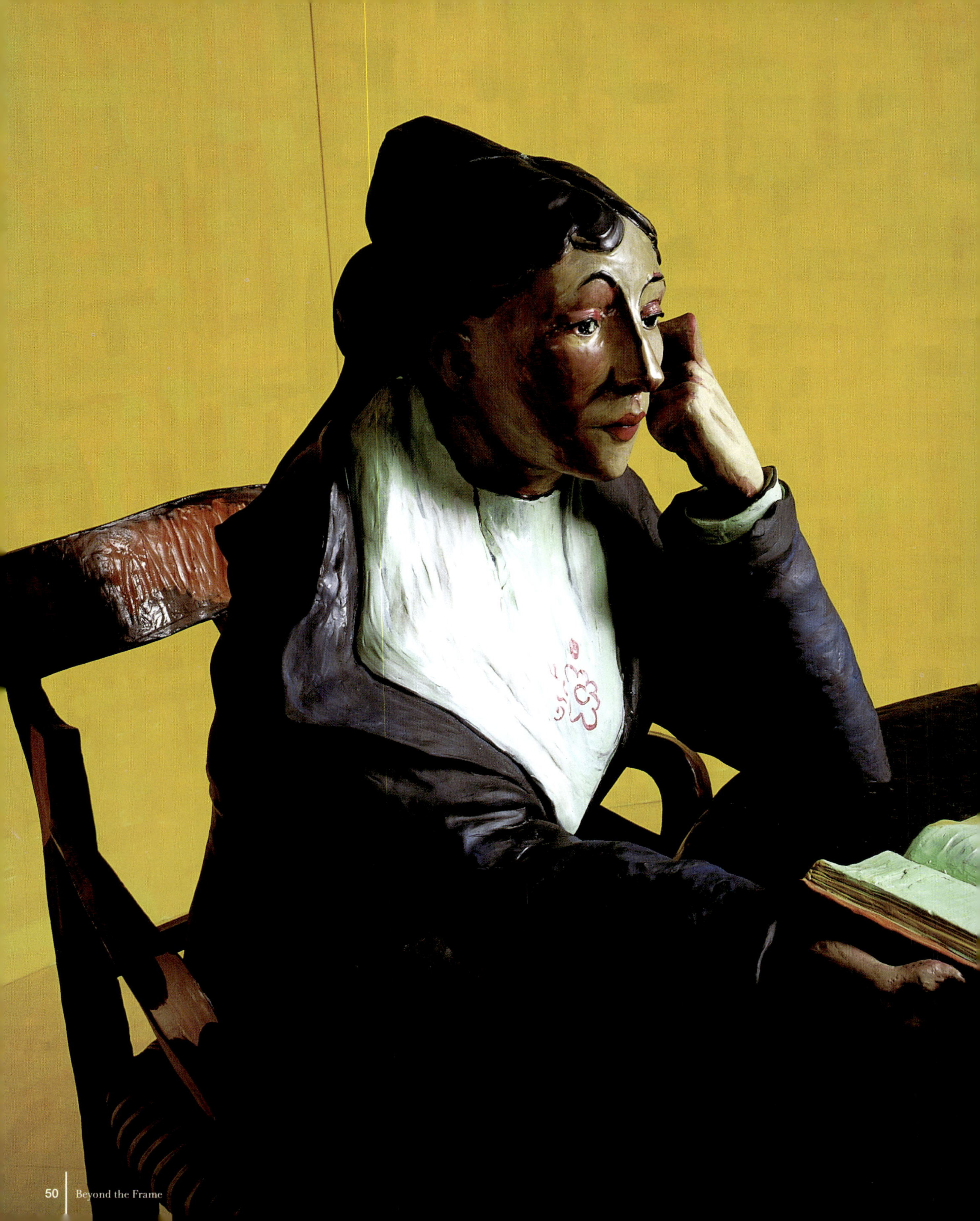

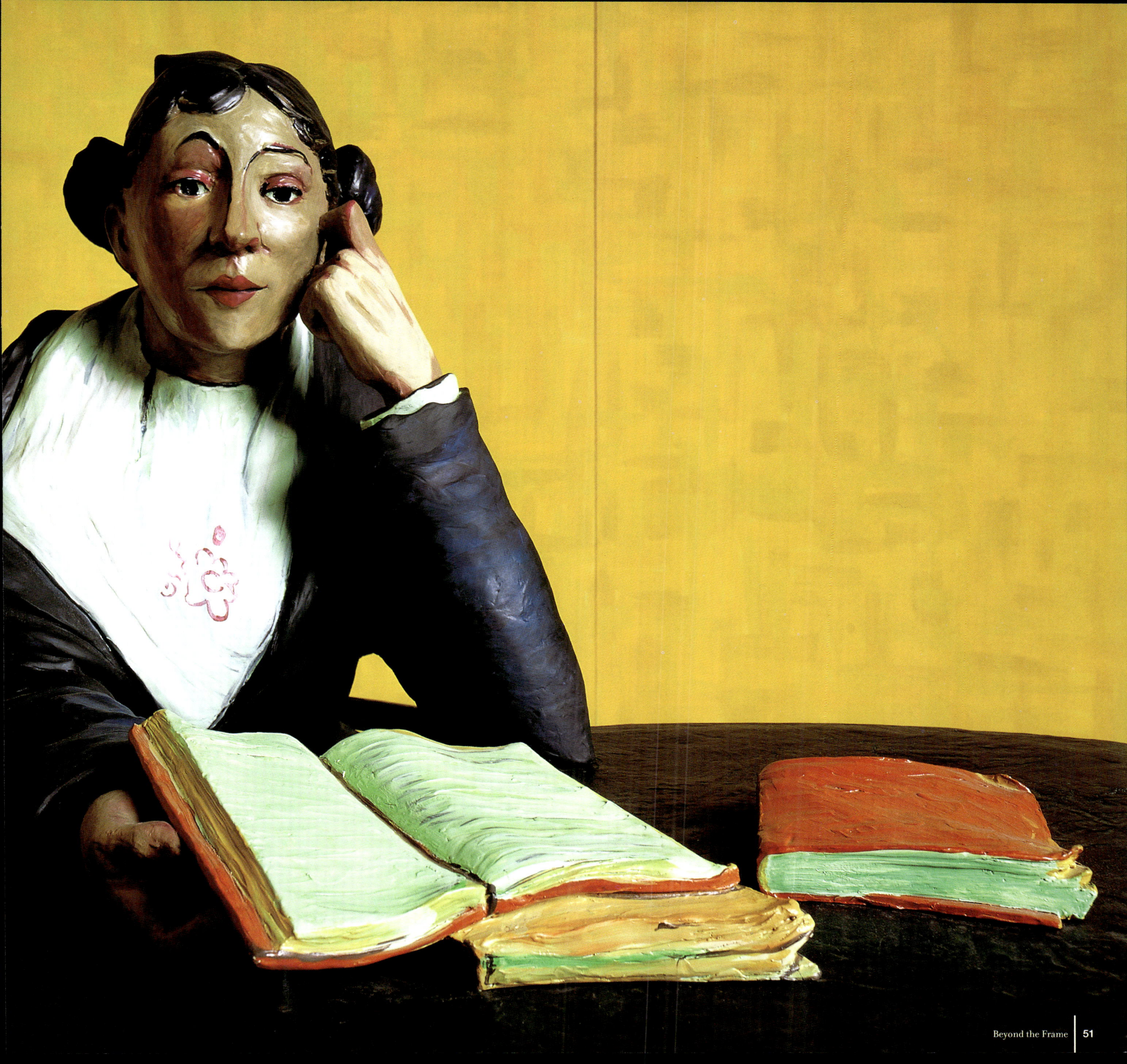

Family Secret

J. Seward Johnson, Jr.

after

Two Sisters (On the Terrace) 1881

Pierre-Auguste Renoir

Art Institute of Chicago

> "Originally called *Two Sisters*, this painting was dismissed by the critics with coarse jokes. It has since become one of the best known and best loved by Renoir. The models are sitting on the terrace of the Fournaise restaurant, and the work is now known more by the site than by the sisters."

—Anne Distel

In *Family Secret* there is a woman in a red hat and a child and I never could figure out what is really going on. When I had the thing in production everyone was talking about the piece. I couldn't think of a name. It was named *The Beauty of Time and Space* which I just hated. So I retitled it *Family Secret*. That leaves it to everyone's imagination. The audience can take it from there.

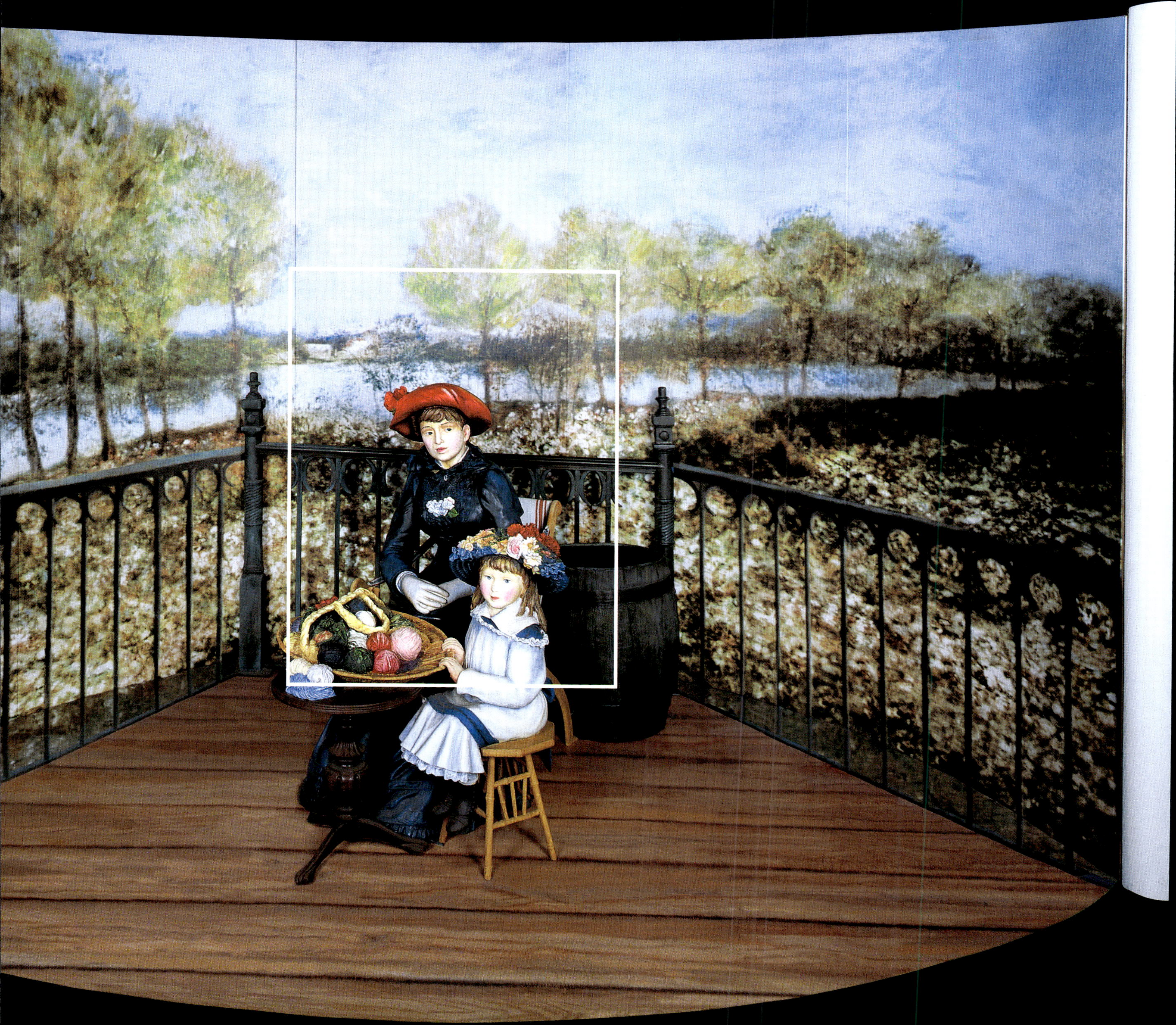

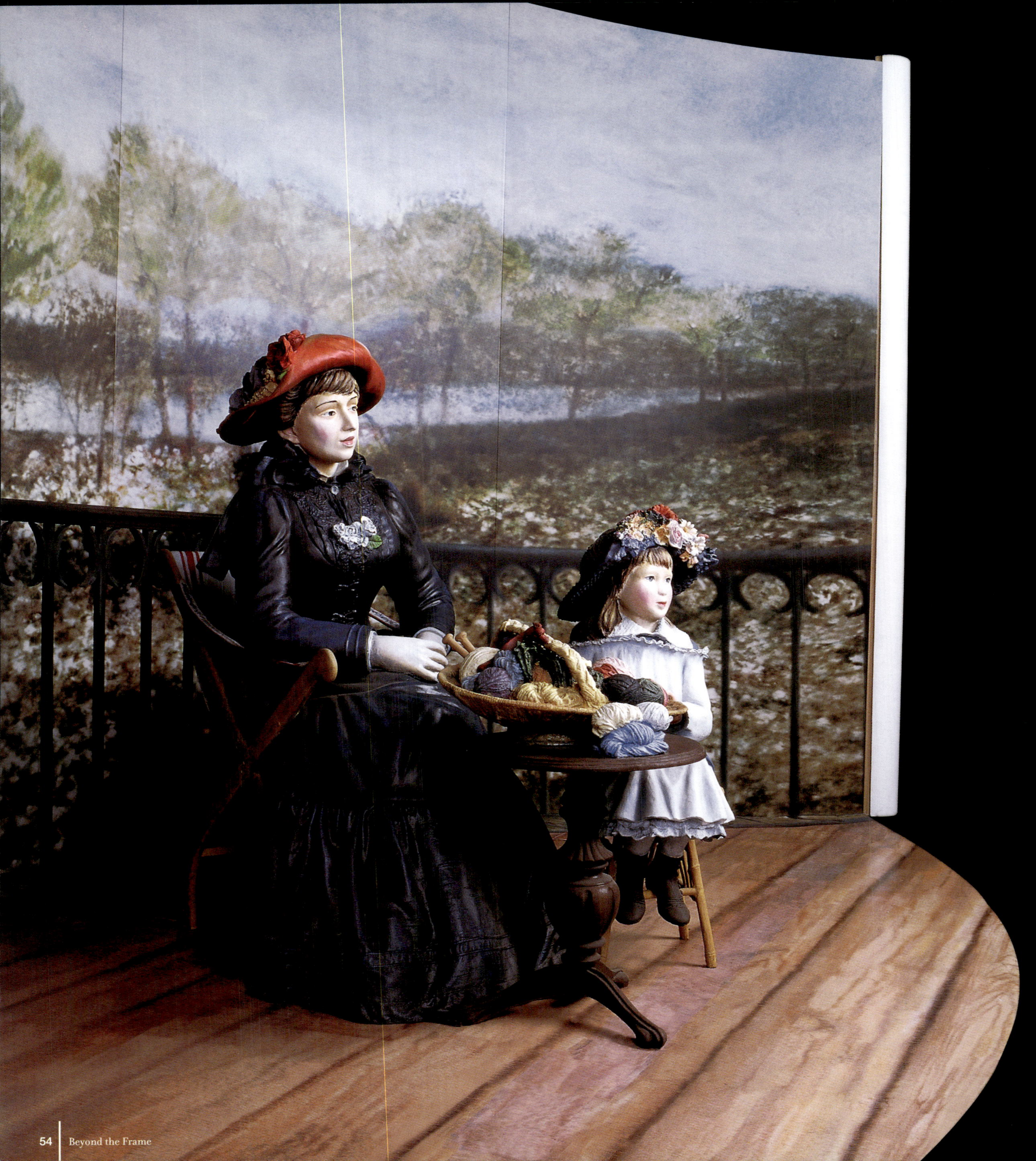

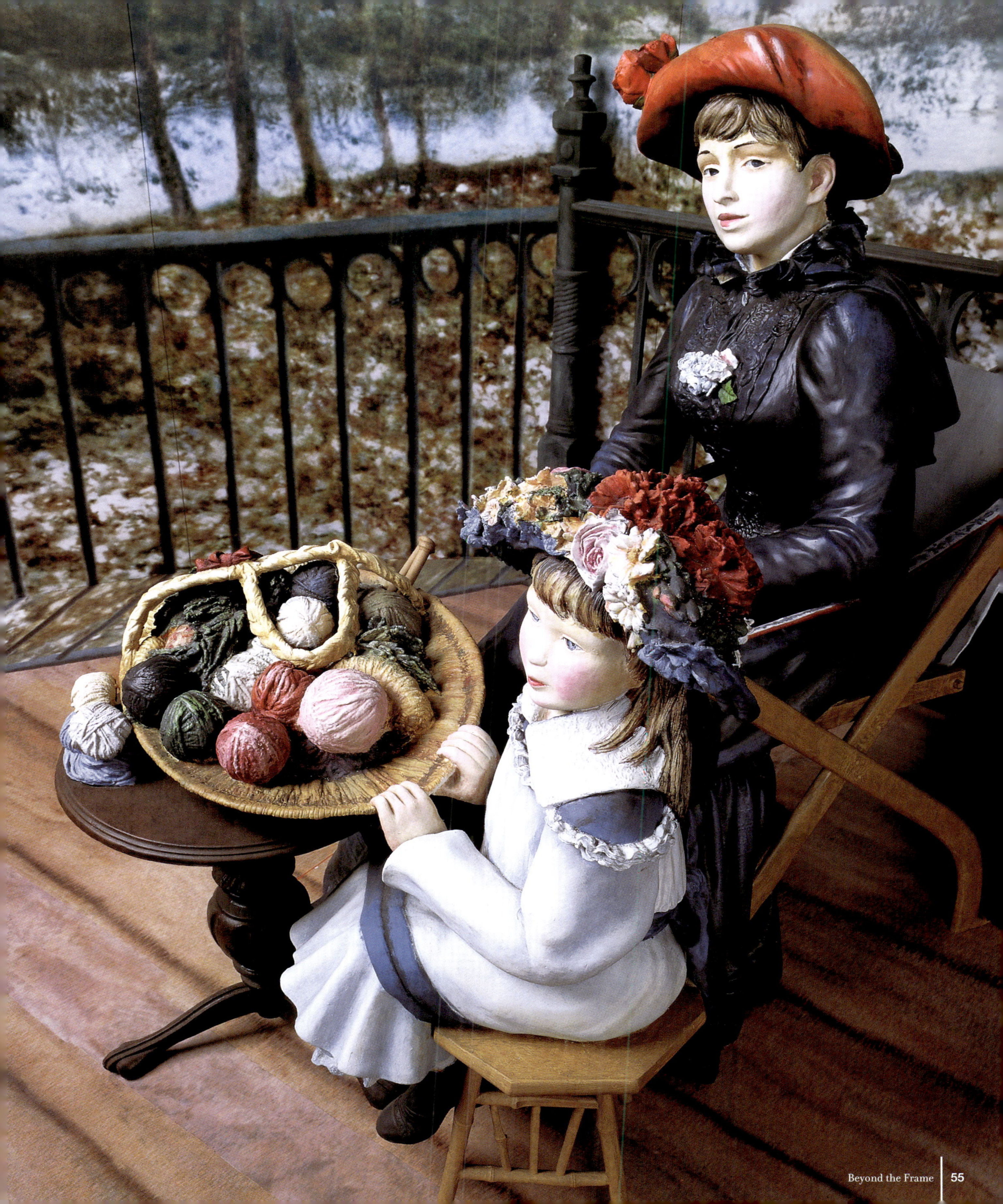

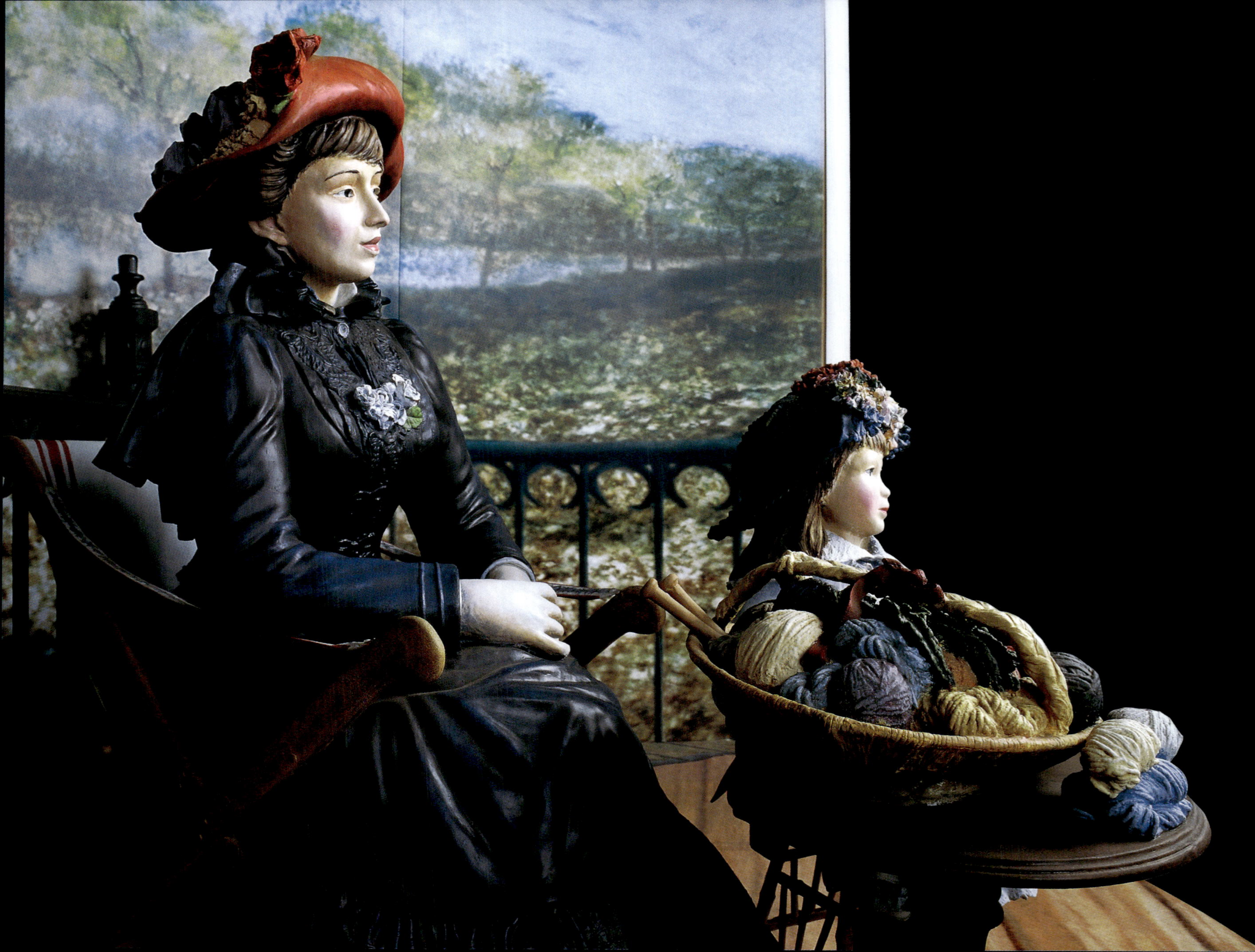

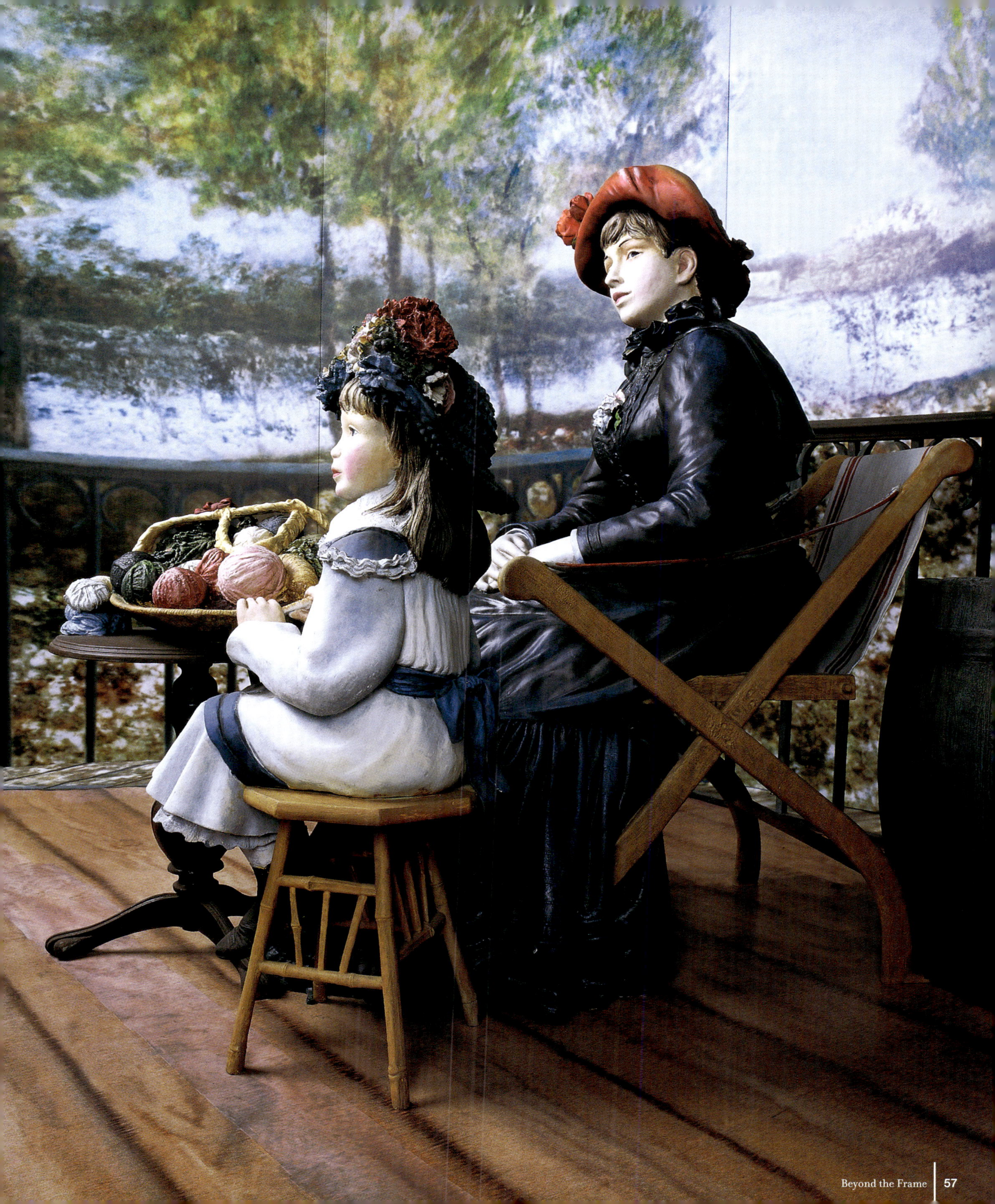

Déjeuner Déjà Vu

J. Seward Johnson, Jr.

after

Le Déjeuner sur l'herbe 1863

Edouard Manet

Musée d'Orsay

> "First of all the famous *Déjeuner sur l'herbe*, rejected by the jury that stupidly did not understand that this is not a woman naked, but a women undressed, which is quite different."

—Fervacques

> "To exhibit is to find friends and allies for the struggle."

—Edouard Manet

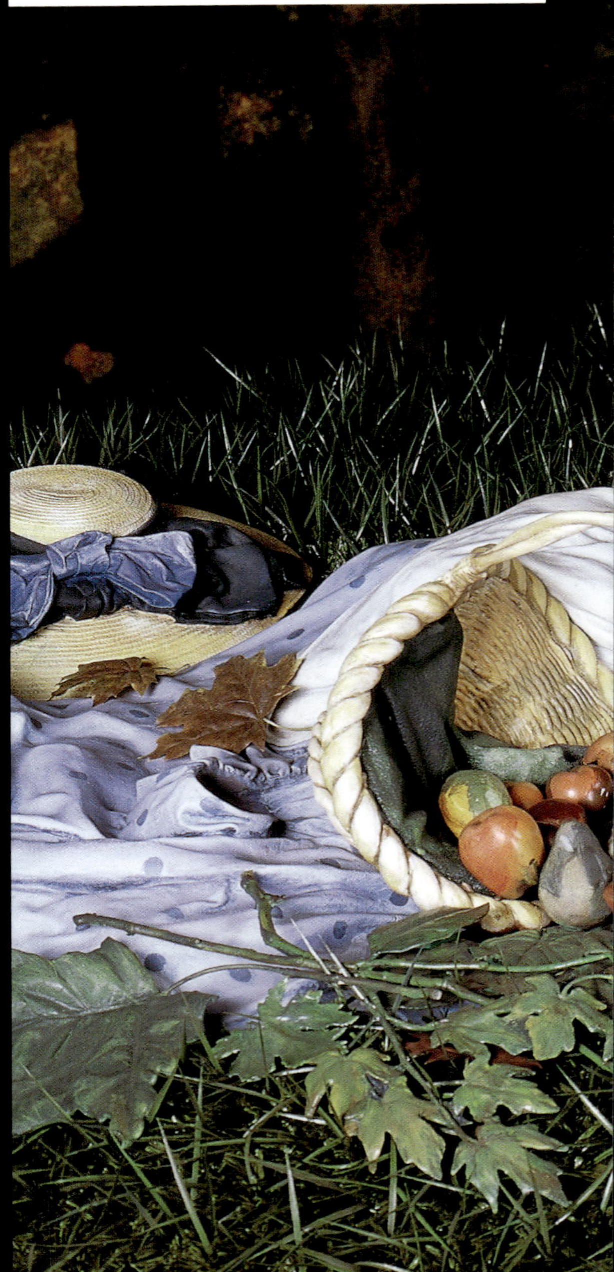

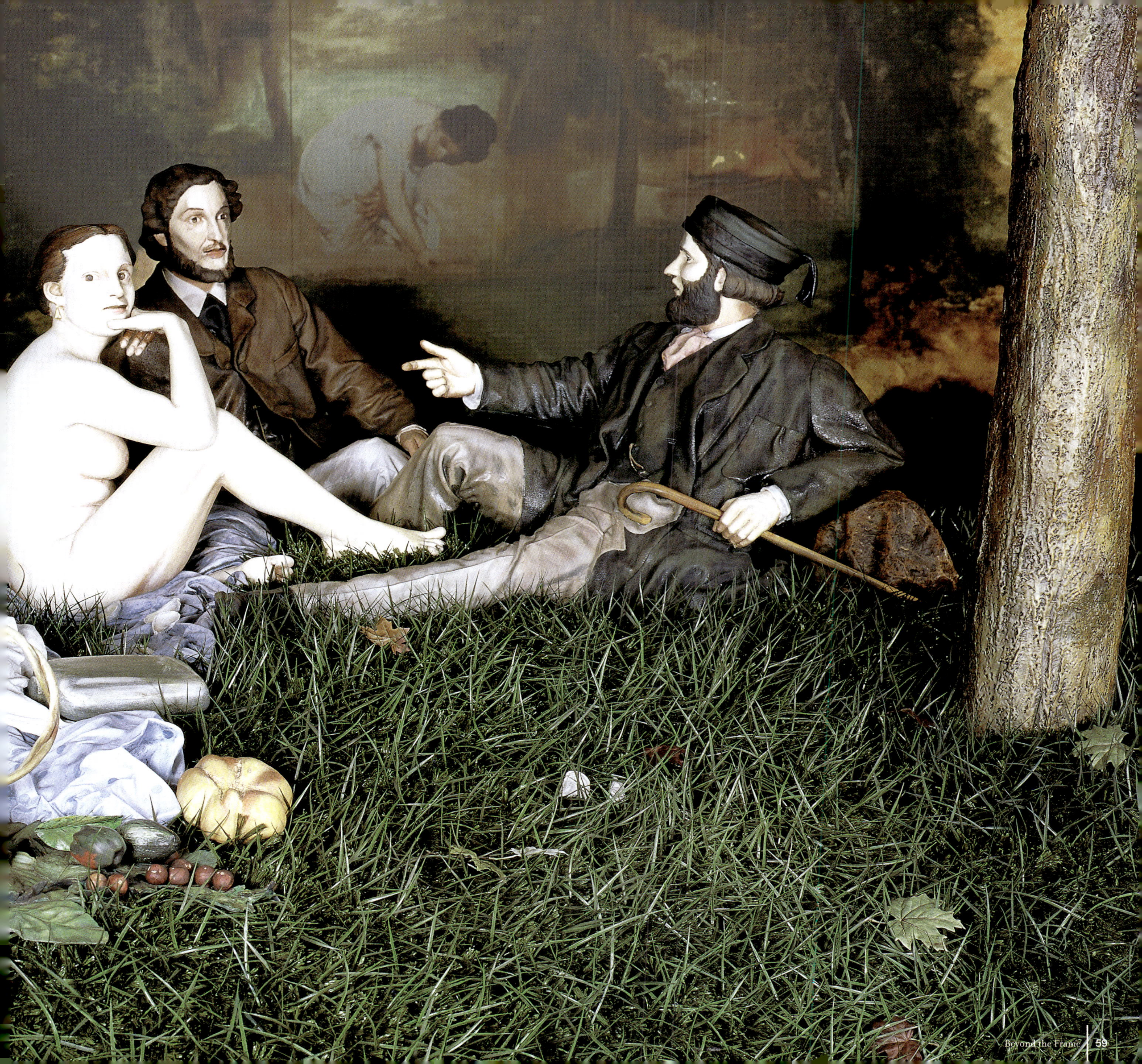

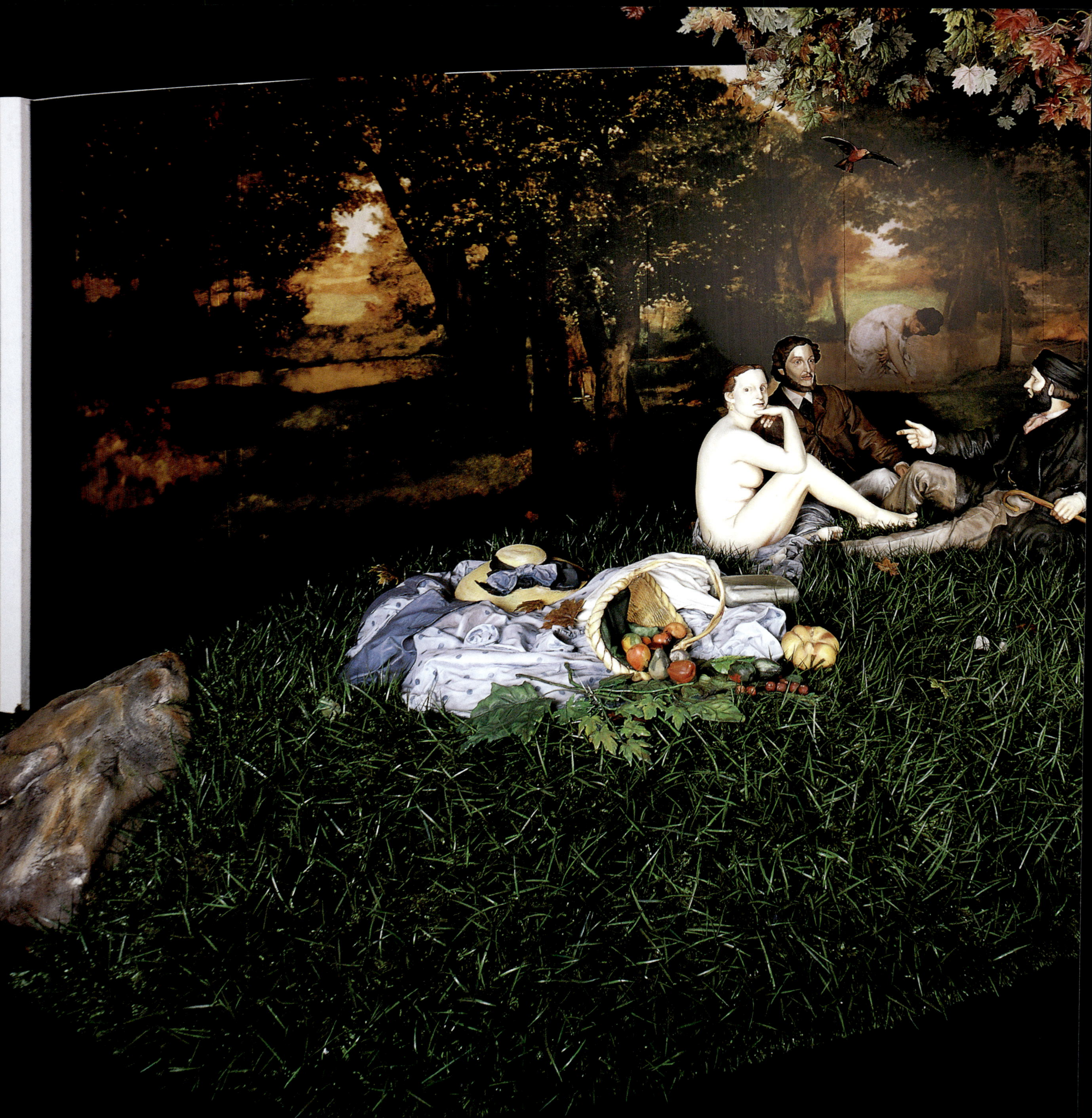

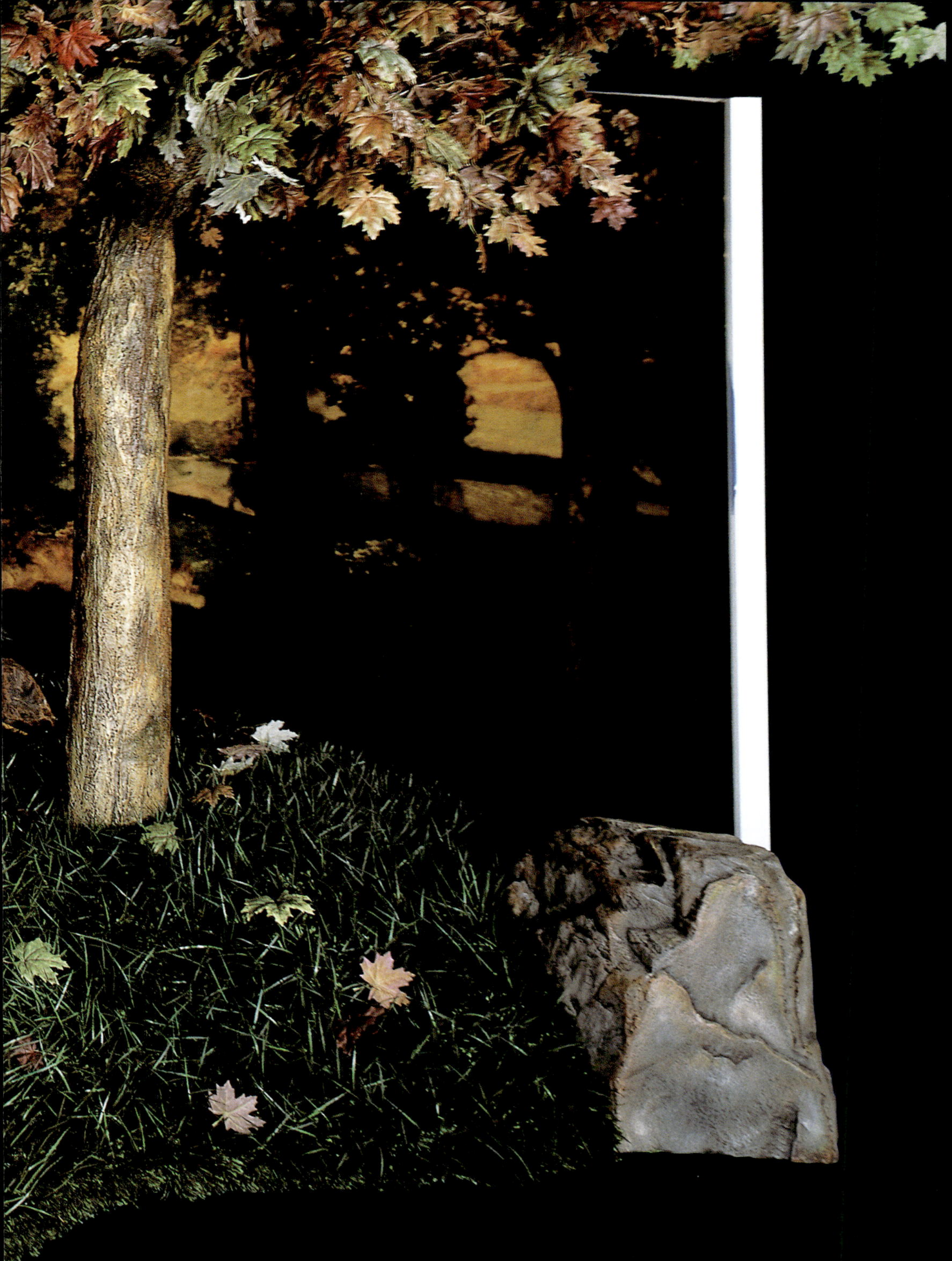

I want my work to disappear into the landscape and then take the viewer by surprise. After he gets over the shock of being fooled it becomes an emotional discovery. Then he owns the sculpture. People often revisit their favorites. They become like friends.

—J. Seward Johnson, Jr.

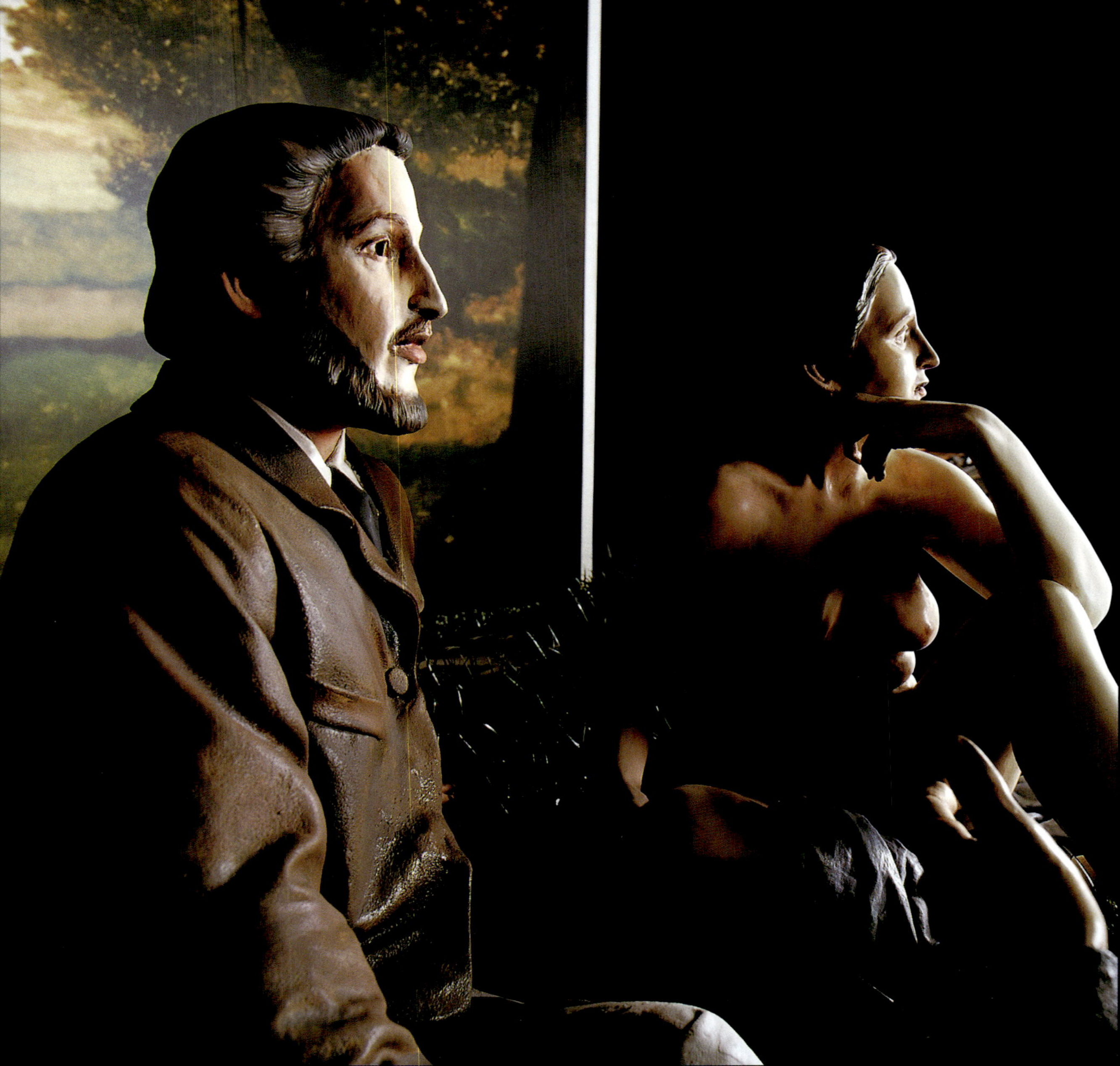

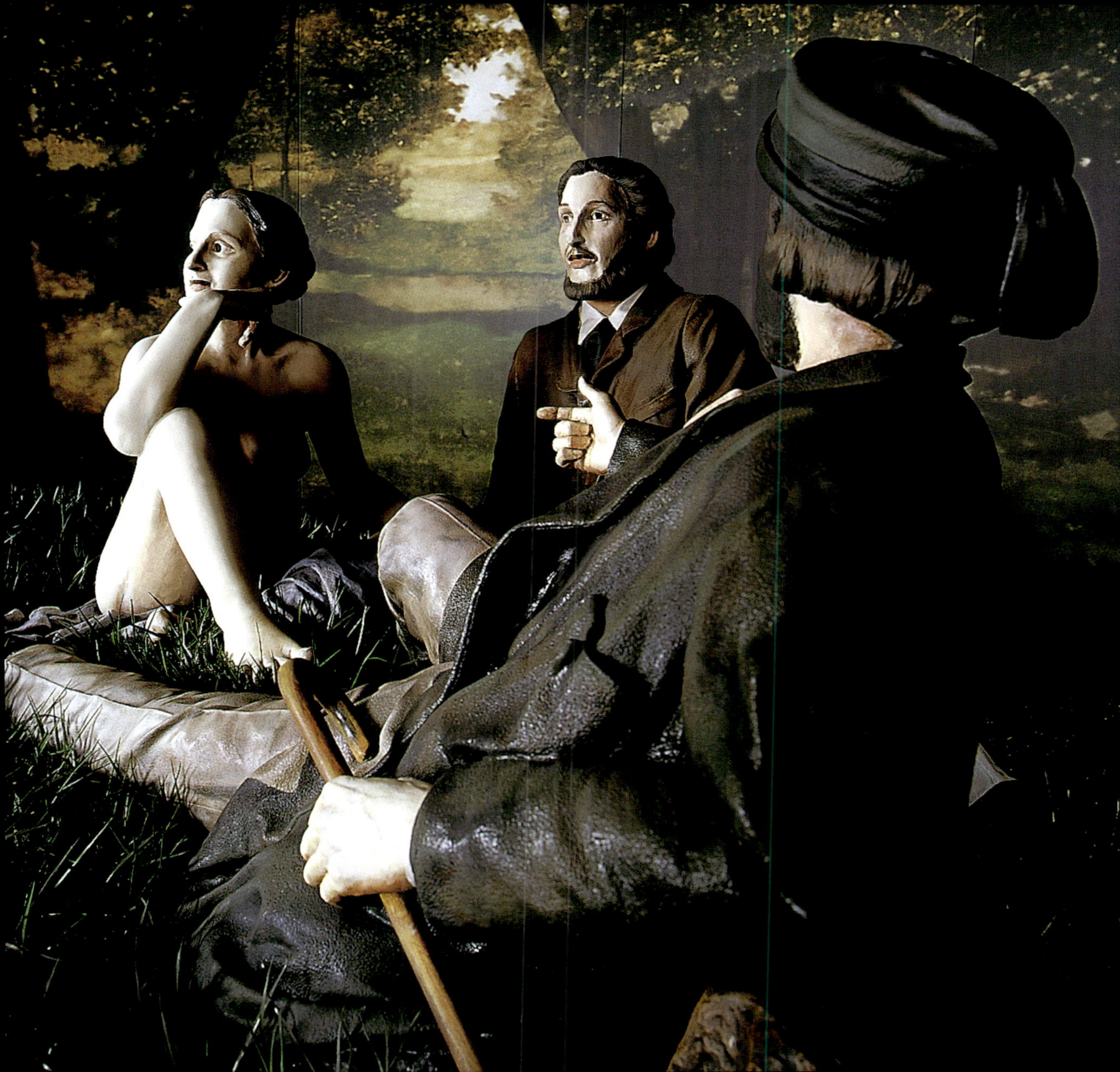

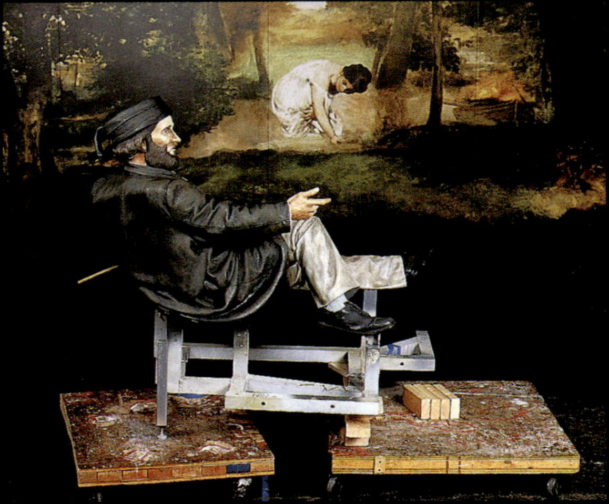
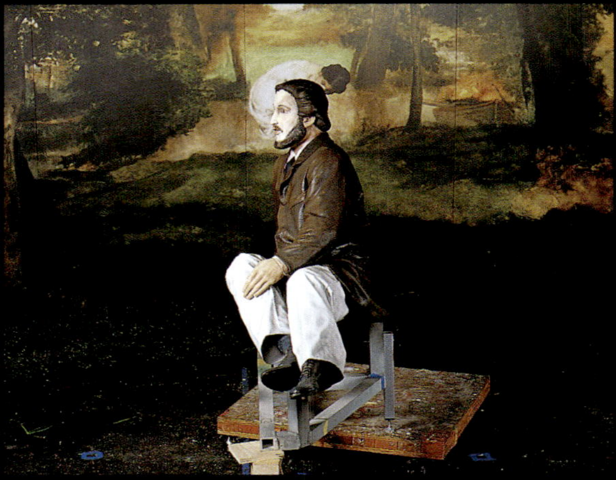
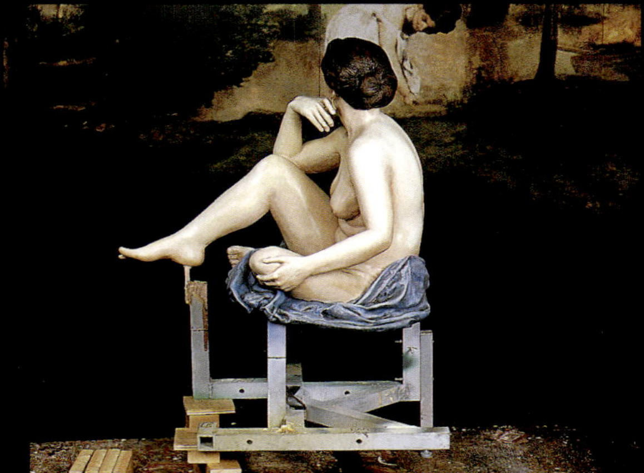

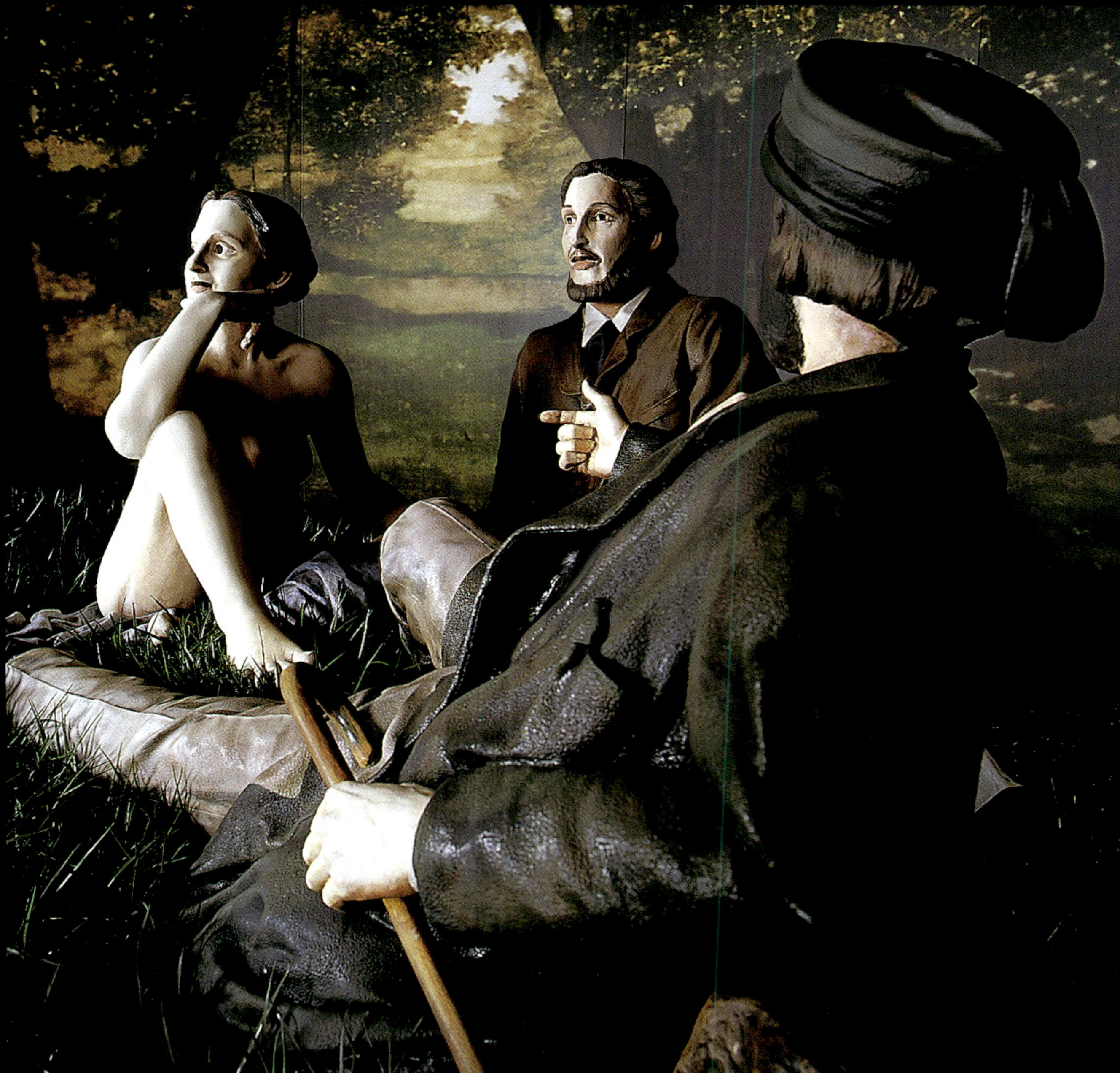

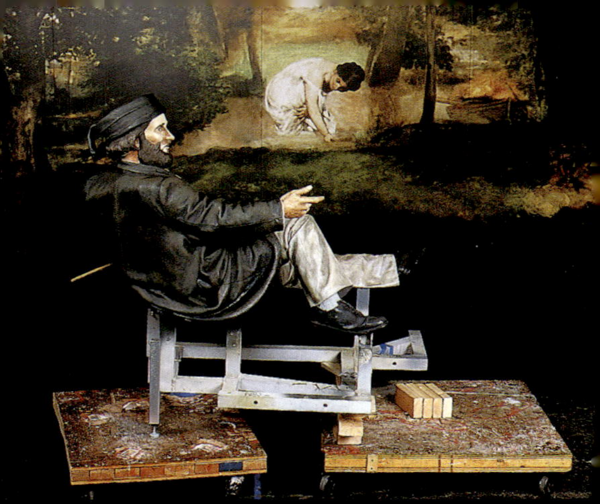

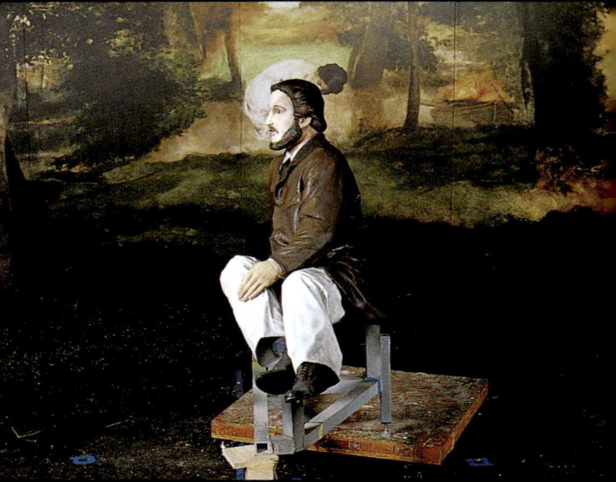

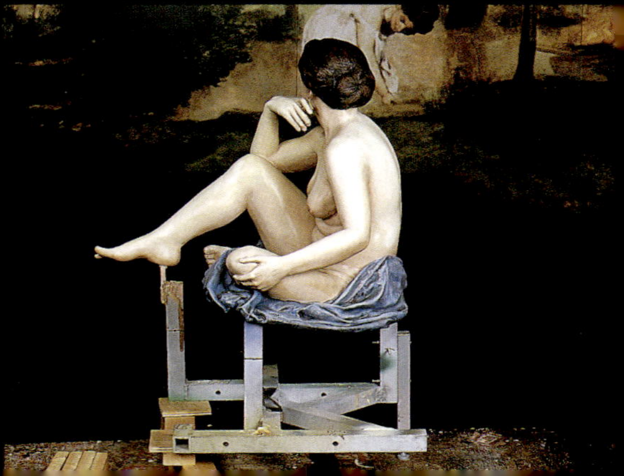

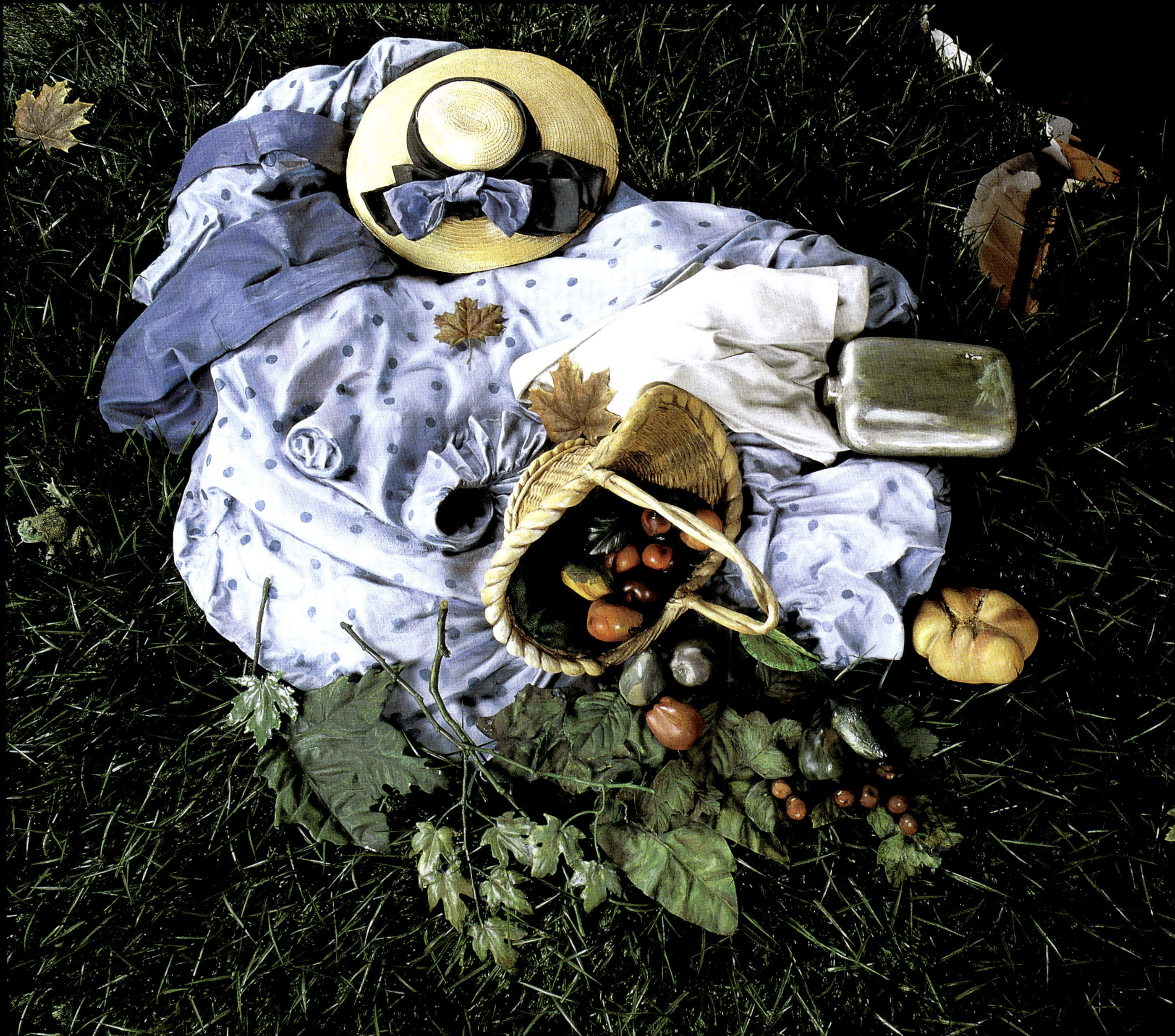

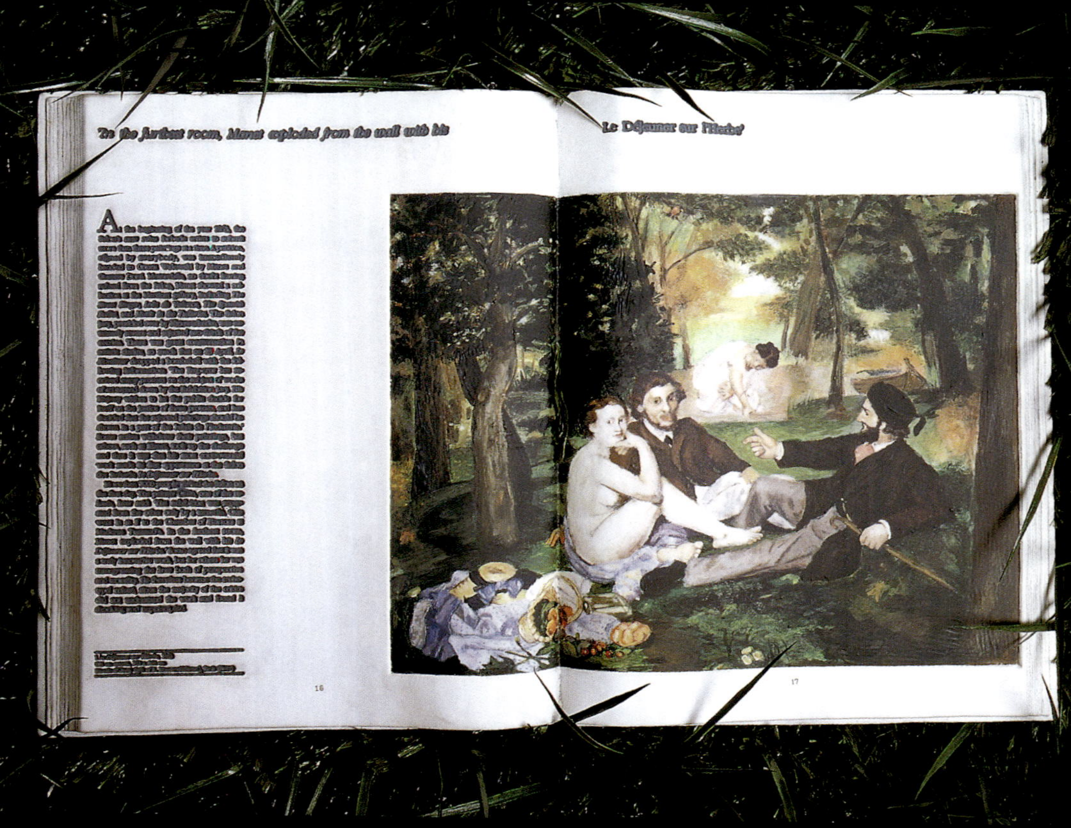

situation makes her much more naked. Manet was making a statement about that. In my piece a book shows the e, and it looks as if they are doing a tableau vivant based on the book.

Seward Johnson, Jr.

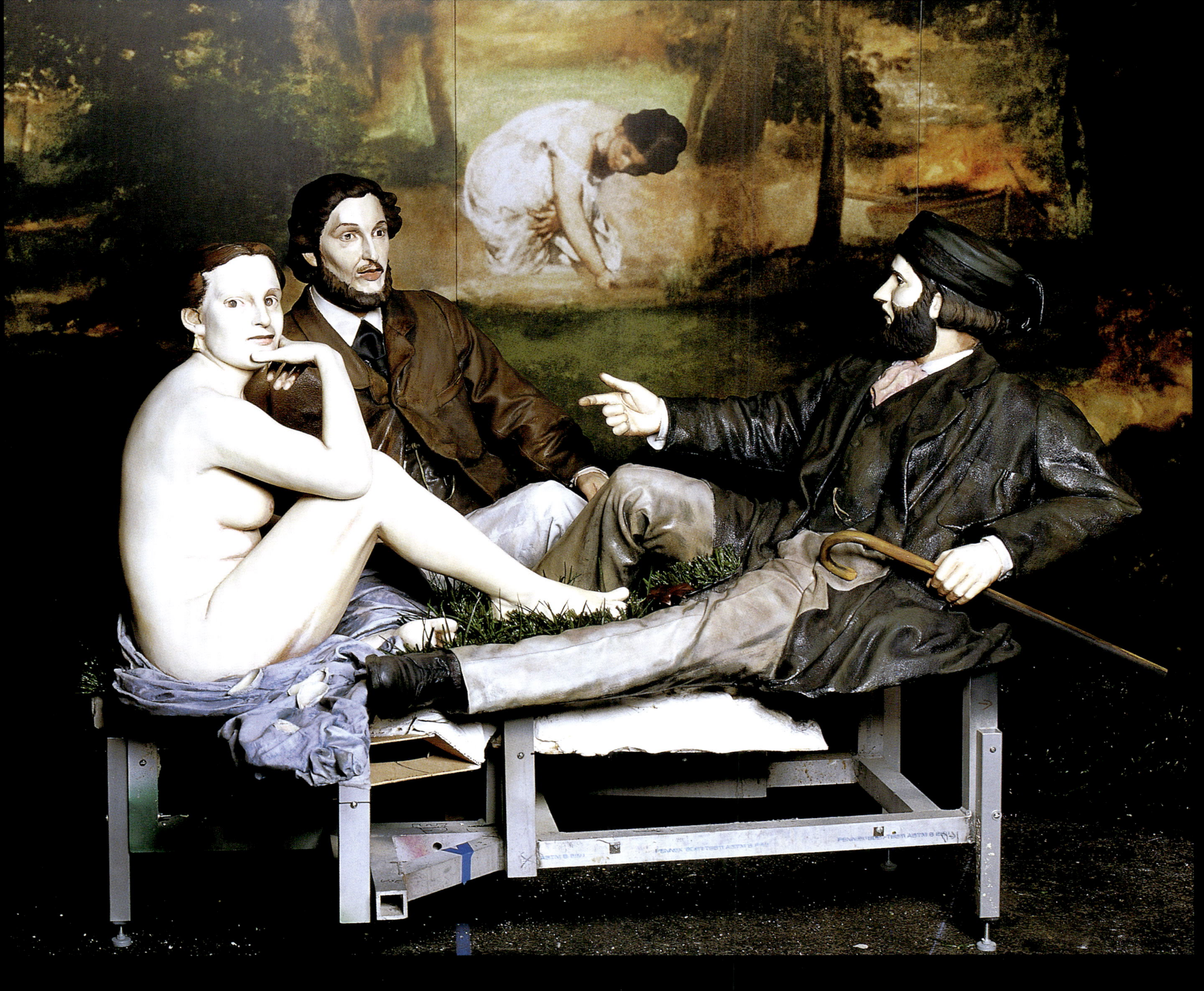

Sailing the Seine

J. Seward Johnson, Jr.

after

Argenteuil 1874

Edouard Manet

Musée des Beaux-Arts de Tournai

> "Boatmen came from various walks of life, but the women they brought with them all belonged to the class of second-rate ladies of pleasure. Such as the one in Argenteuil."

—Théodore Duret

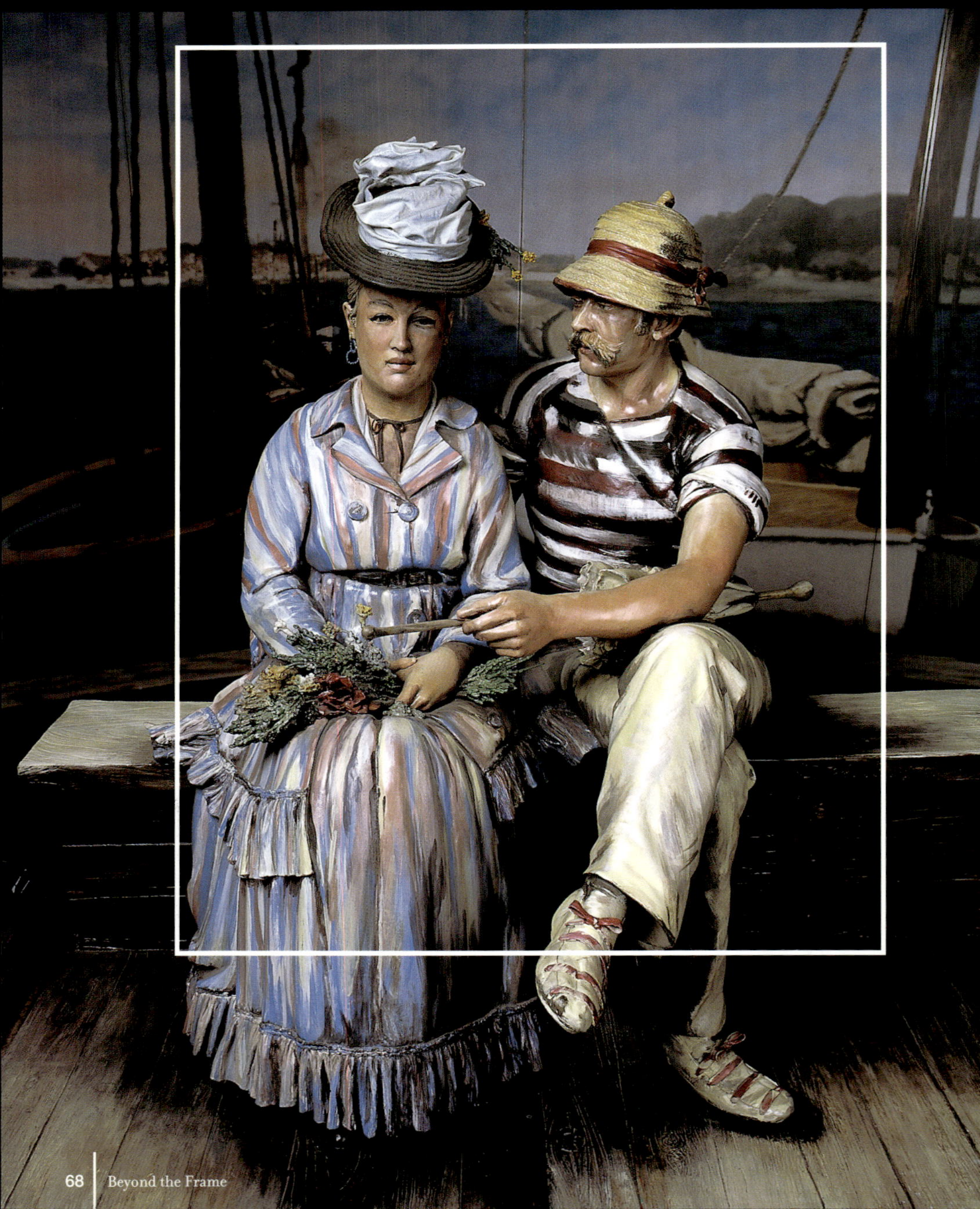

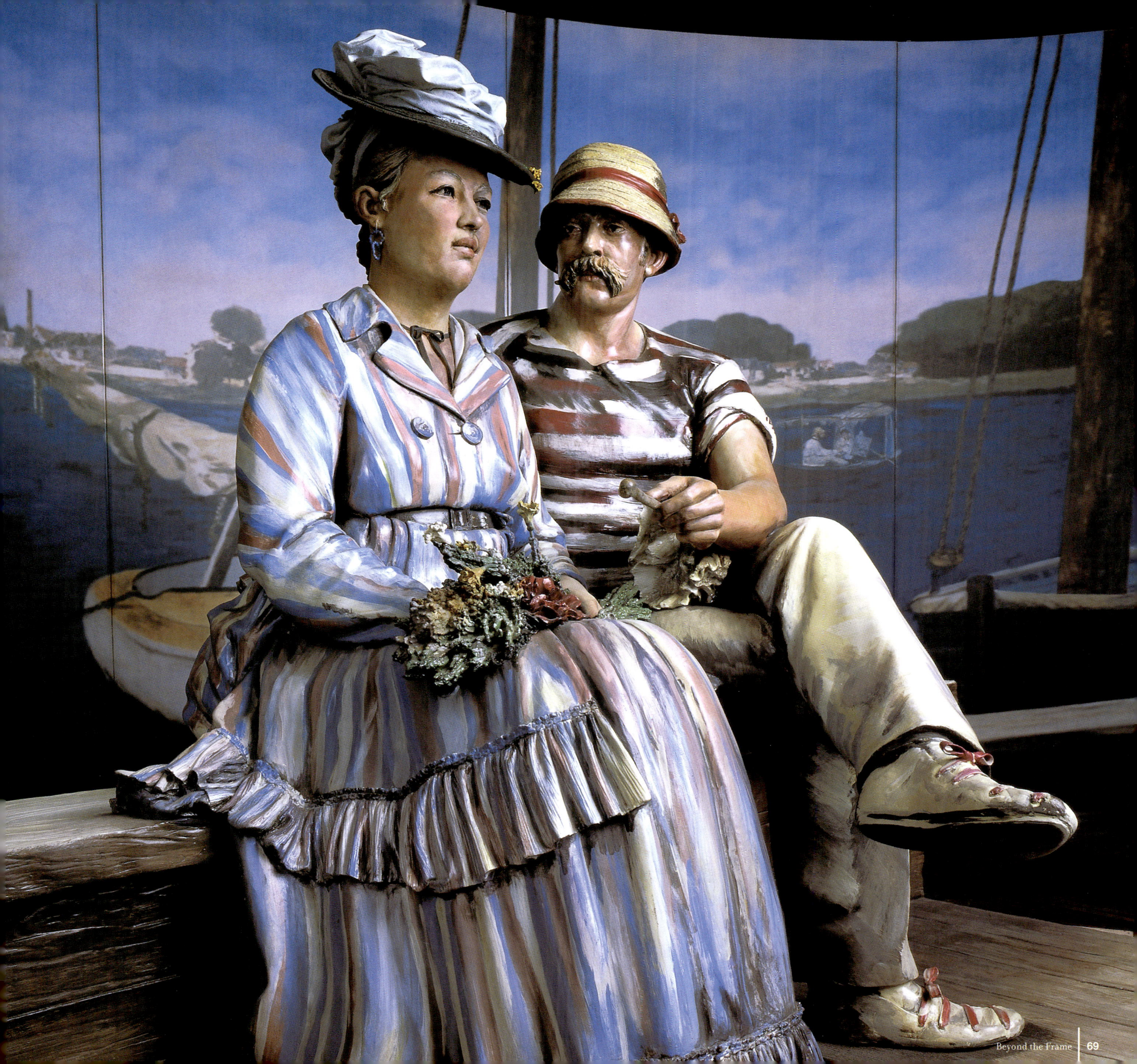

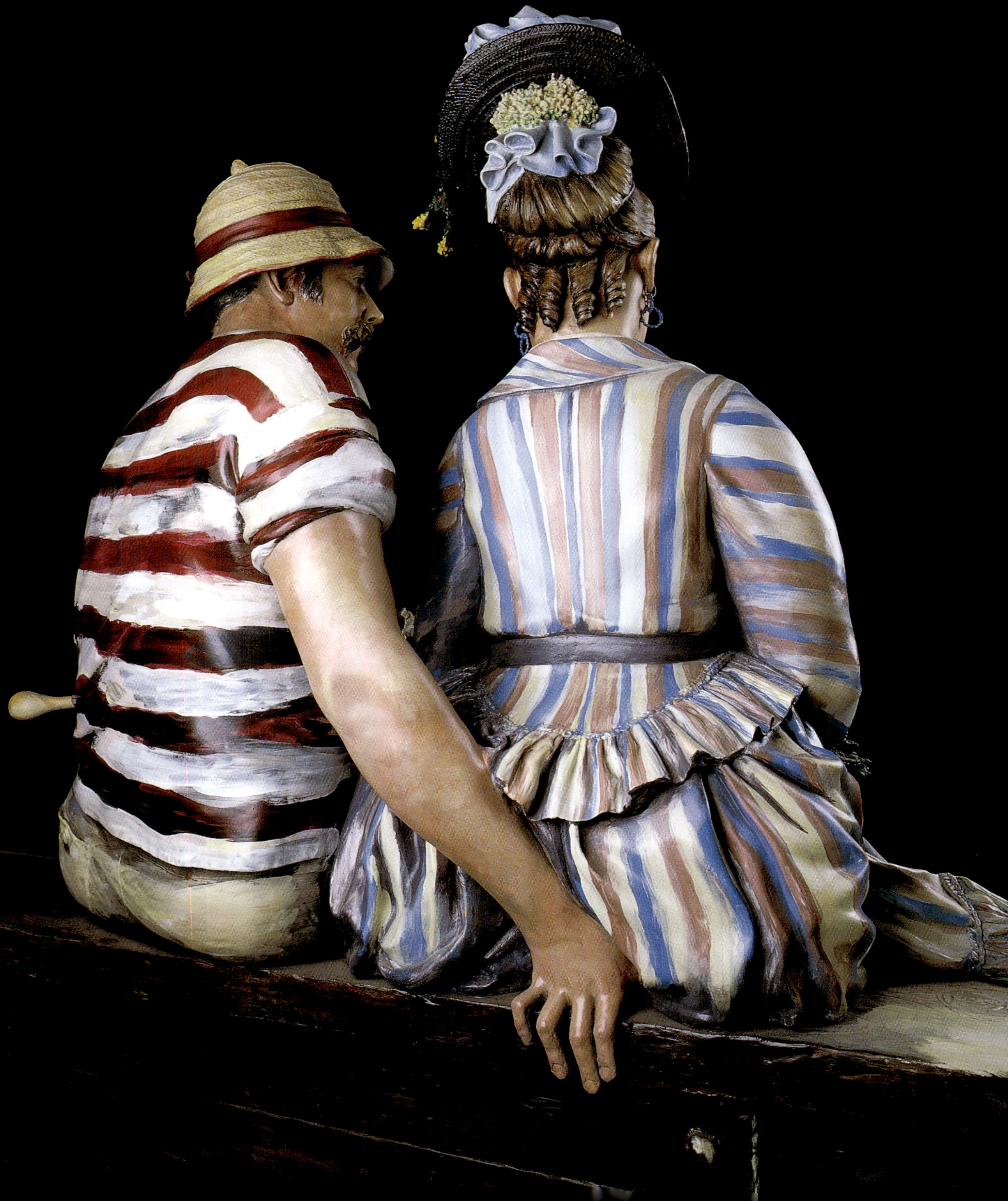

If we had been there to see what else the artist saw but didn't paint we would have seen the relationship between the man and woman. And so I decide what it is and put it in. It is subversive, but it is fair game.

J. Seward Johnson, Jr.

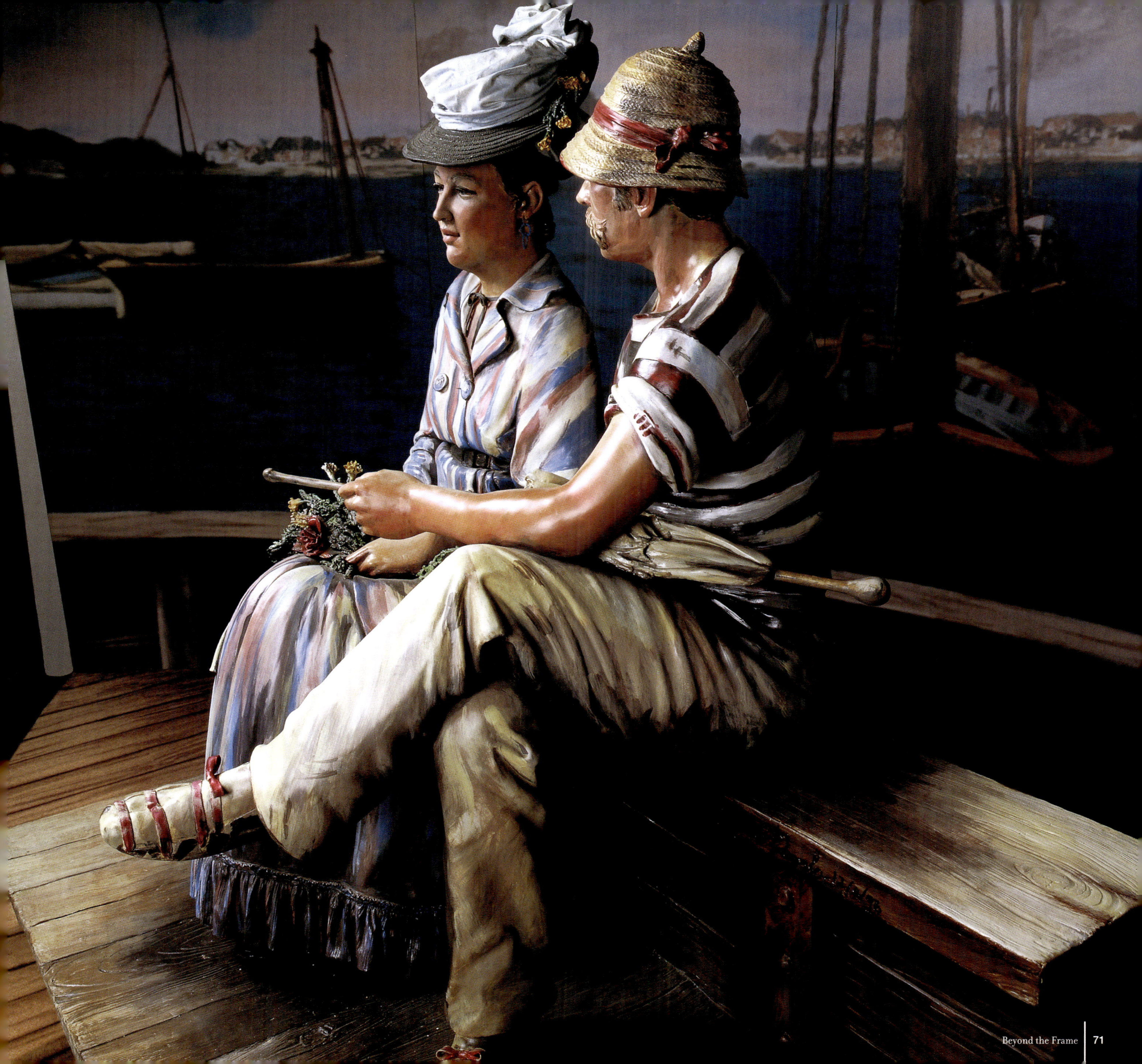

La Promenade

J. Seward Johnson, Jr.

after

Paris Street; A Rainy Day 1887

Gustave Caillebotte

The Art Institute of Chicago

> "These anonymous figures, almost uniformly dressed in grey or black, are as monotonous as the street itself. They appear listless, spiritless, without direction, aptly described by Varnedoe as strolling somnambulants."
>
> —Anne Distel

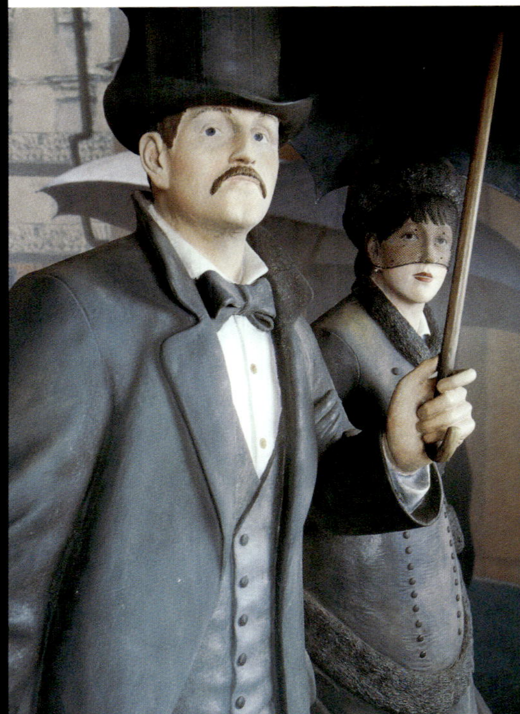

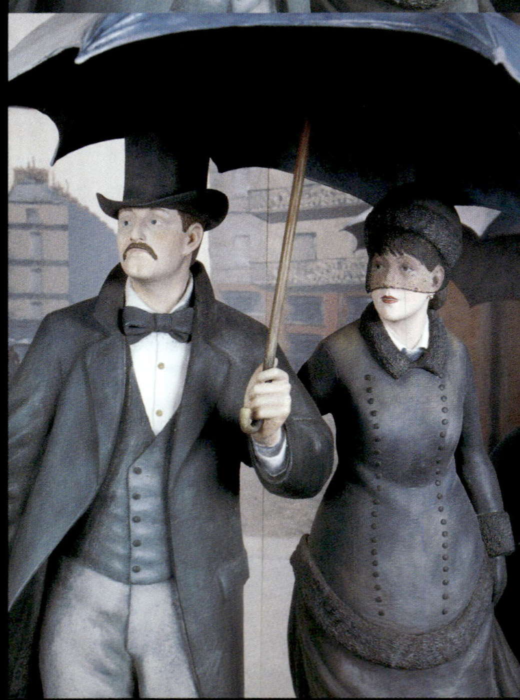

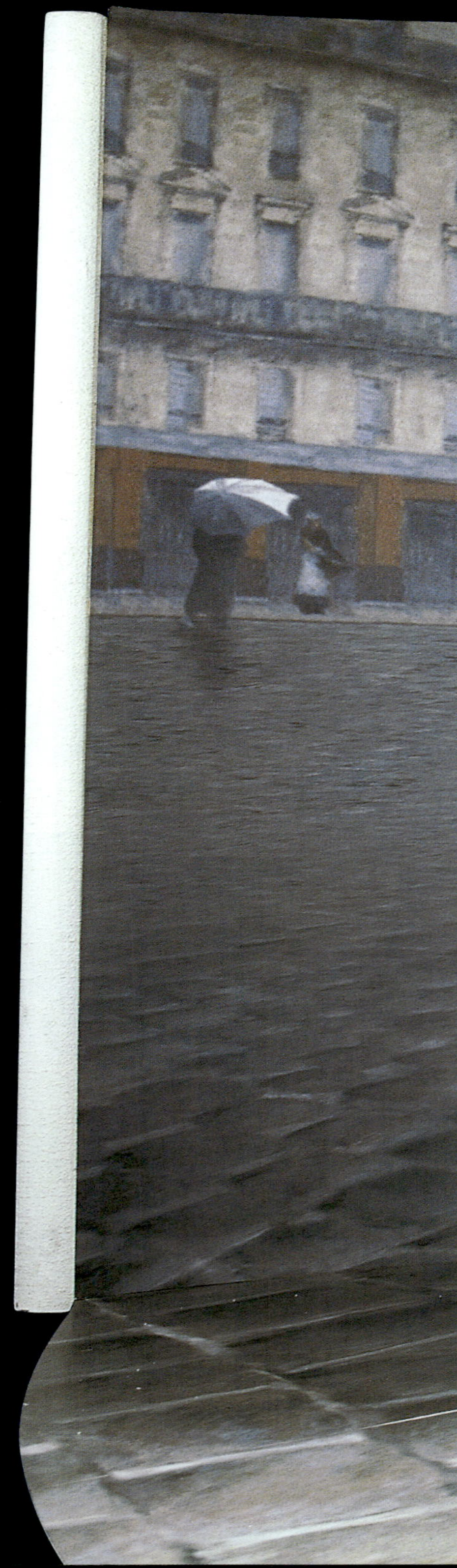

There is always a point, a sweet spot where you see the painting first, and then from there you can get in amongst them and have your picture taken, and involve yourself with the people.

—J. Seward Johnson, Jr.

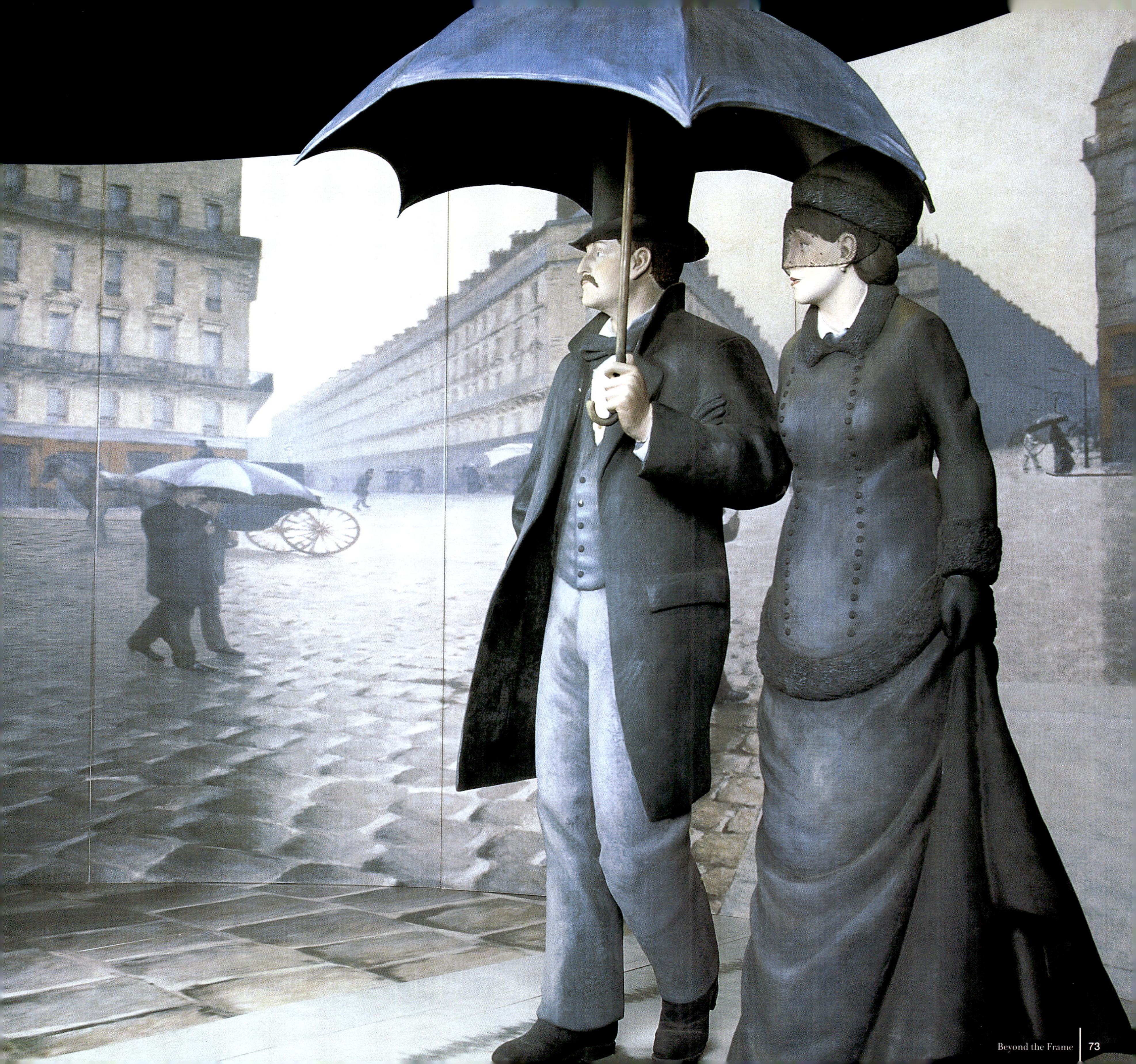

We like to remember the civility of people in the nineteenth century, and the pace of life. When they look at my work people can concentrate on the world they know. And then be surprised and delighted by my interpretation of it.

—J. Seward Johnson, Jr.

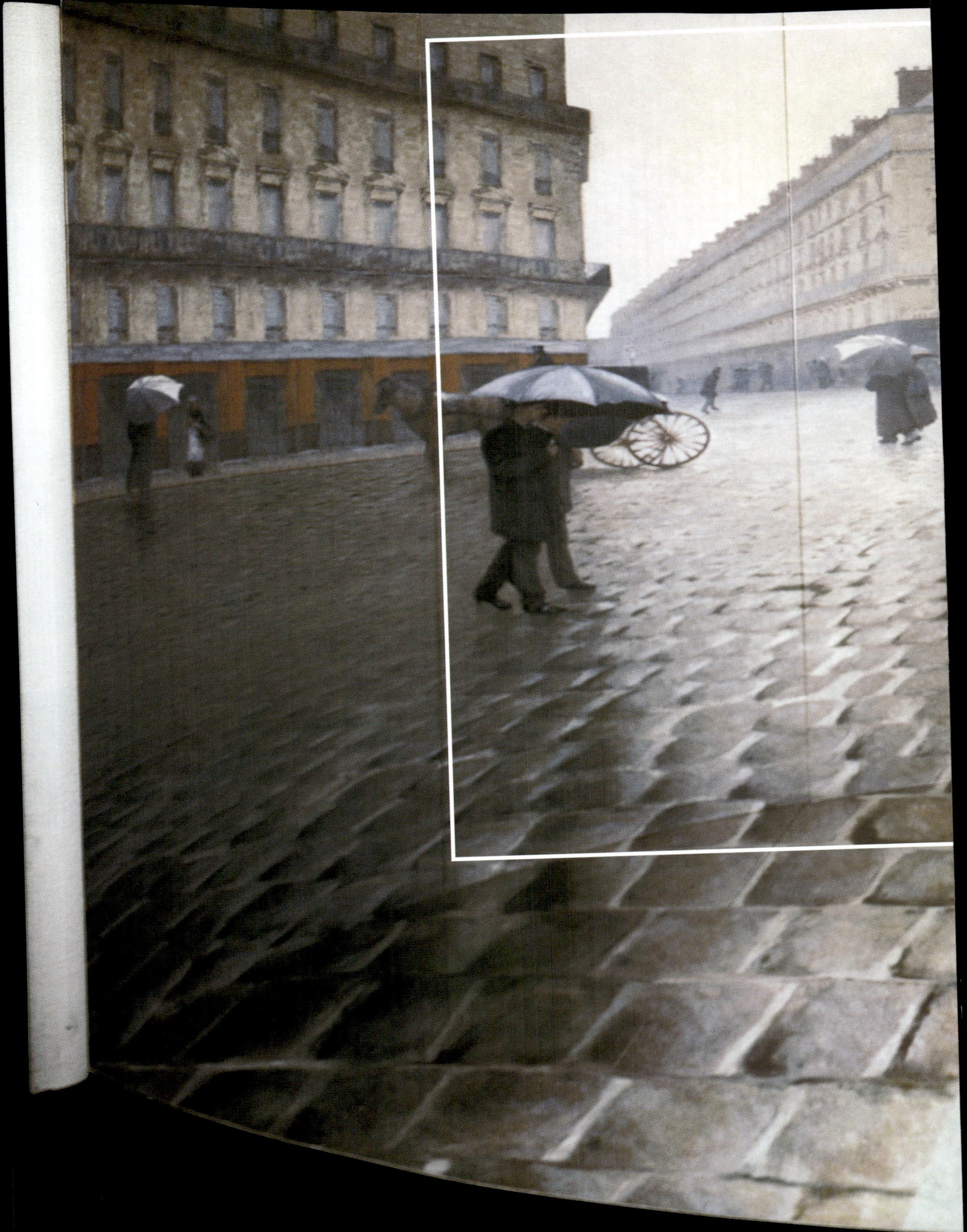

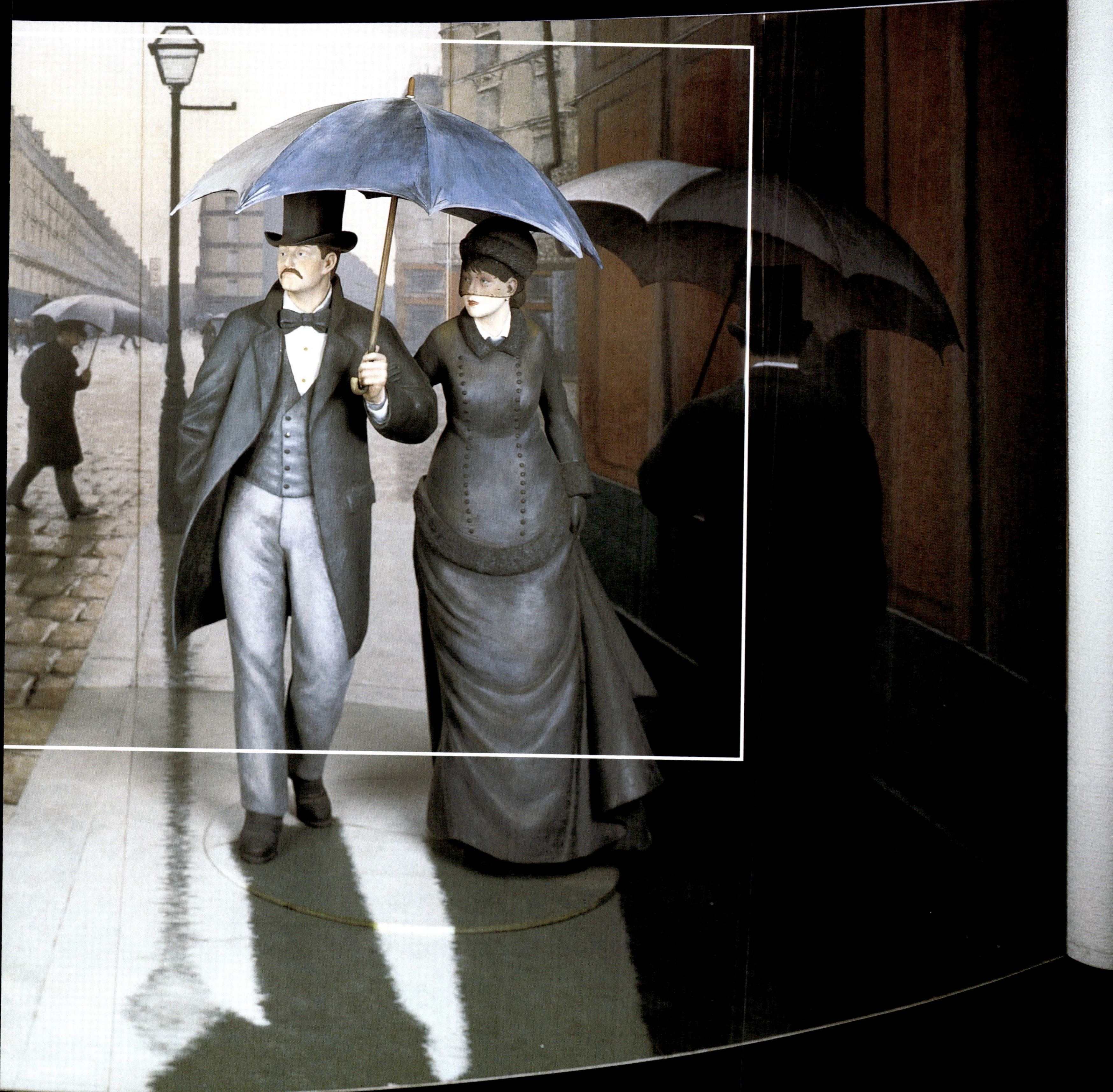

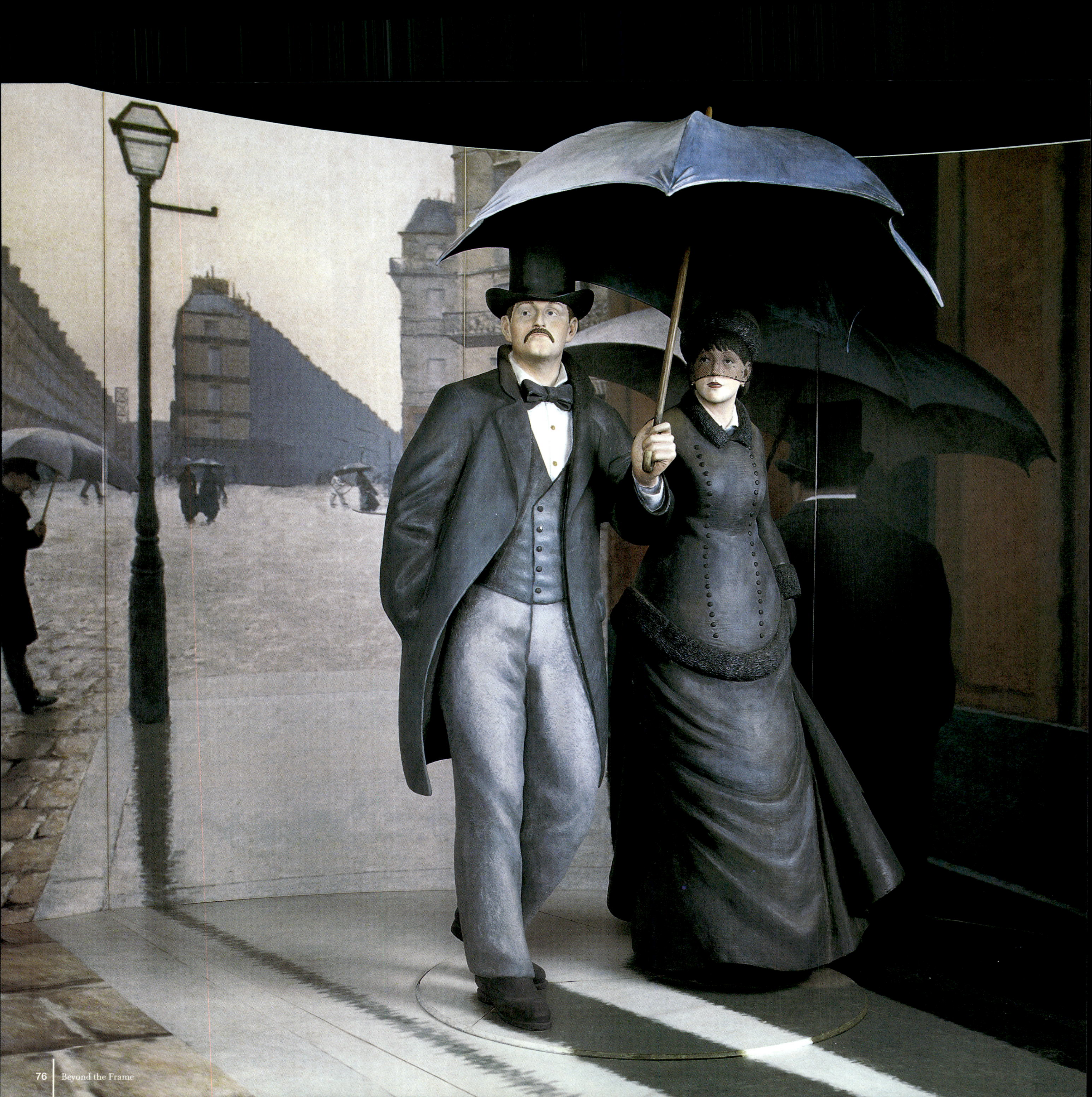

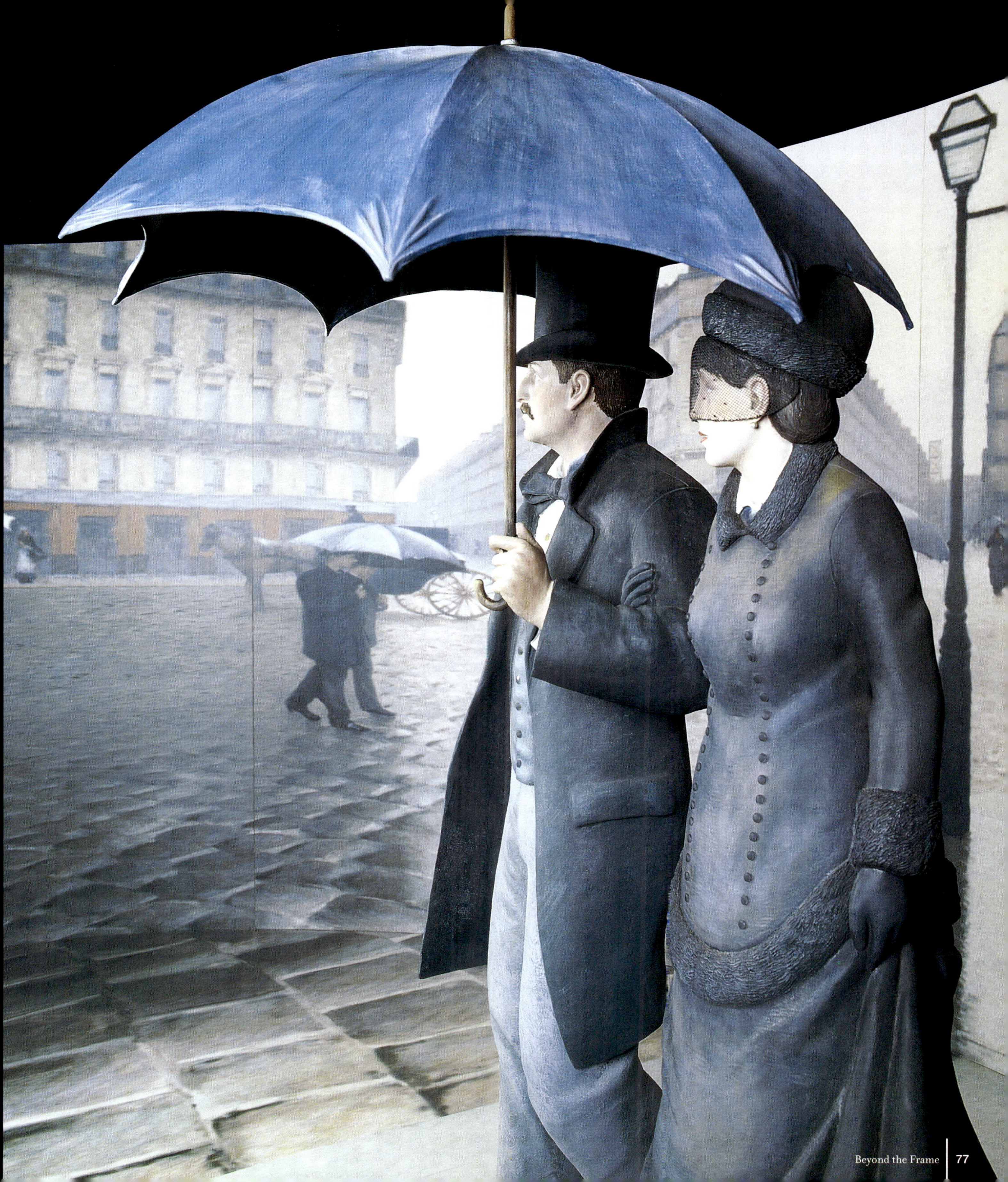

A Thought to Consider

J. Seward Johnson, Jr.

after

In the Winter Garden 1879

Edouard Manet

Nationalgalerie, Staatliche Museen zu Berlin

> "Manet's men and women live imprisoned in their respective inner monologues; even when people share the same spot, the same space, there is an invisible barrier between them."

—Werner Hofmann

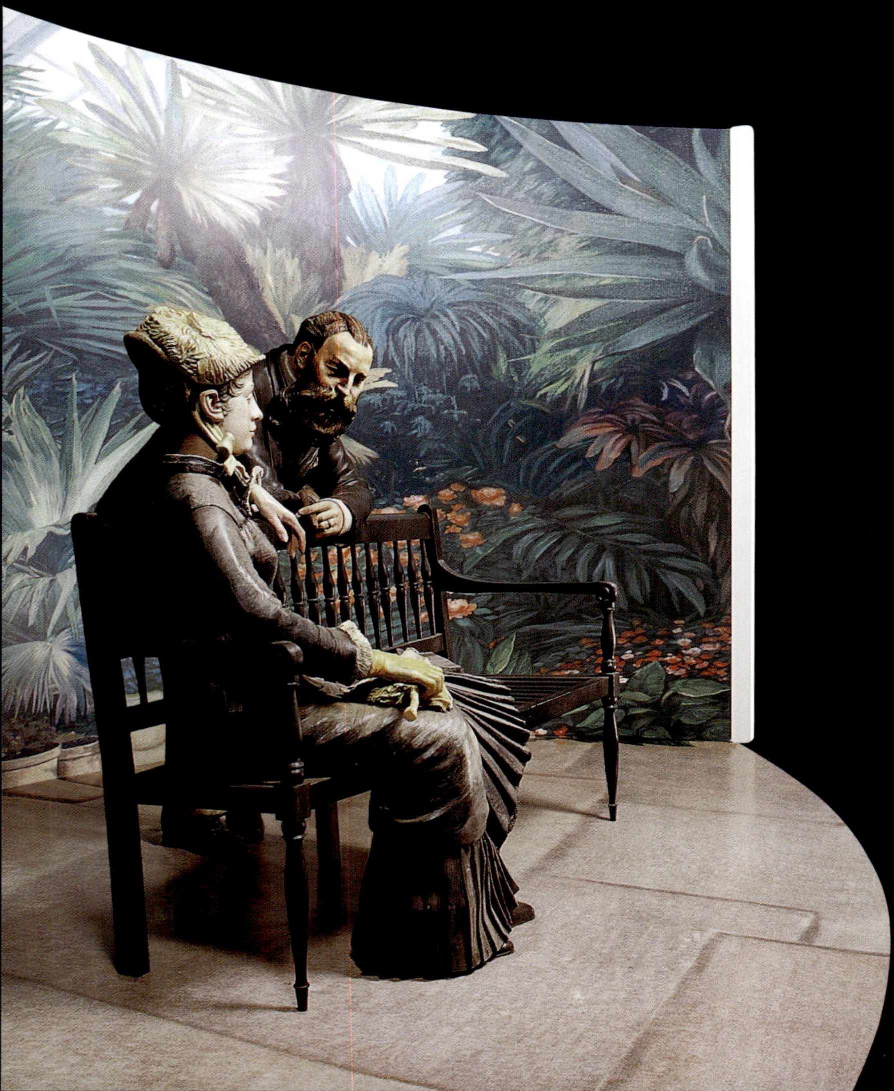

When the artist is having fun he is creating his life. And that is what I am doing. I learned so much about the work. I read about Manet and built my knowledge about the painting, getting to know every square centimeter of it.

—J. Seward Johnson, Jr.

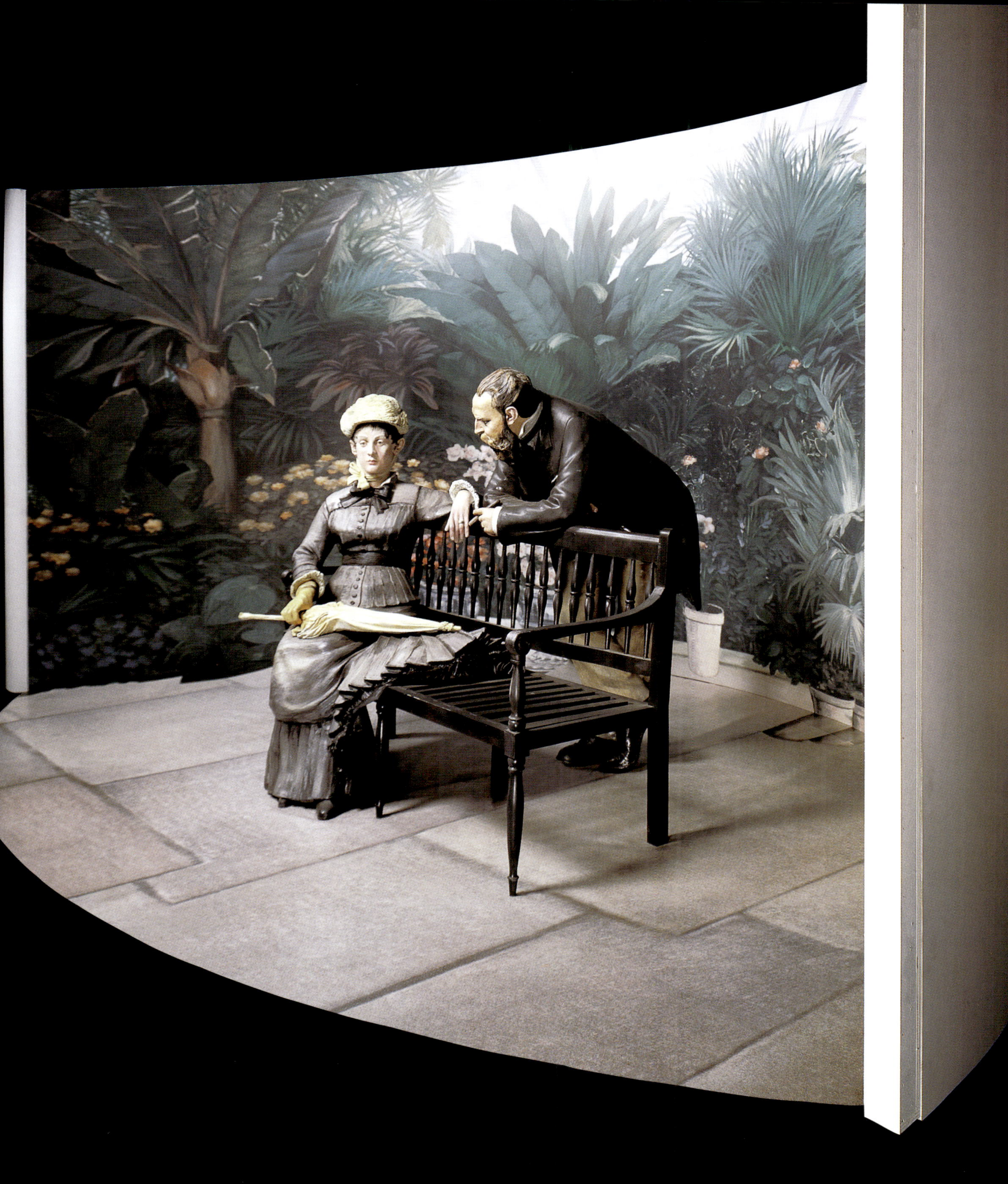

> "Figures in Manet's work are lonely in crowds, disconnected in pairs, totally oblivious to each other, or subtly detached."

—B. Collins

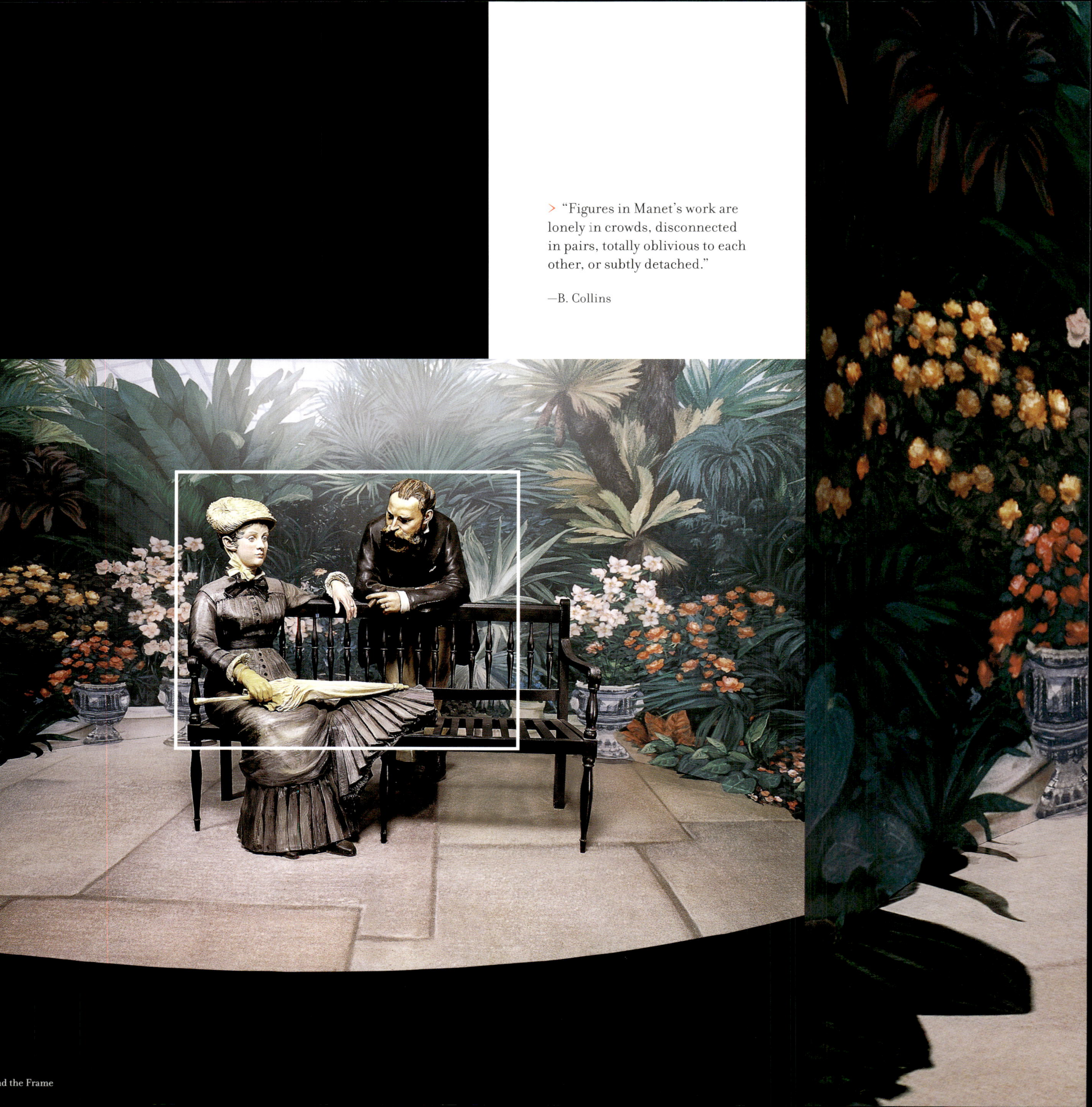

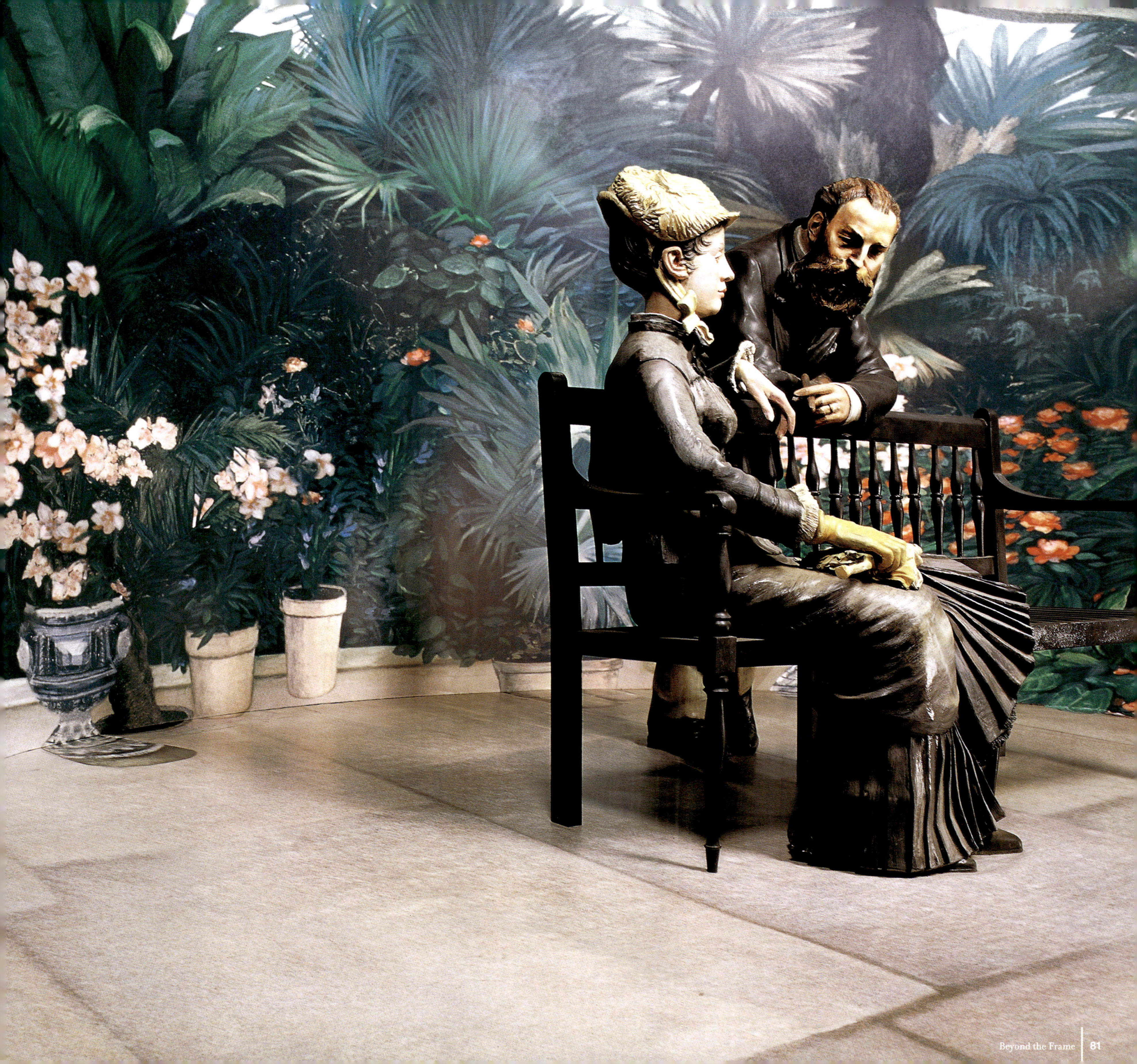

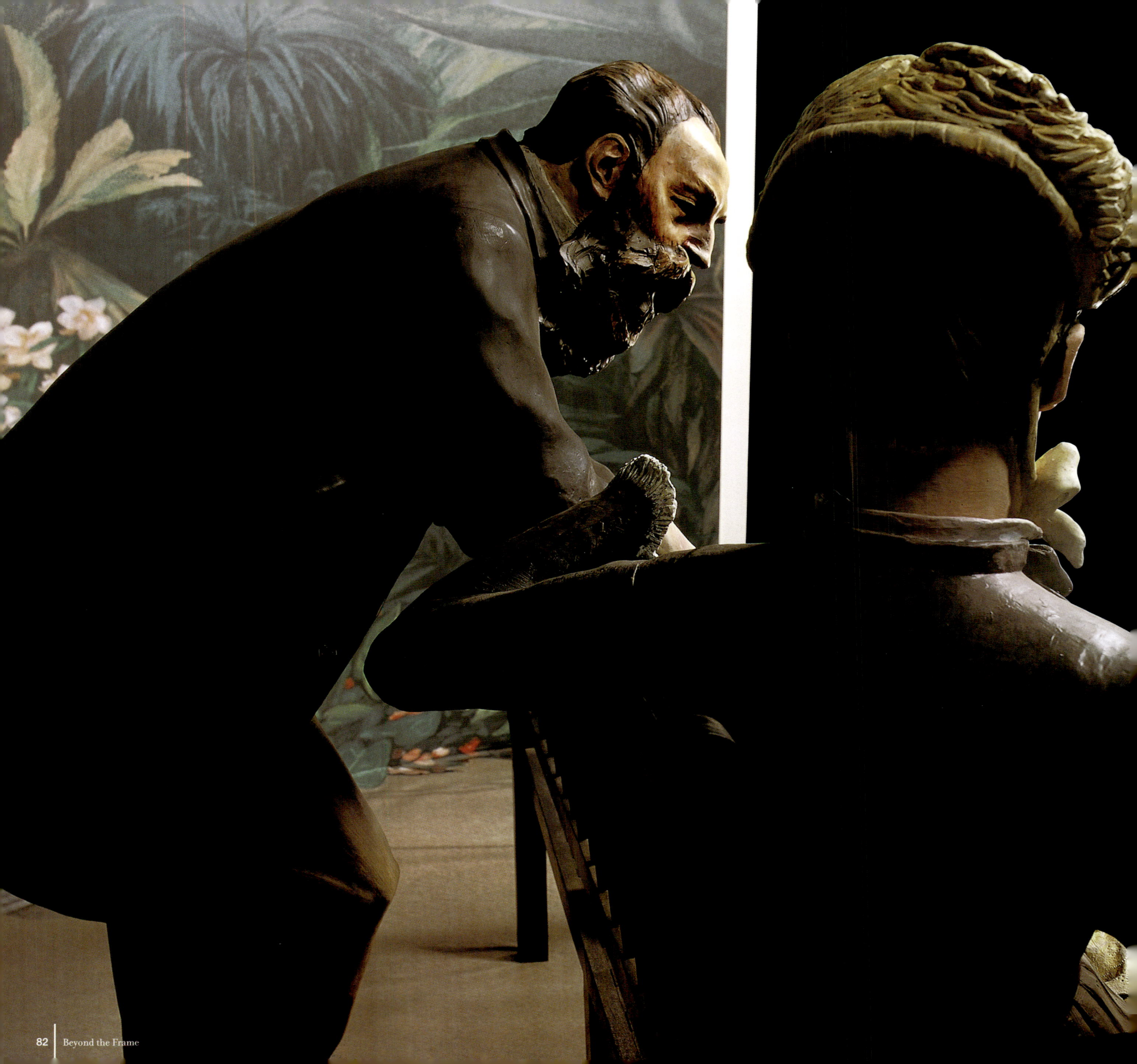

> "She is self-possessed, lost in thought. There is not a hint of flirtation anywhere. In fact, during the moment of the painting, the woman ignores her companion, who, it turns out, is her husband."

—Eunice Lipton

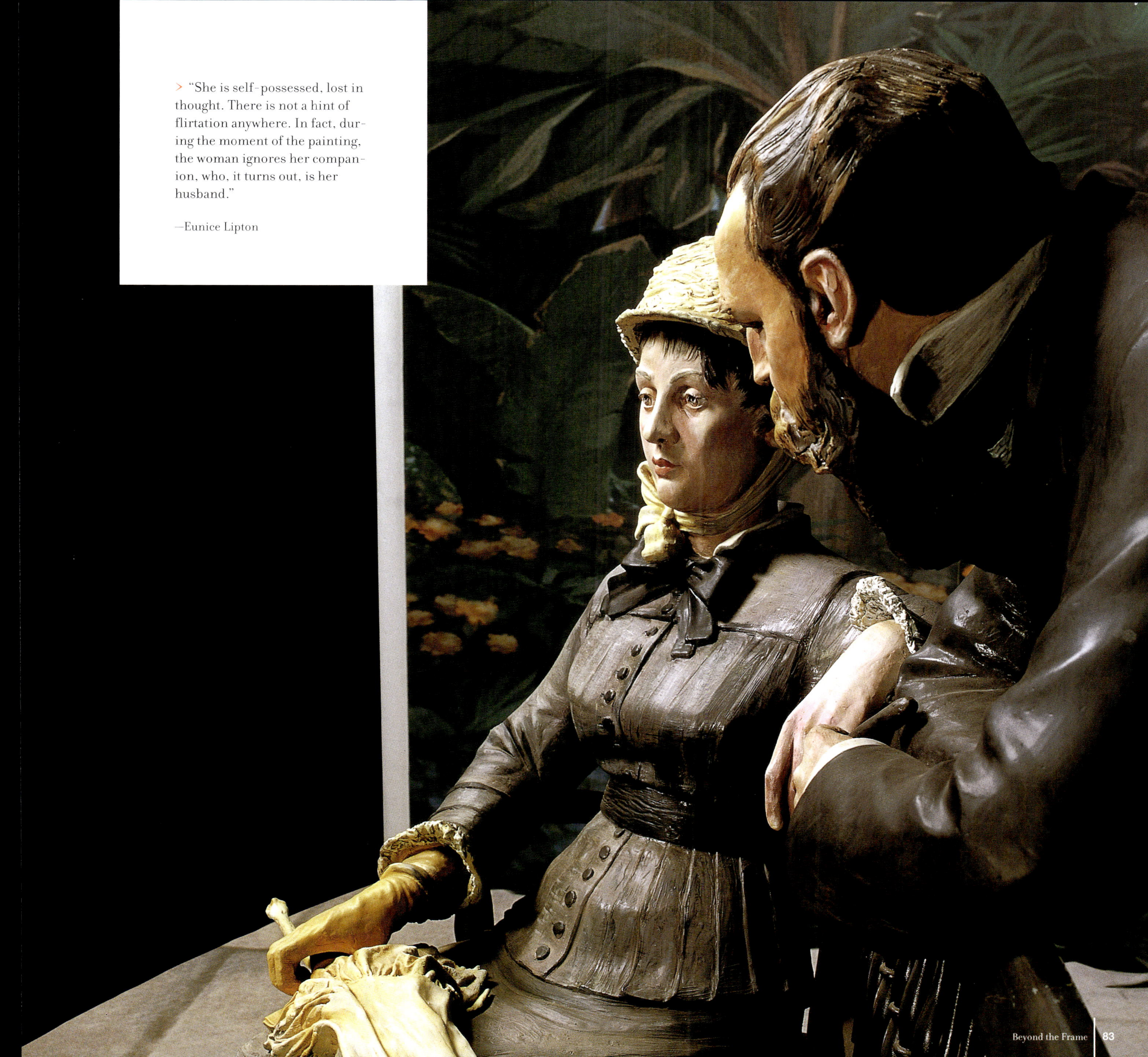

Were You Invited?

J. Seward Johnson, Jr.

after

Luncheon of the Boating Party 1880–81

Pierre-Auguste Renoir

The Phillips Collection, Washington, DC

> "On his own terms Renoir compresses into one image the example of the past and vitality of the present. This duality is the foundation of Renoir's best work and is nowhere more eloquently and successfully expressed than in *Luncheon of the Boating Party*."

—Elizabeth Steele

> "Much of the painting's success lies in the convincing interaction that Renoir creates among his sitters. Their arrangement in twos and threes leads the eye back and forth across the table and through the composition to the rear of the balcony. It is the complexity of the scene that makes the painting so intriguing, and it demonstrates the painter's mastery of strong compositional skills."

—Elizabeth Steele

> *Un Déjeuner à Bougival* [*Luncheon of the Boating Party*] is a charming work, full of gaiety and spirit, its wild youth caught in the act, radiant and lively, frolicking at high noon in the sun, laughing at everything, seeing only today and mocking tomorrow. For them eternity is in their glass, in their boat, and in their songs. It is fresh and free without being too bawdy.

— Paul de Charry

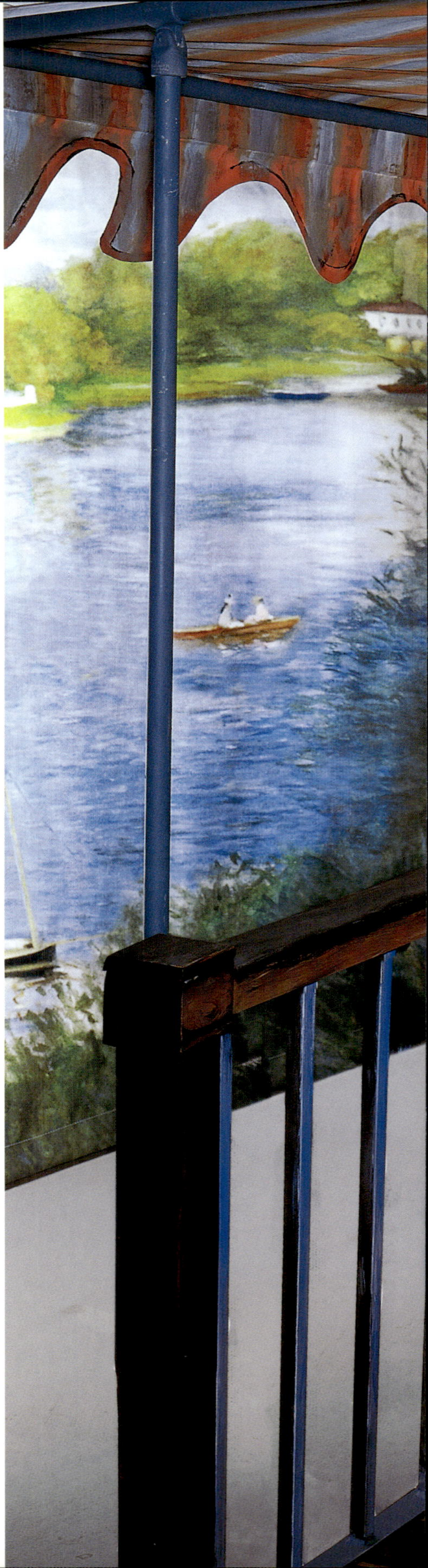

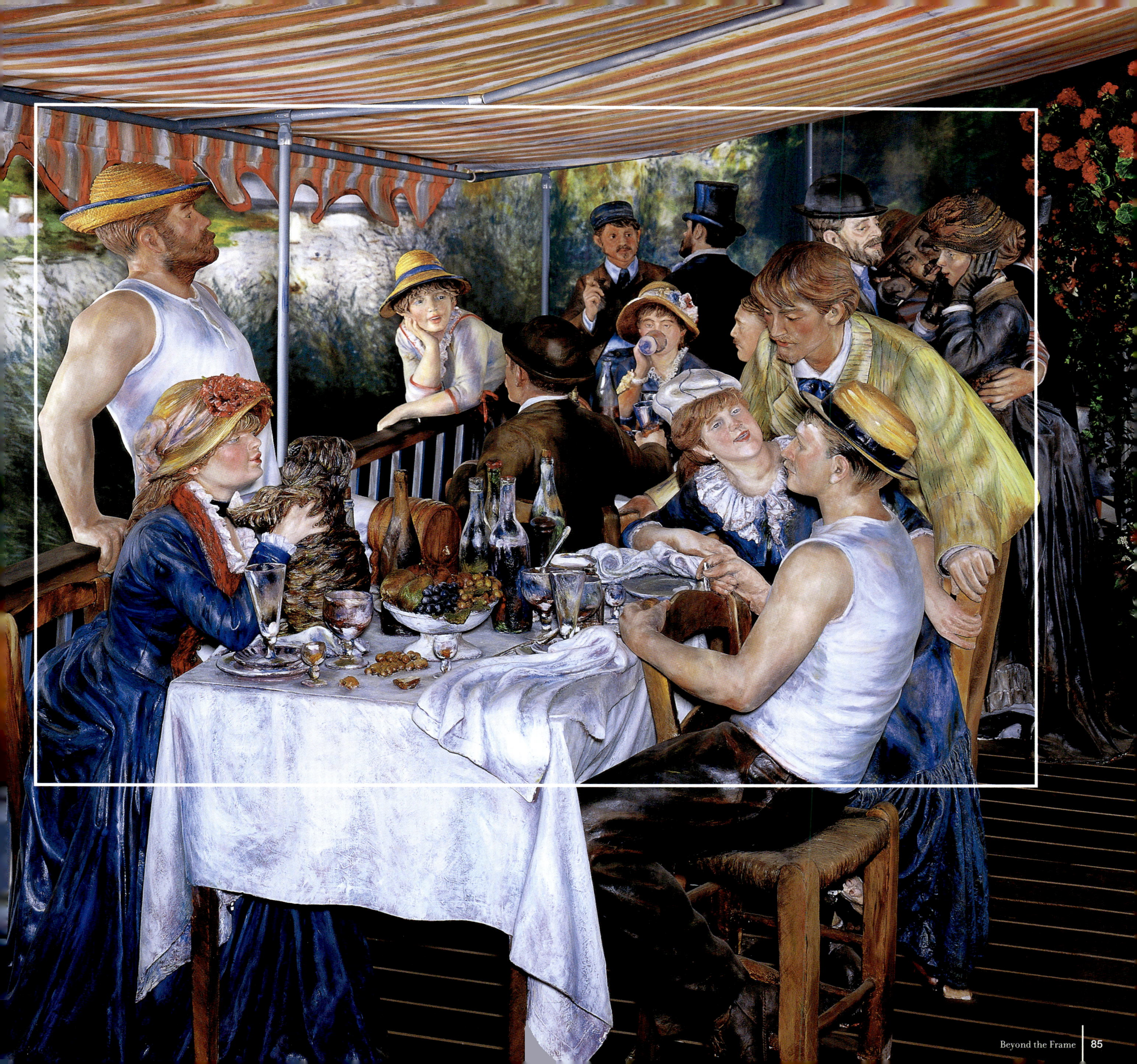

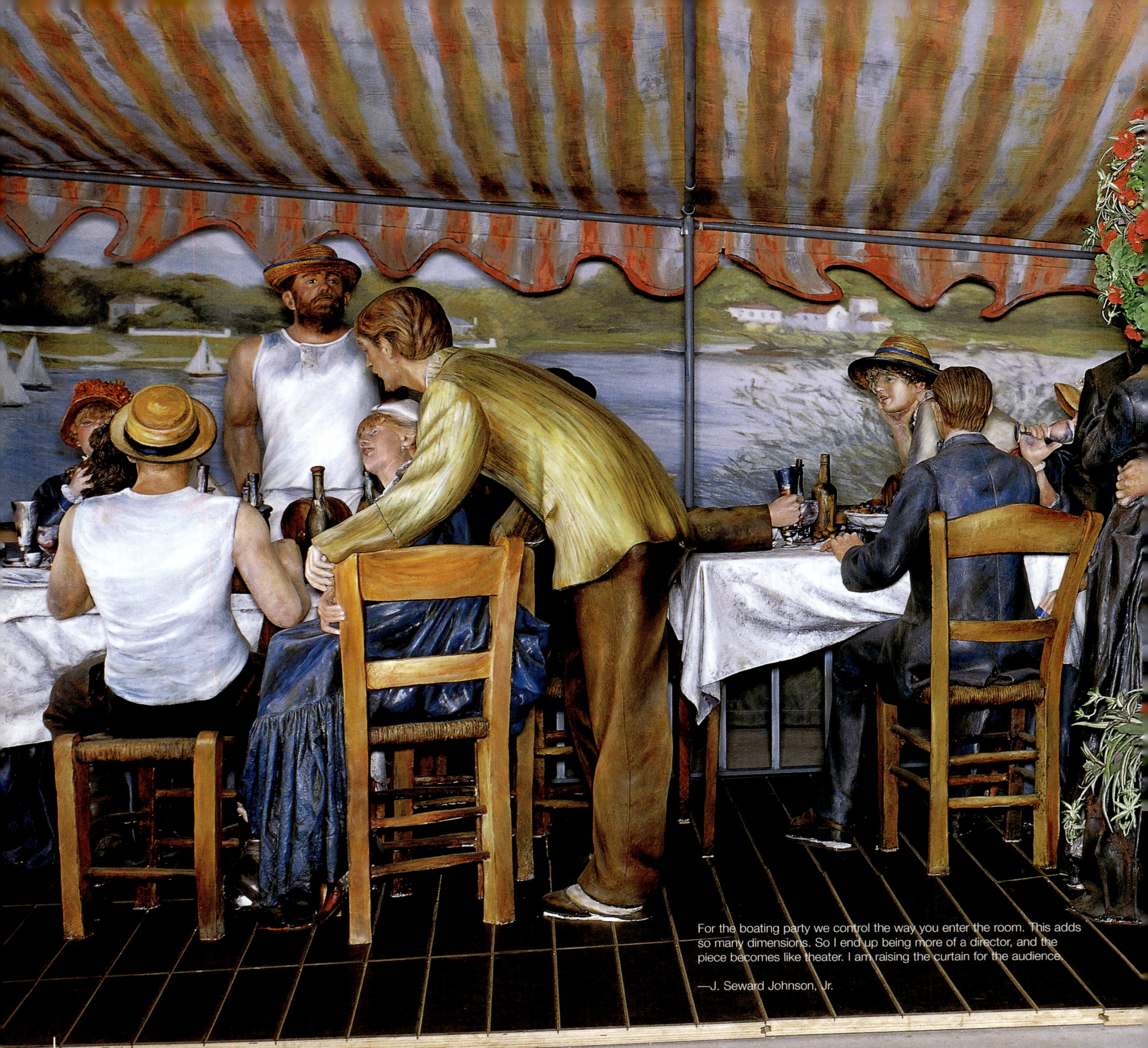

For the boating party we control the way you enter the room. This adds so many dimensions. So I end up being more of a director, and the piece becomes like theater. I am raising the curtain for the audience.

—J. Seward Johnson, Jr.

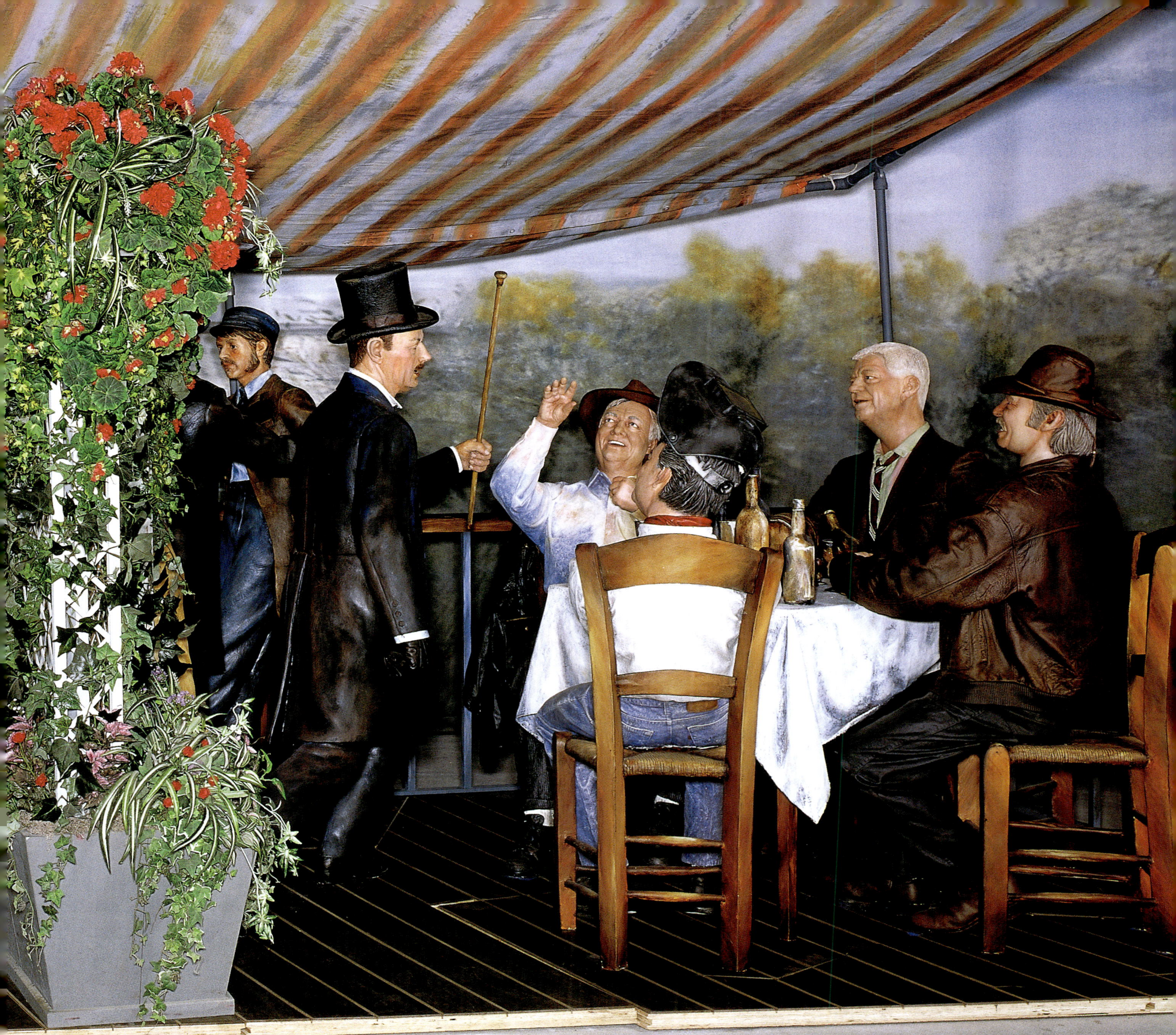

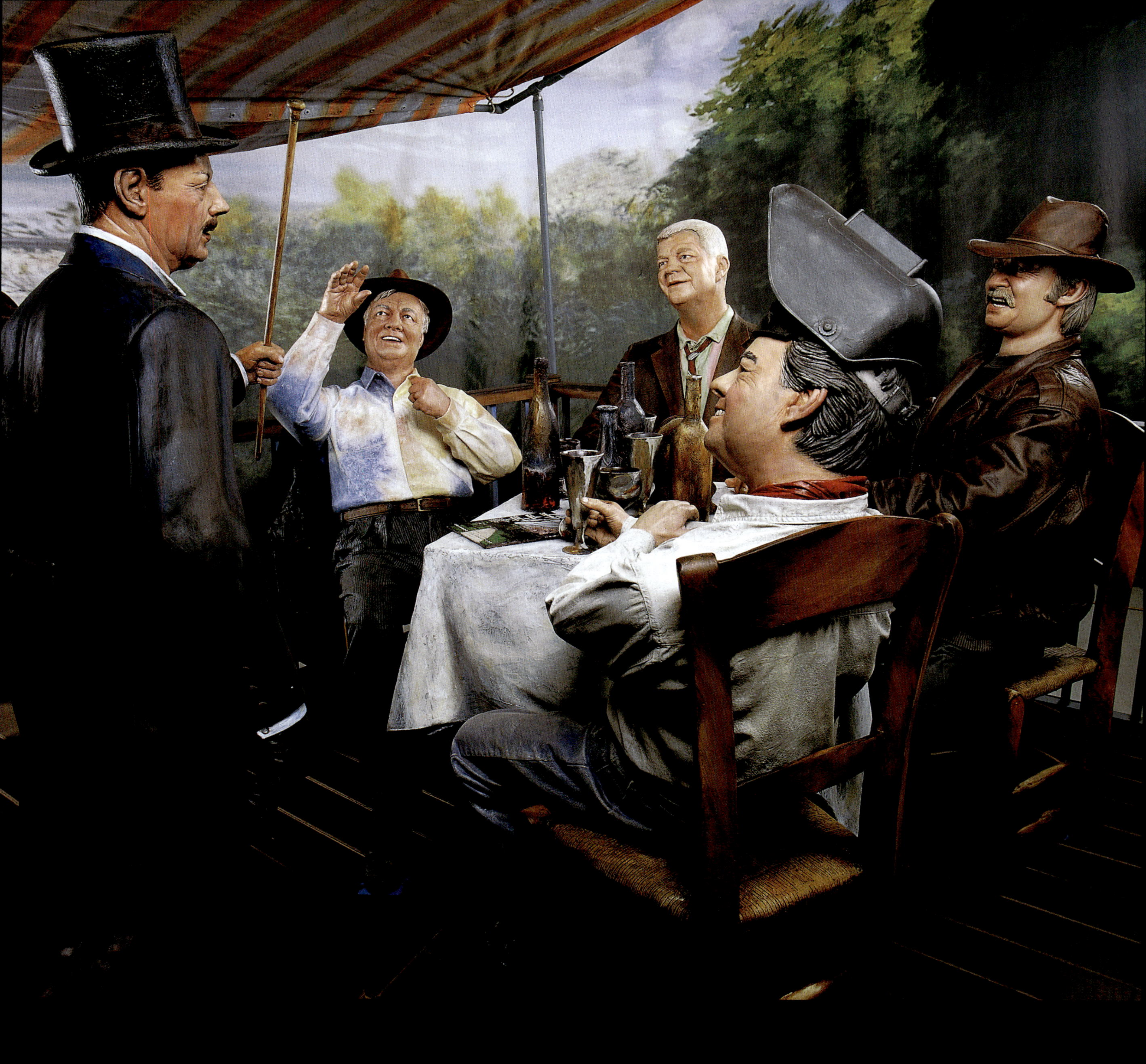

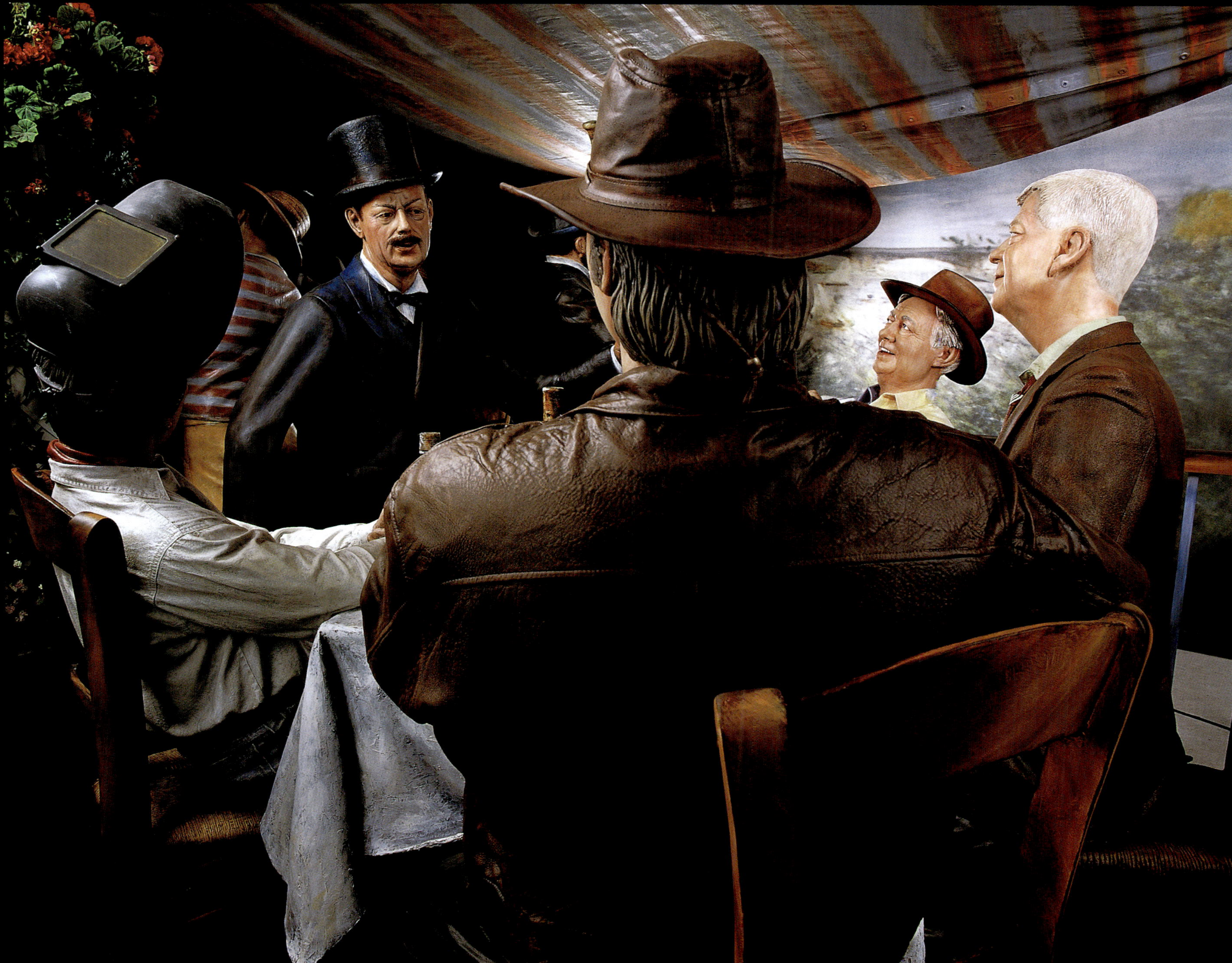

In the modern section I put twice as many bottles. We were drinking up all of Renoir's wine. We are the coarse interlopers. Crashers. Artists will be artists and party where they can. I love being playful with it. Renoir's painting shows an informal gathering, so my gathering is even more informal. I painted our figures in a twentieth-century way, the nineteenth-century figures are more painterly, like Renoir's.

—J. Seward Johnson, Jr.

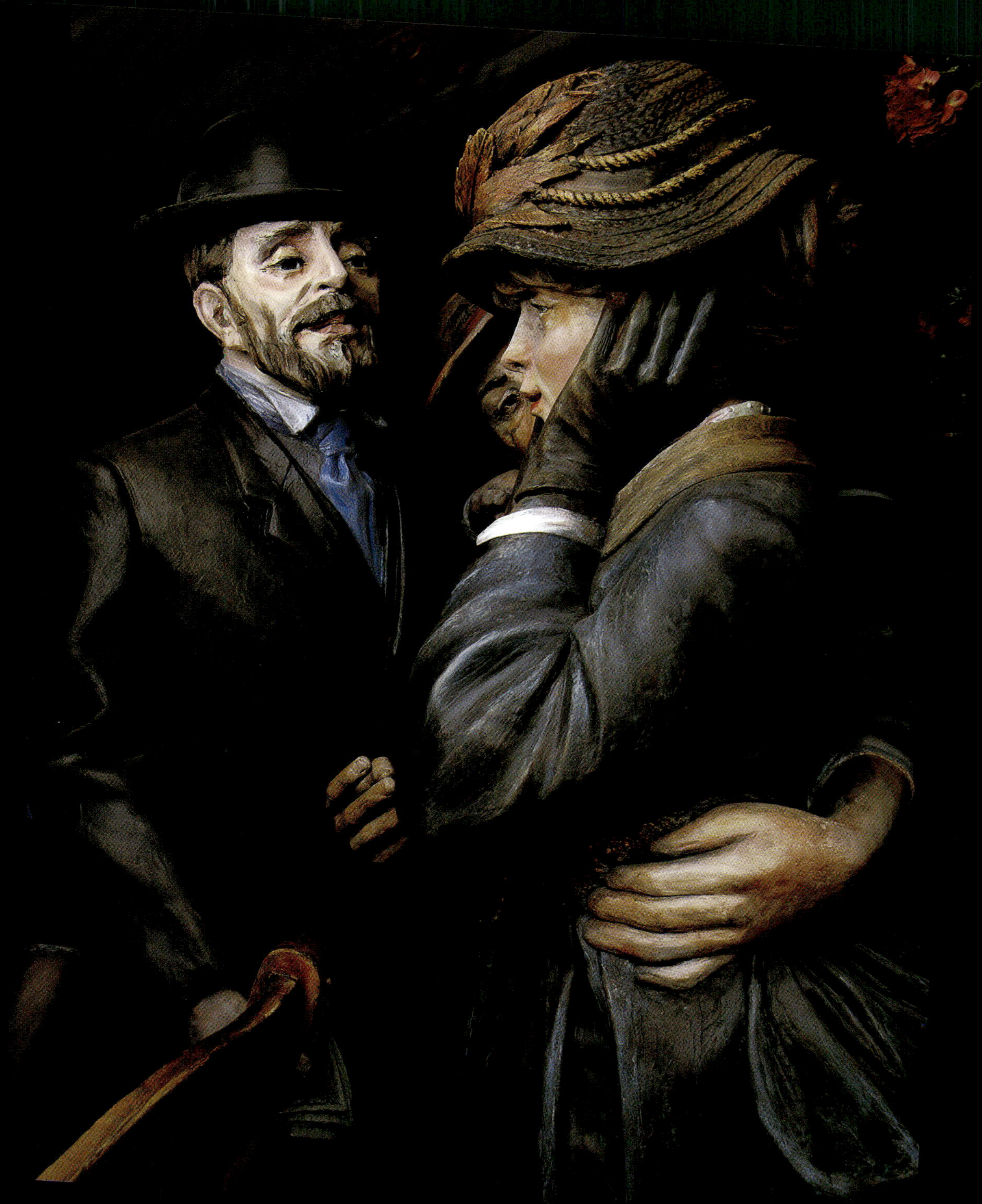

The men were coming on so aggressively that she wanted to cover her ears. They were proposing something she didn't want to hear.

—J. Seward Johnson, Jr.

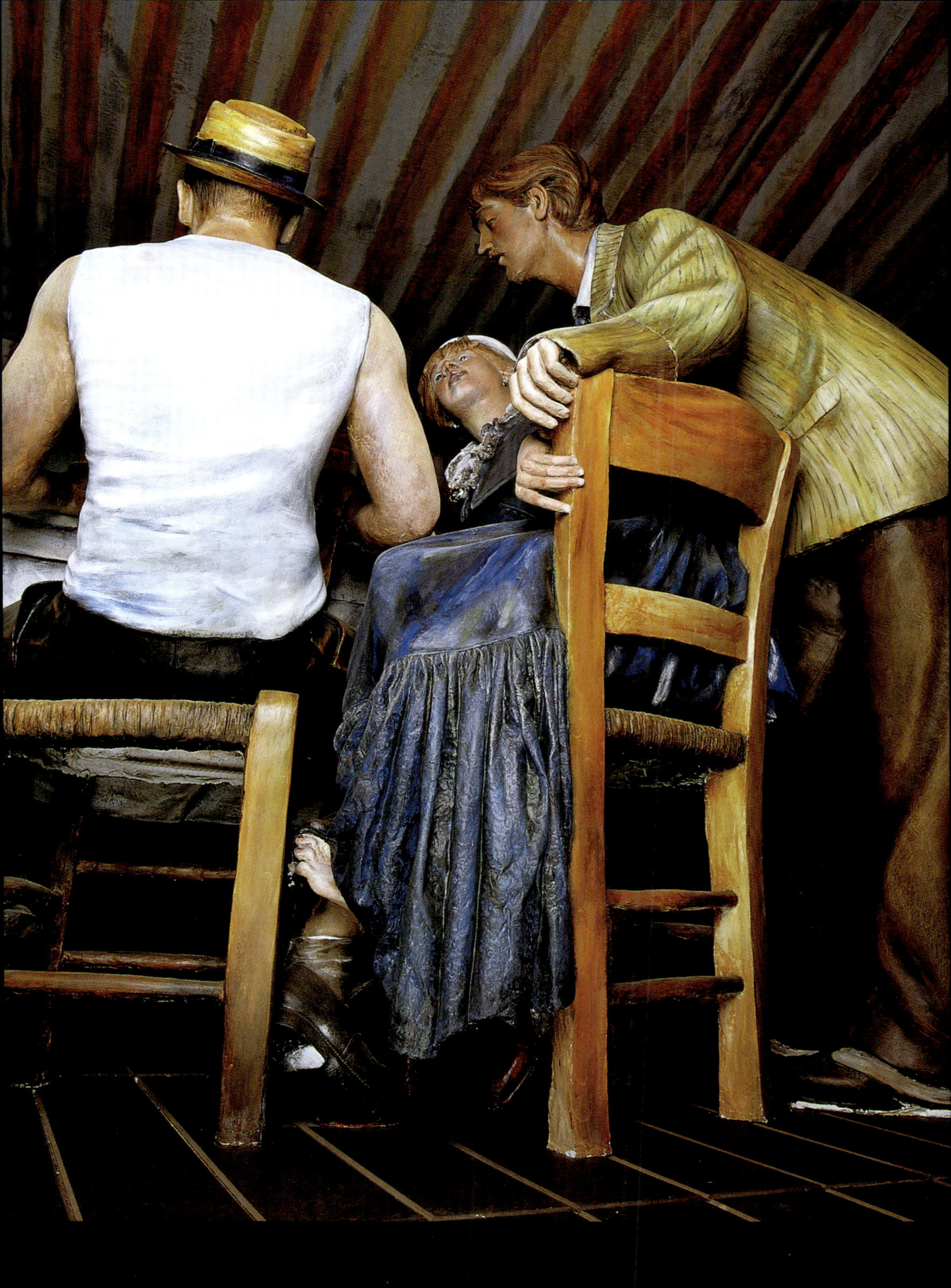

Caillebotte is sitting there and the woman next to him is one of Renoir's models. I have her shoe kicked off and she's running her foot up his leg. My humor comes in the third dimension. Renoir didn't see what was going on. He might have painted that...but he missed it!

Welcome Home

J. Seward Johnson, Jr.

after

The Bedroom 1889

Vincent van Gogh

Art Institute of Chicago

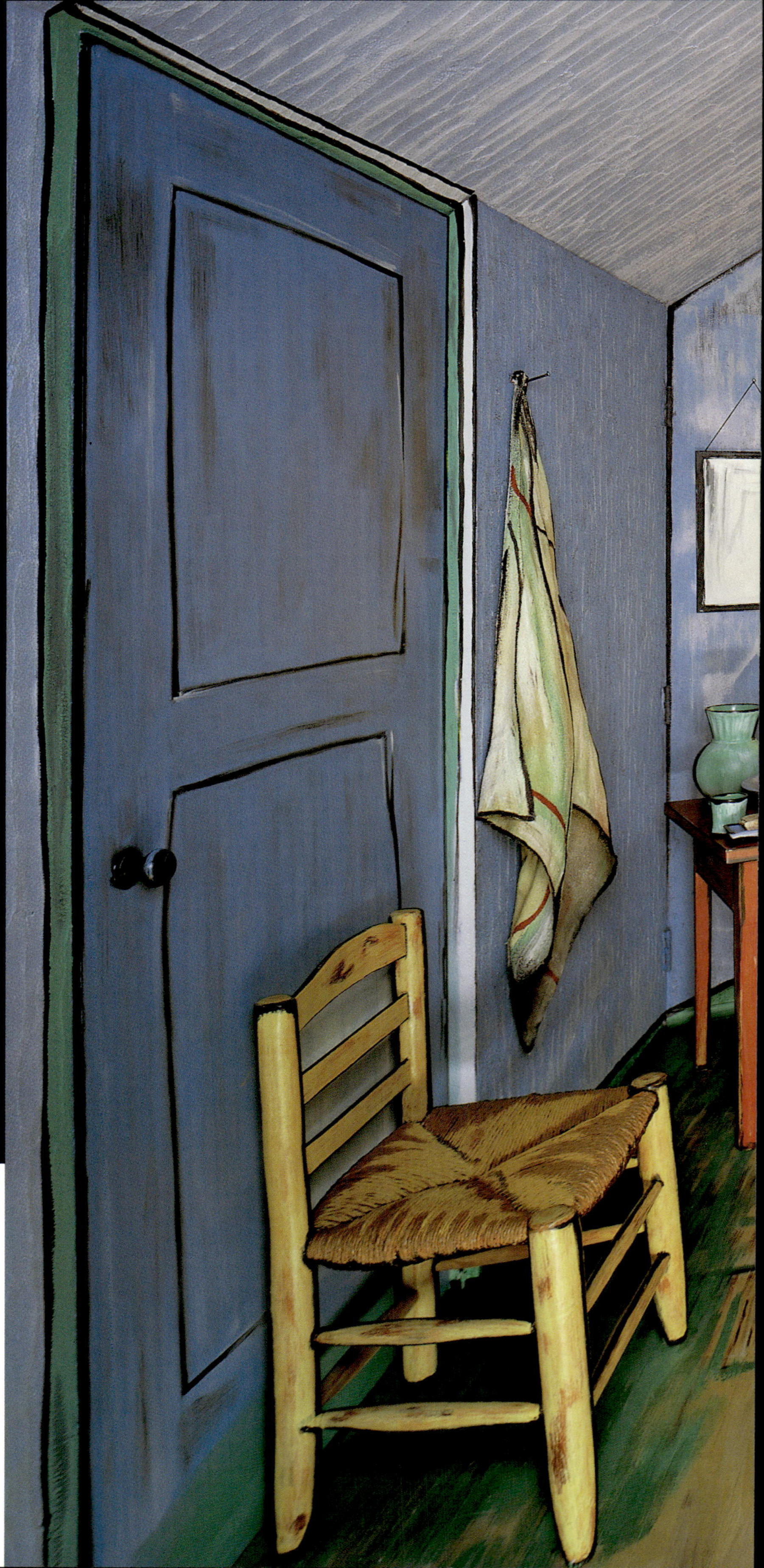

> "Who can deny that *The Bedroom*, painted by van Gogh ... is a kind of wooden womb, a warm room for having pleasant dreams in?"

—Waldemar Januskczak

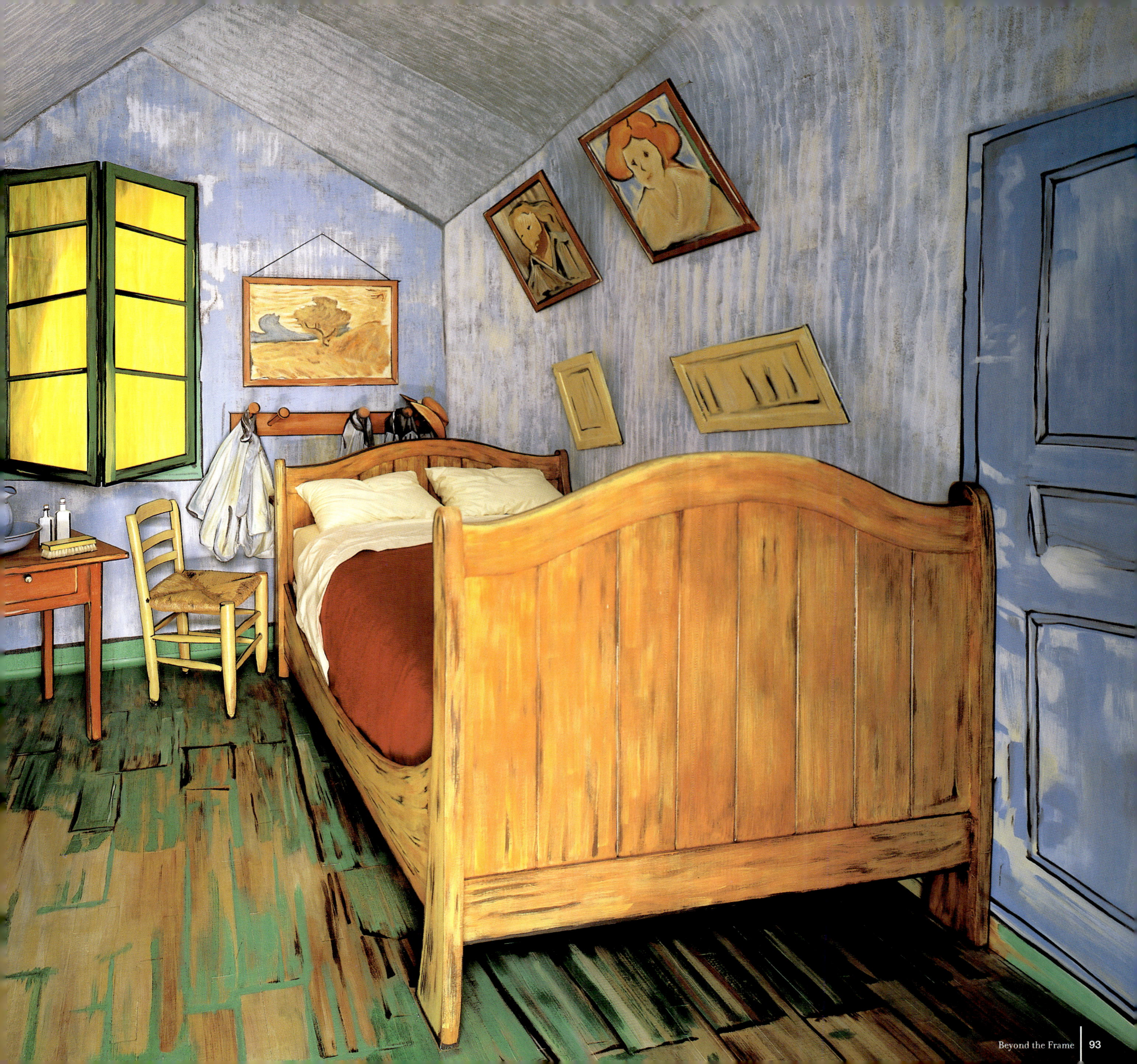

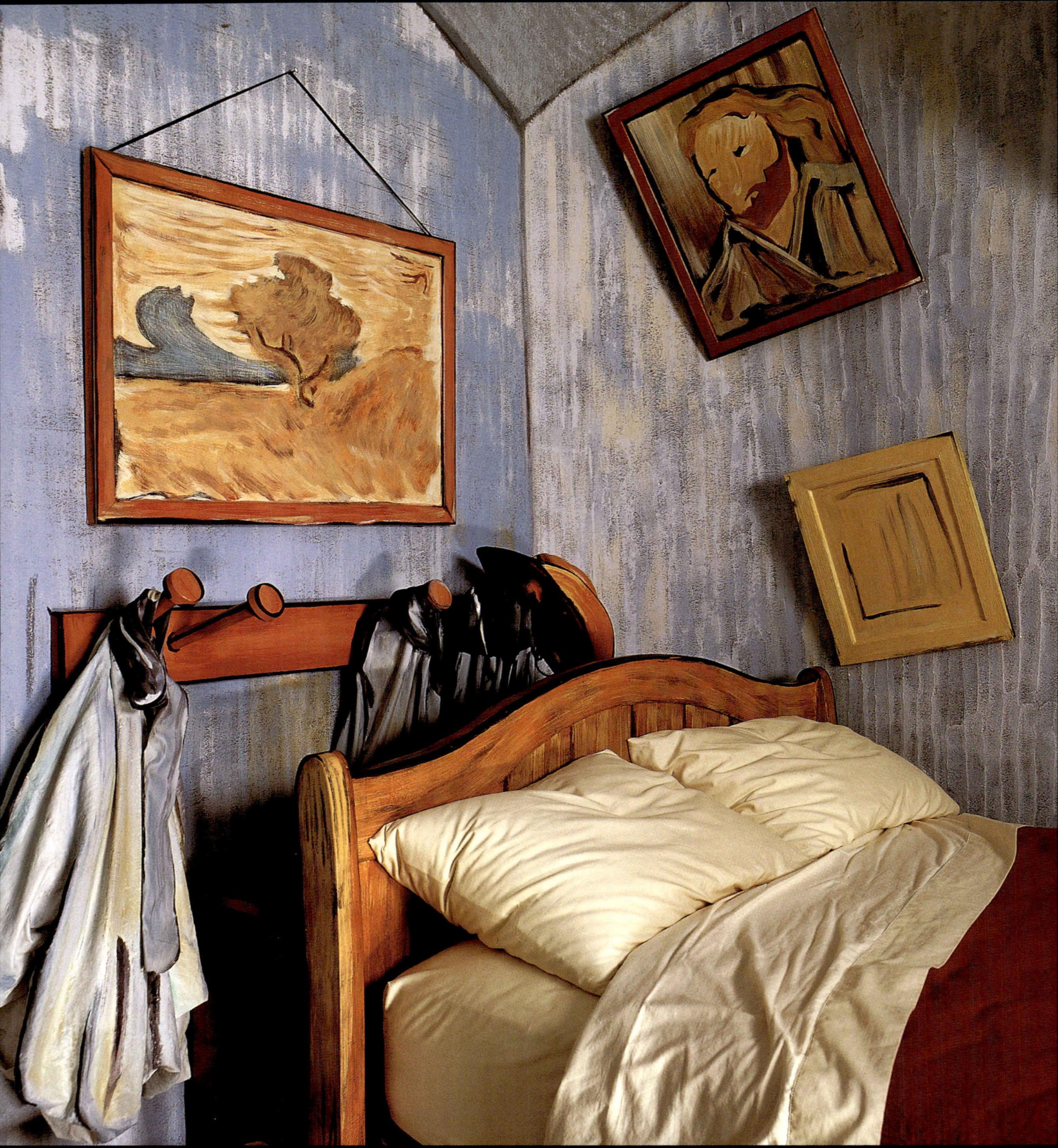

I take naps in here sometimes. Once when I woke up I had so much energy I put on my tap shoes and danced. I am living in my own dream you see.

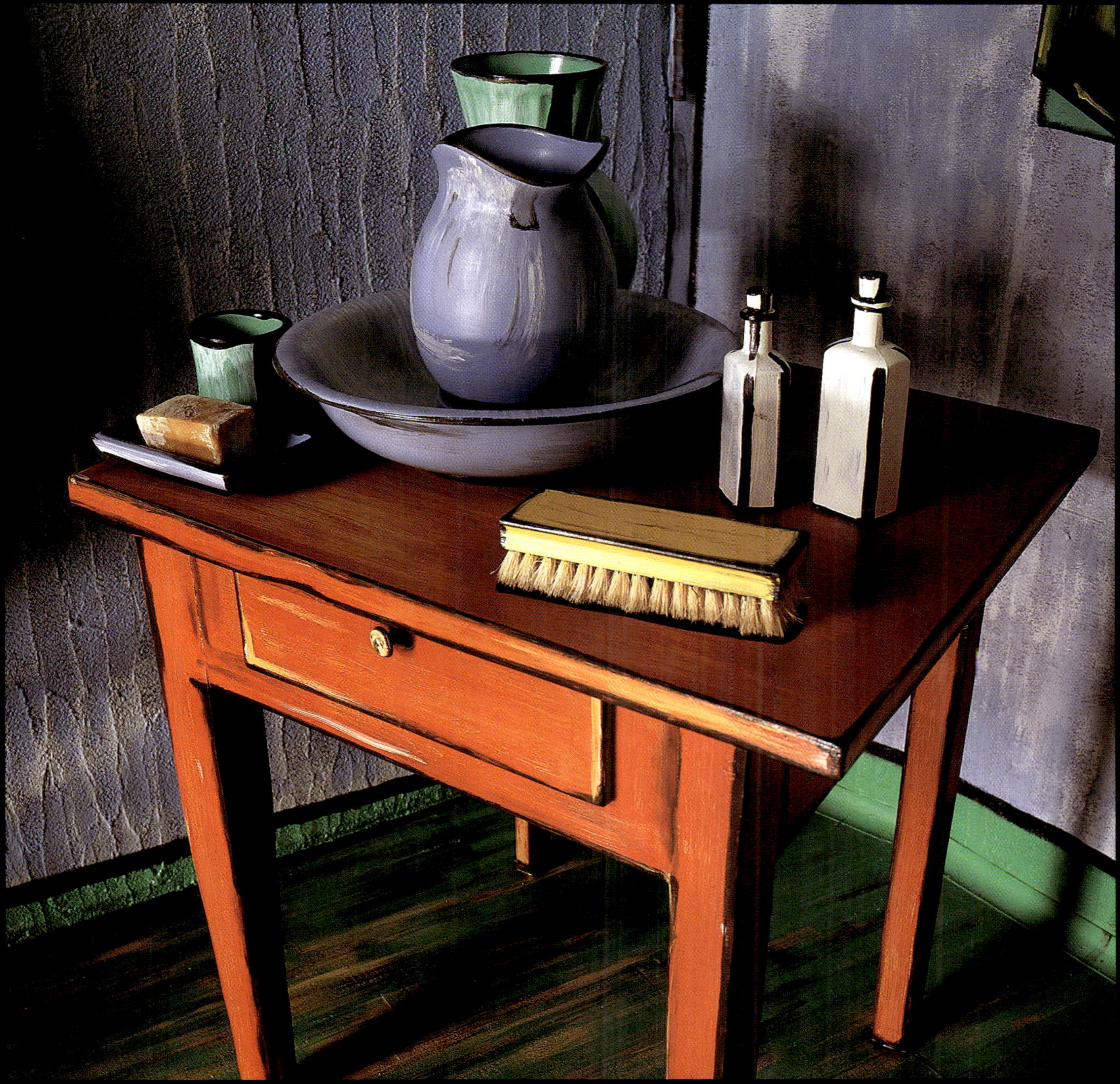

I leave my tap shoes in this little drawer.
—J. Seward Johnson, Jr.

Time for Fun

J. Seward Johnson, Jr.

after

Dance in the Country 1883

Pierre-Auguste Renoir

Musée d'Orsay, Paris

> "One could add to the dancers the literary commentary so dear to the French imagination, but I can see in them only an art that is skilled at painting faces flushed with pleasure, relaxed by delicious fatigue, an art which makes clothing that is cut well and worn well seem elegant and distinguished."
>
> —Philippe Burty

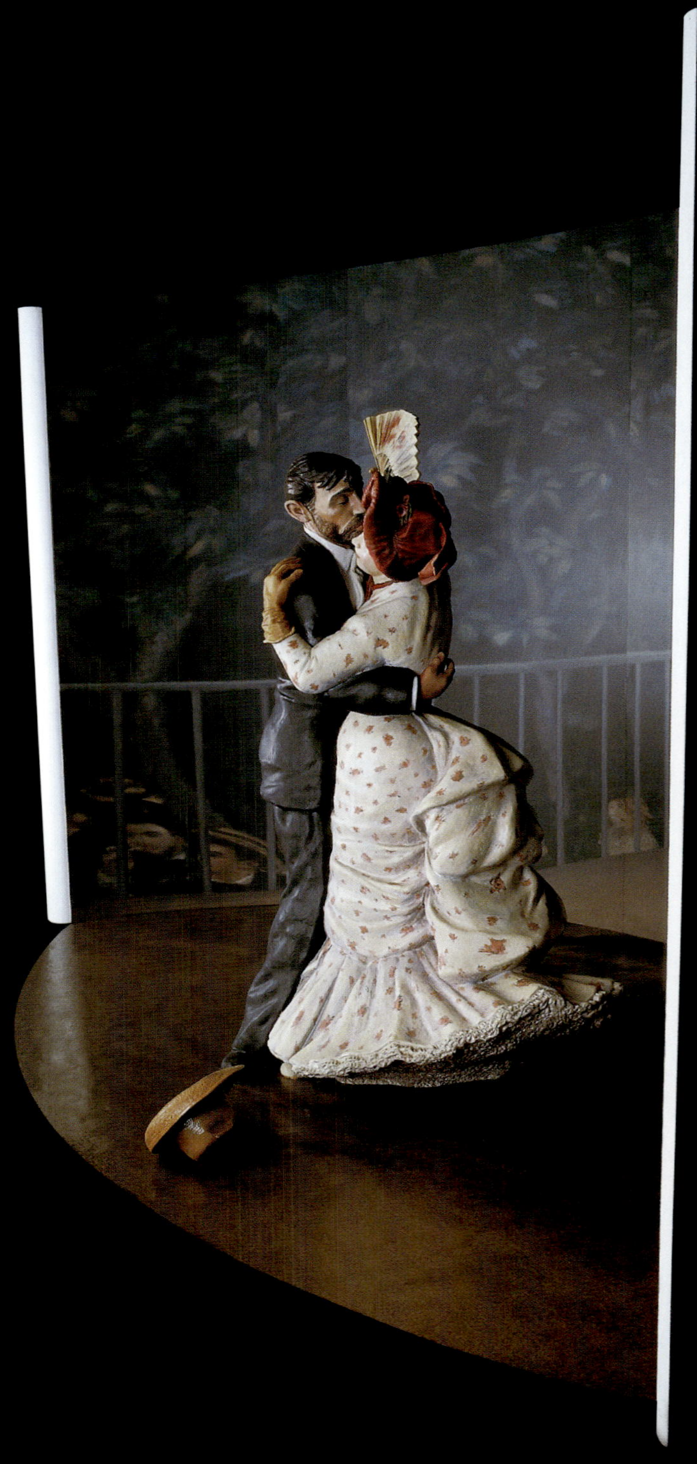

All of my former work celebrated that existential moment where people are taking charge of their lives. The Impressionists were doing the same thing. They put people in nature and celebrated that. It is an existential expression. That is why the paintings are so popular.

—J. Seward Johnson, Jr.

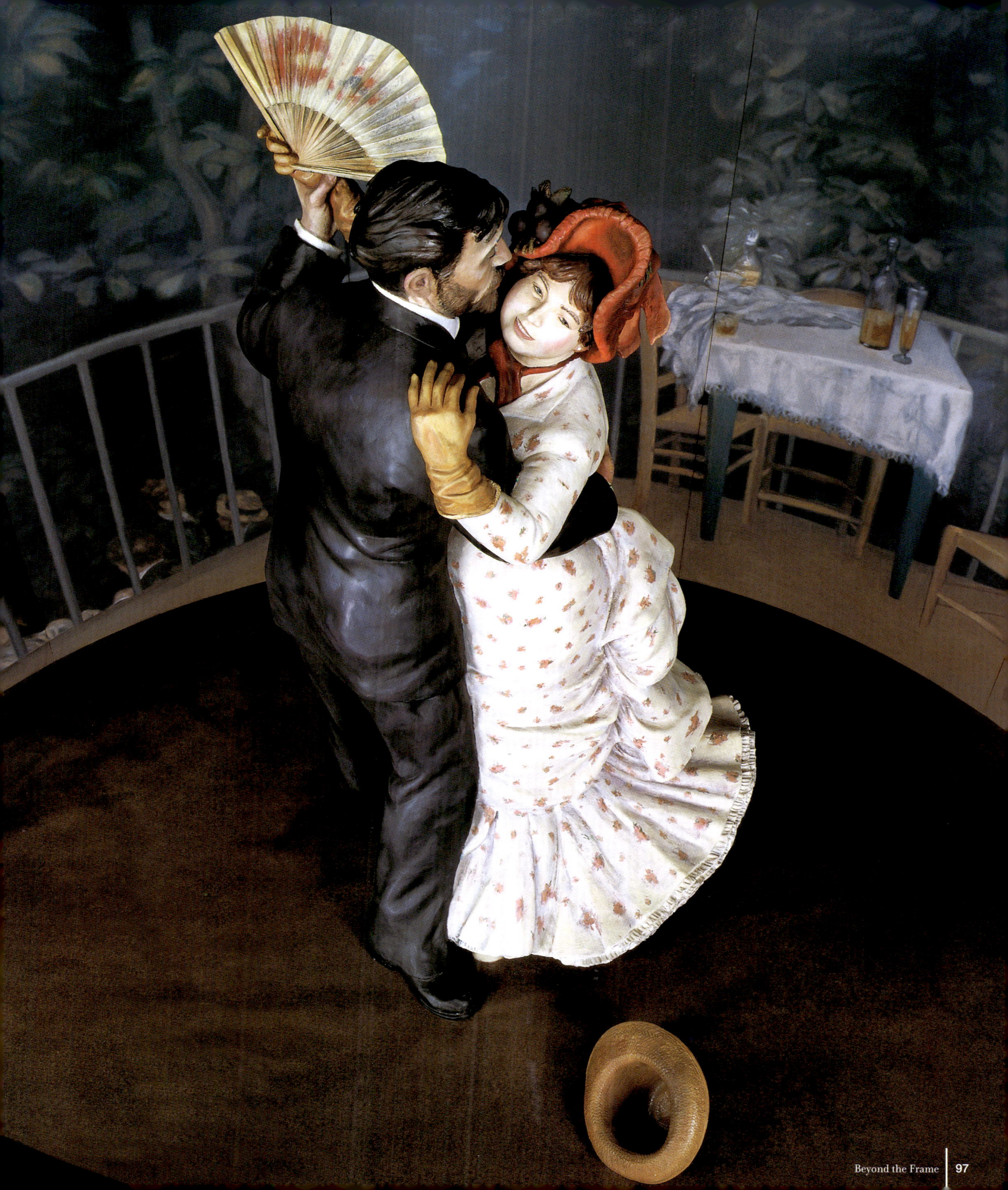

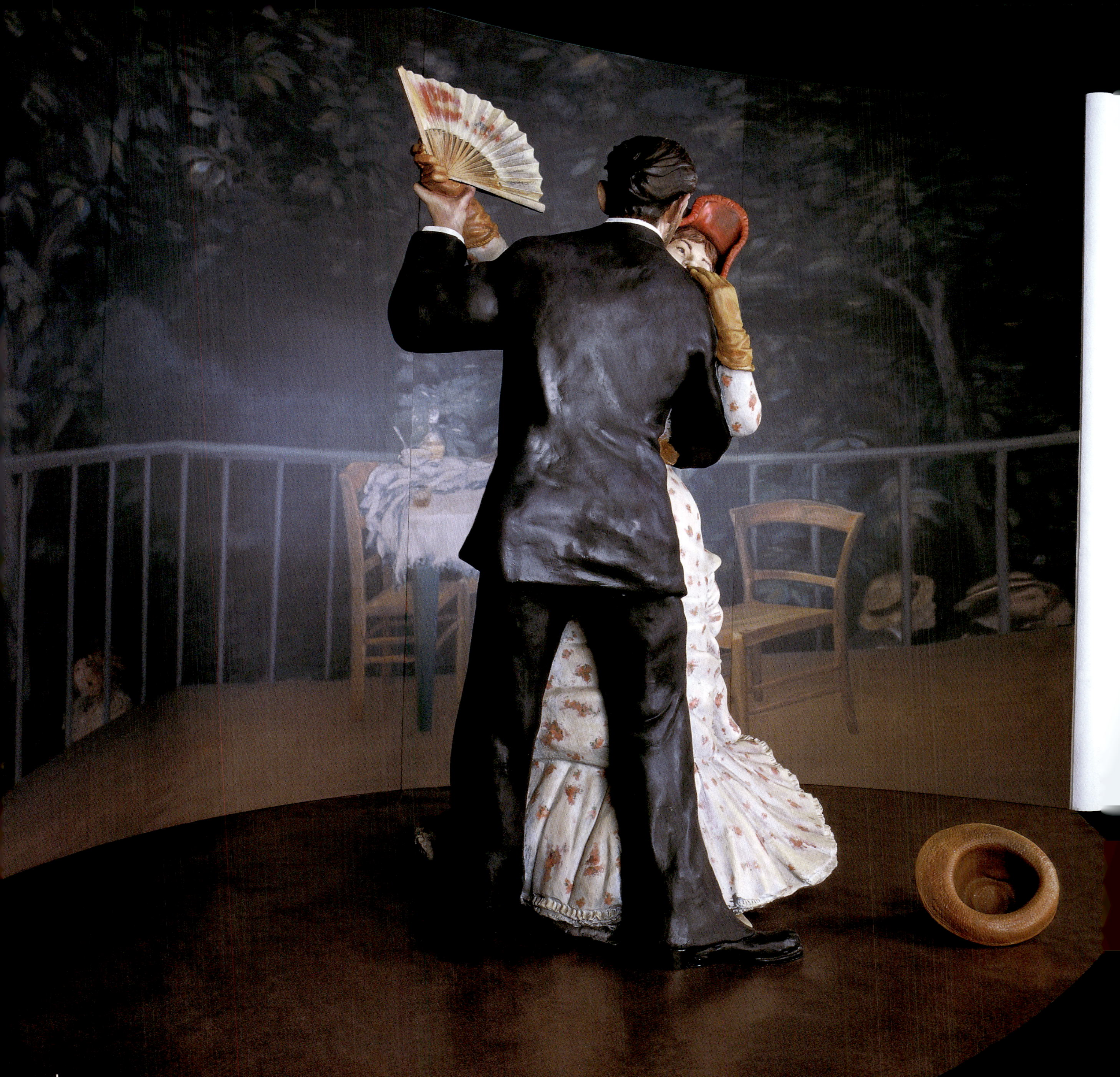

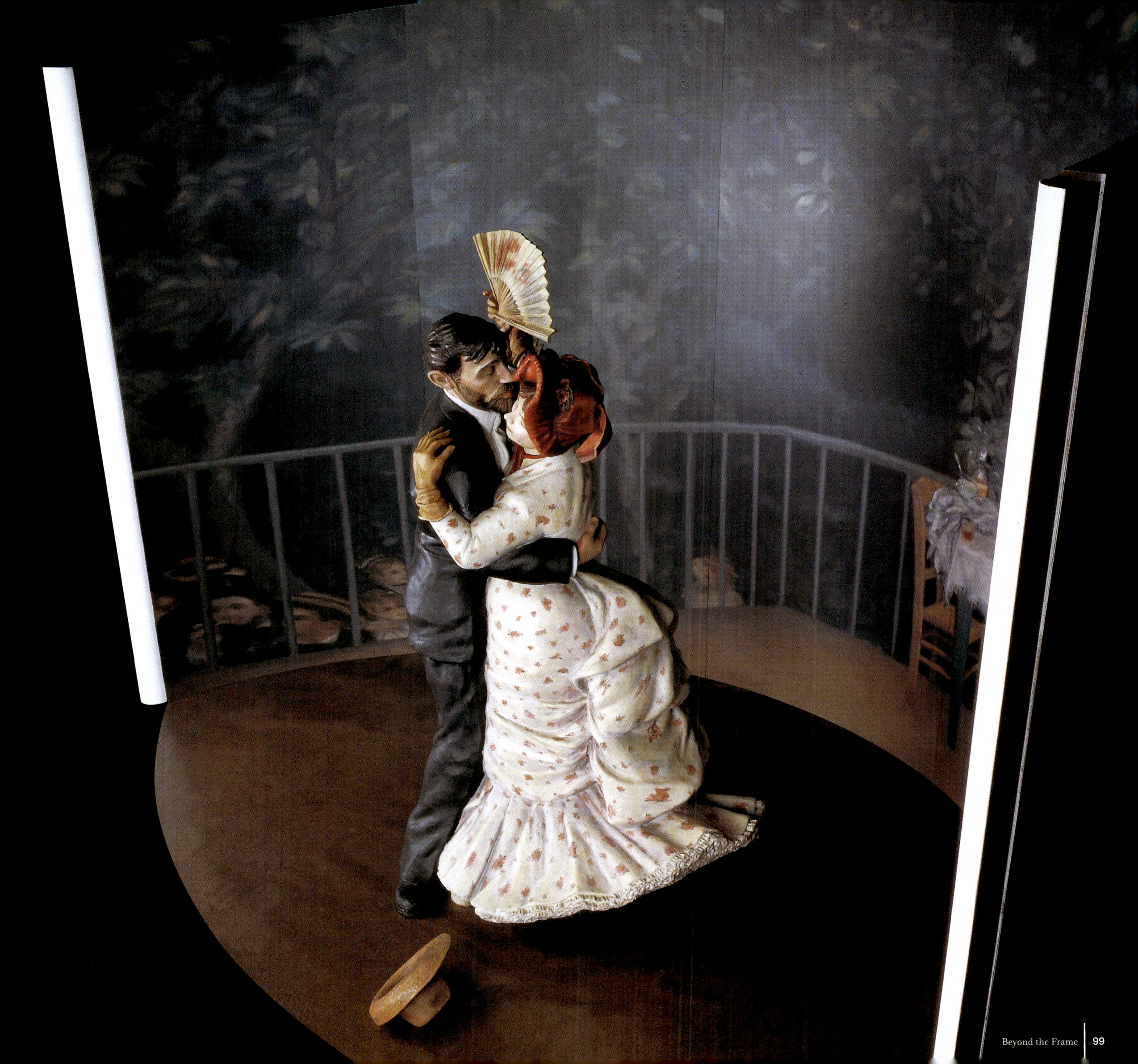

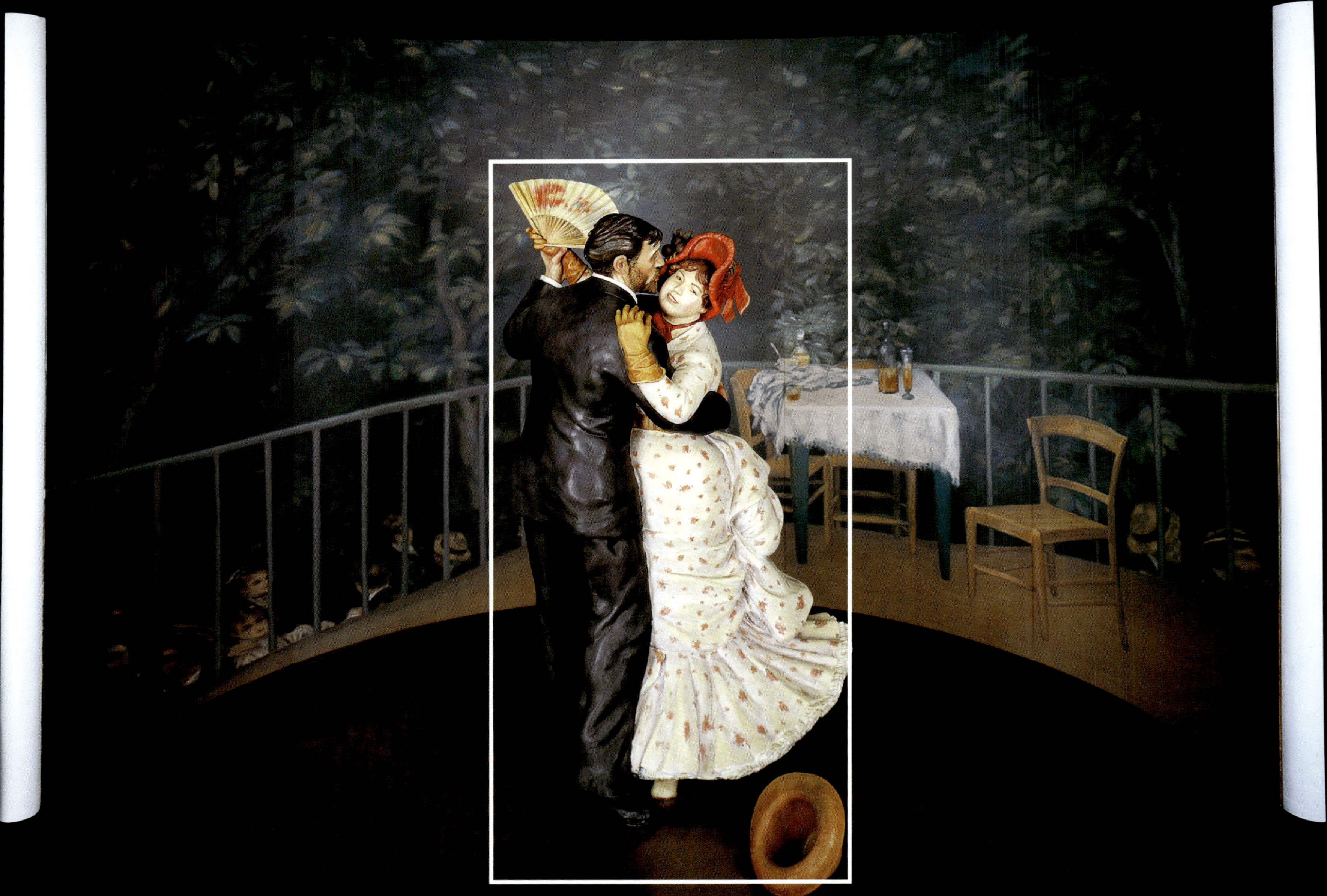

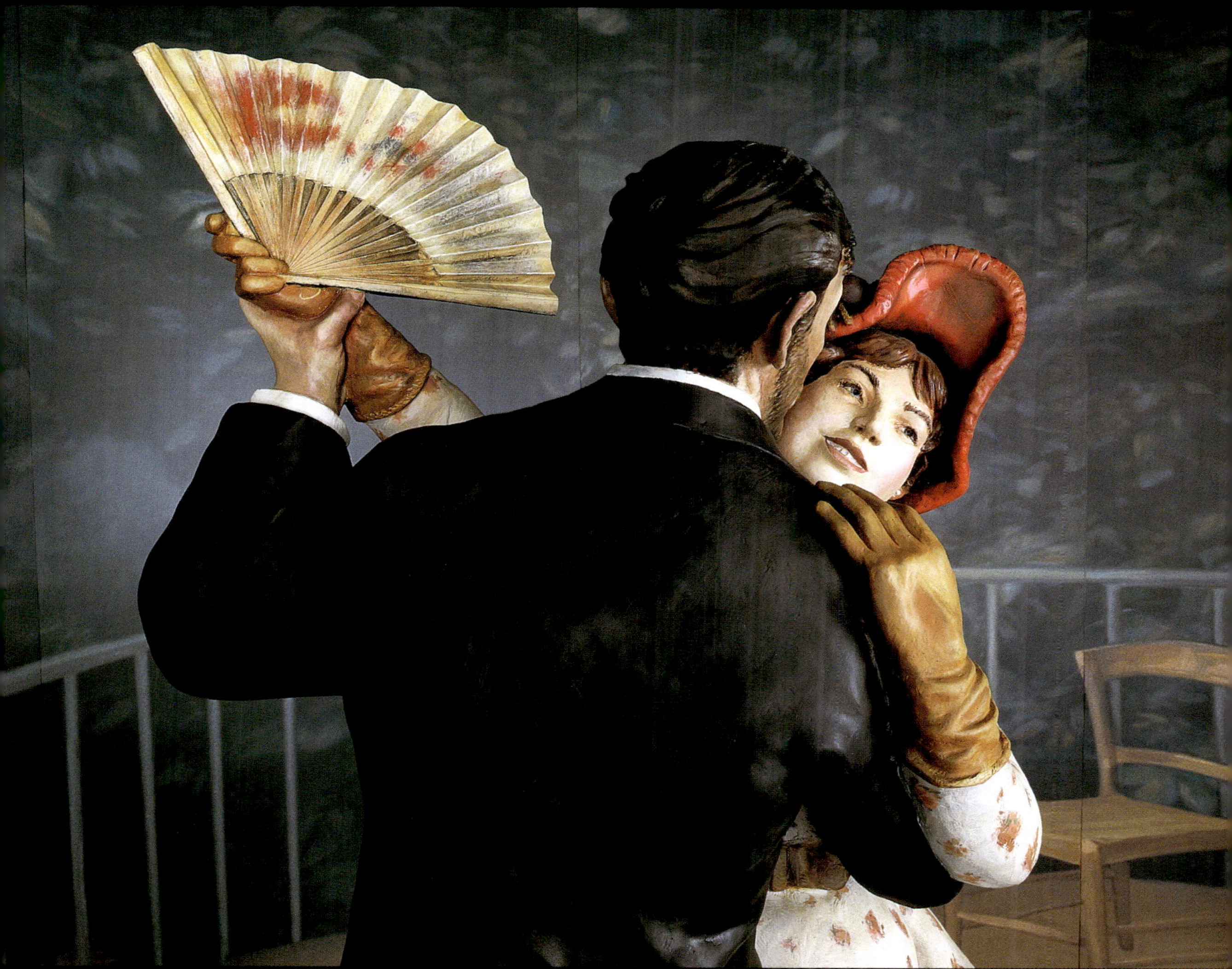

Whispering Close

J. Seward Johnson, Jr.

after

Dance in the City 1883

Pierre-Auguste Renoir

Musée d'Orsay, Paris

"The model is only there to get me going. She enables me to dare things that I couldn't invent without her, also to help me back on course if I go too far."

—Pierre-Auguste Renoir

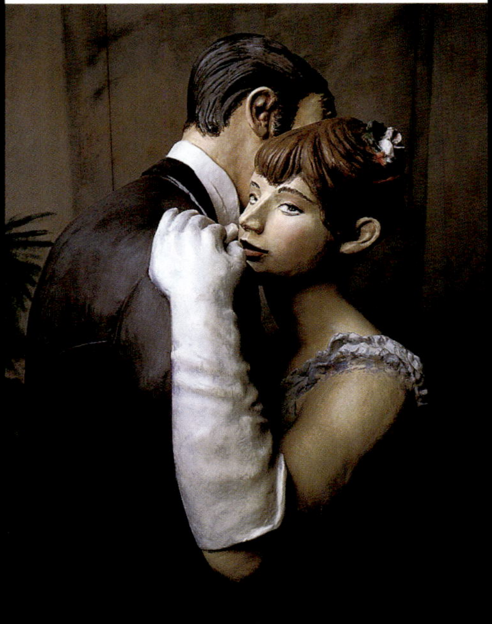

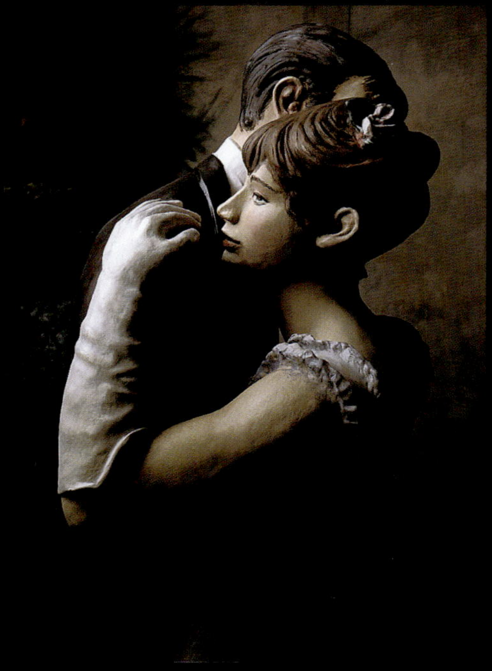

With these works I bow to the French school and to each painting. As much as I am having fun, I have reverence for these paintings. Obviously I am an American sculptor, so these are not French, but I am channeling these paintings and also stealing from them. Artists are always copying each other.

—J. Seward Johnson, Jr.

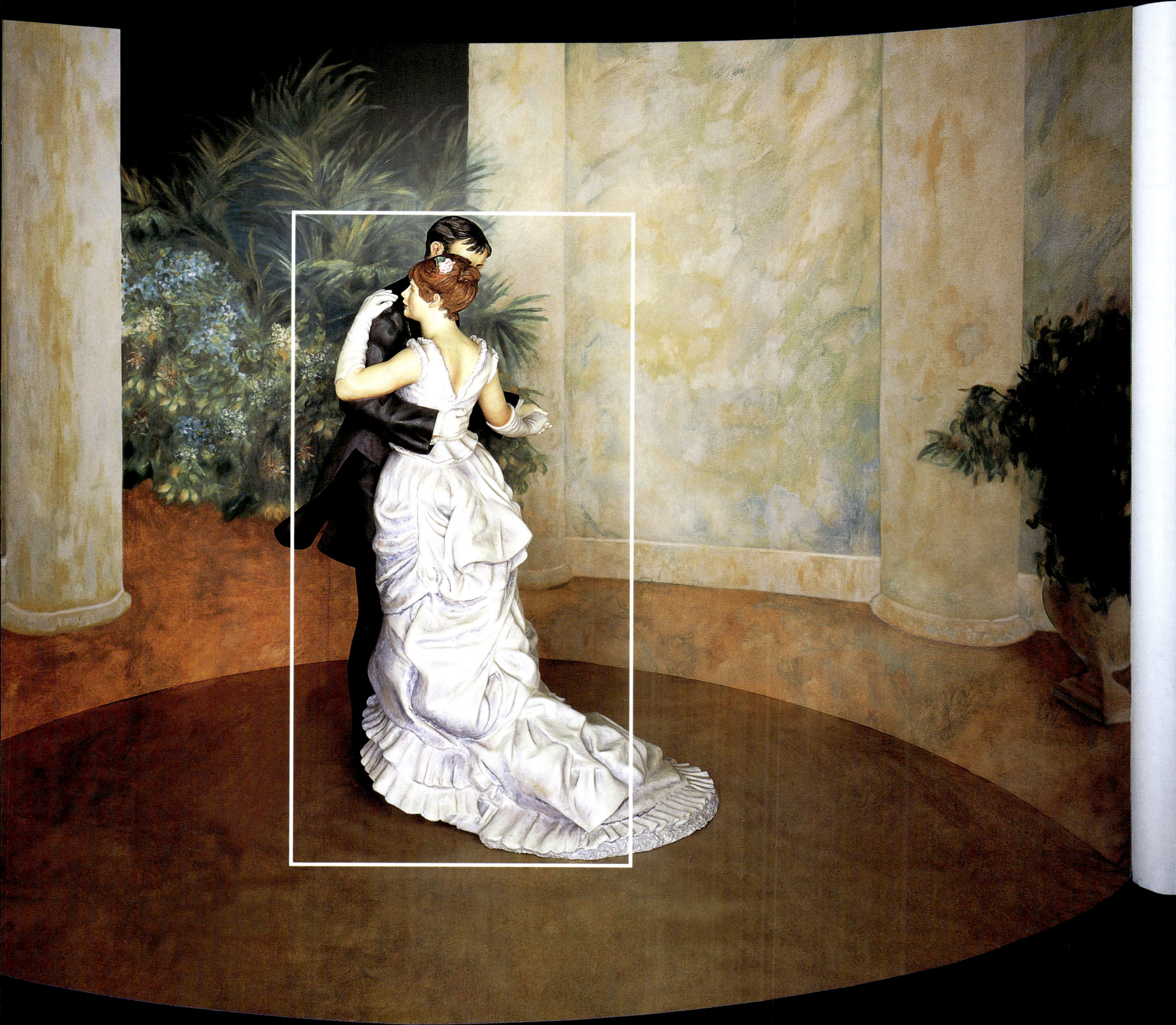

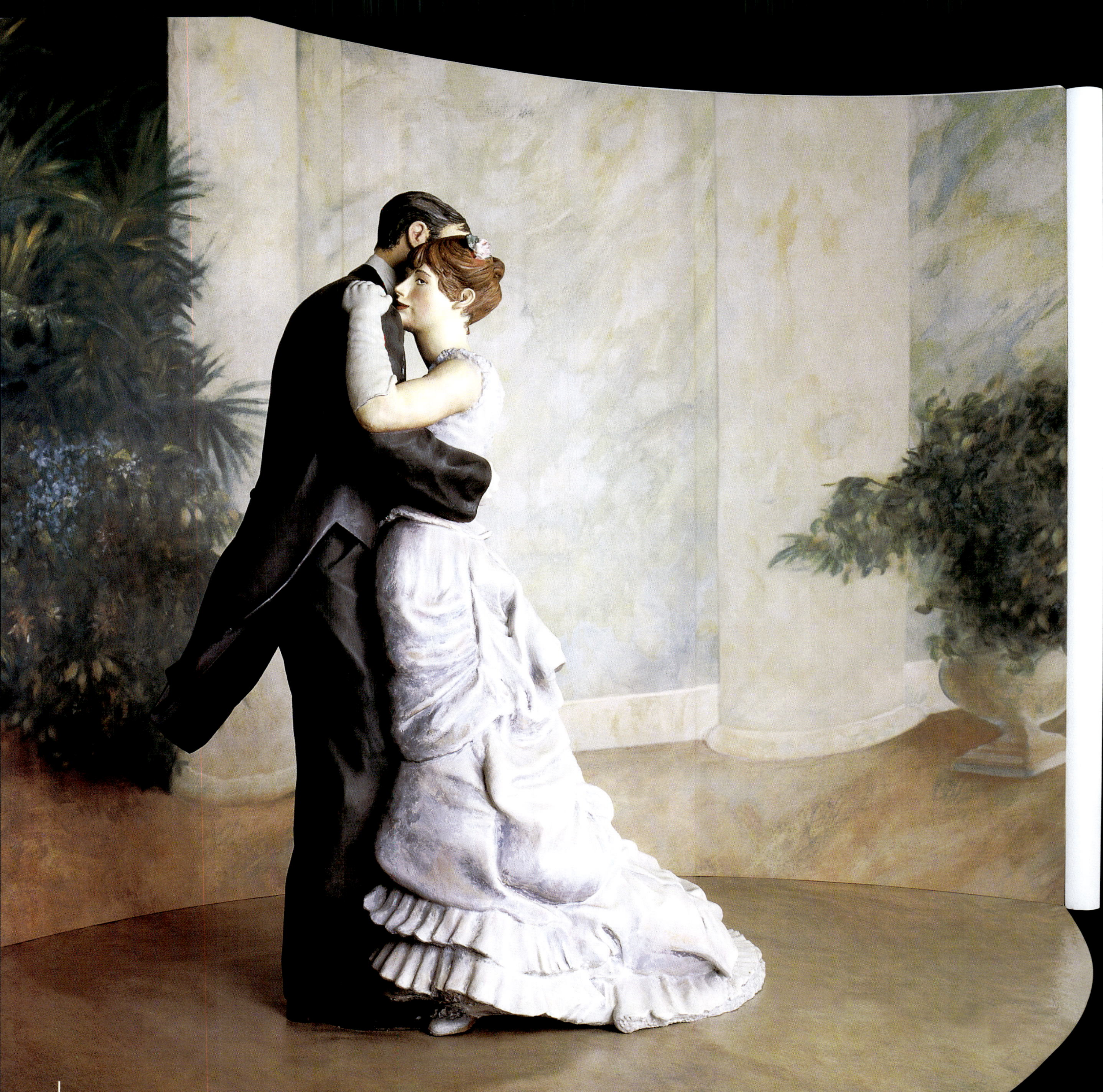

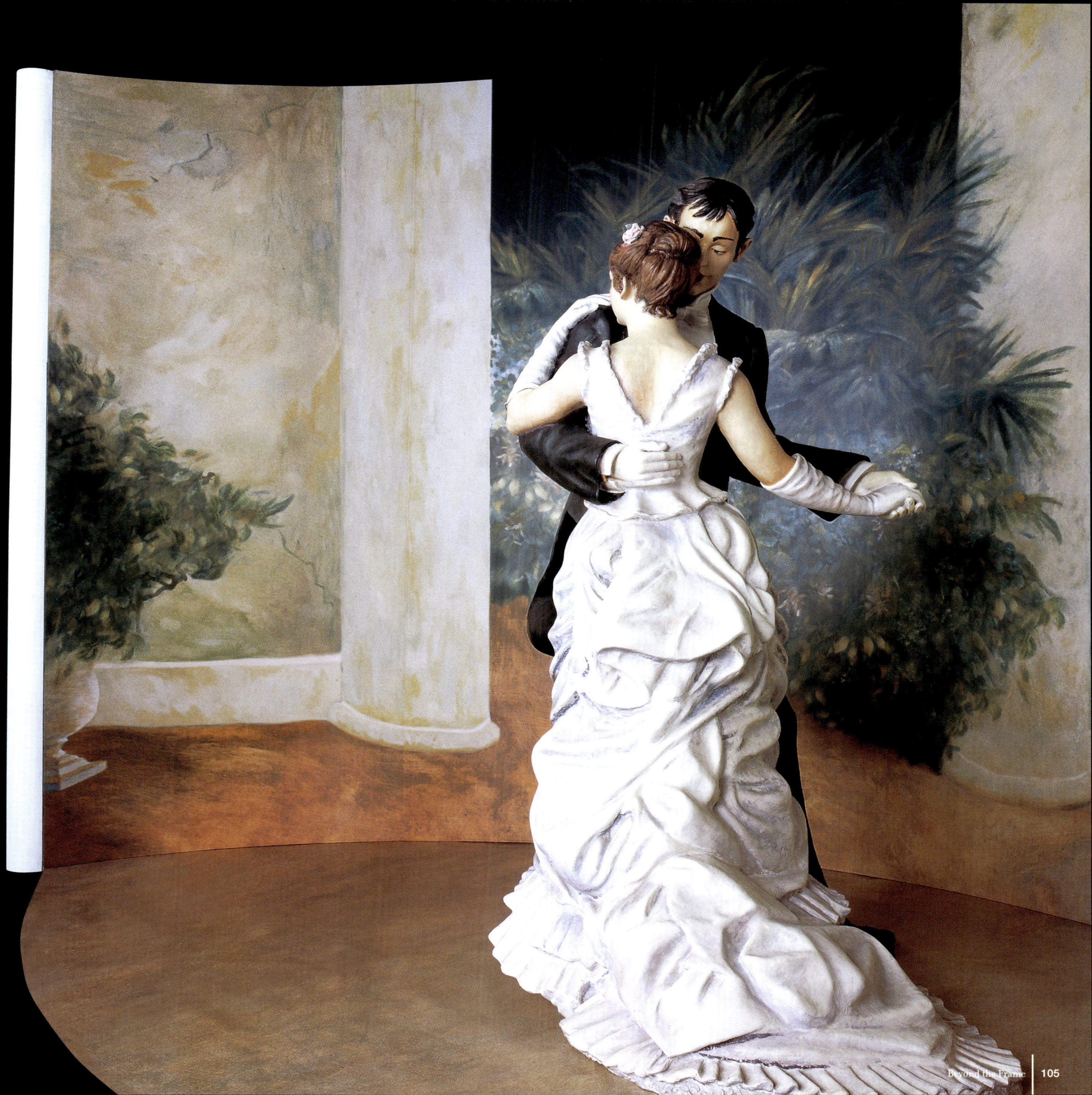

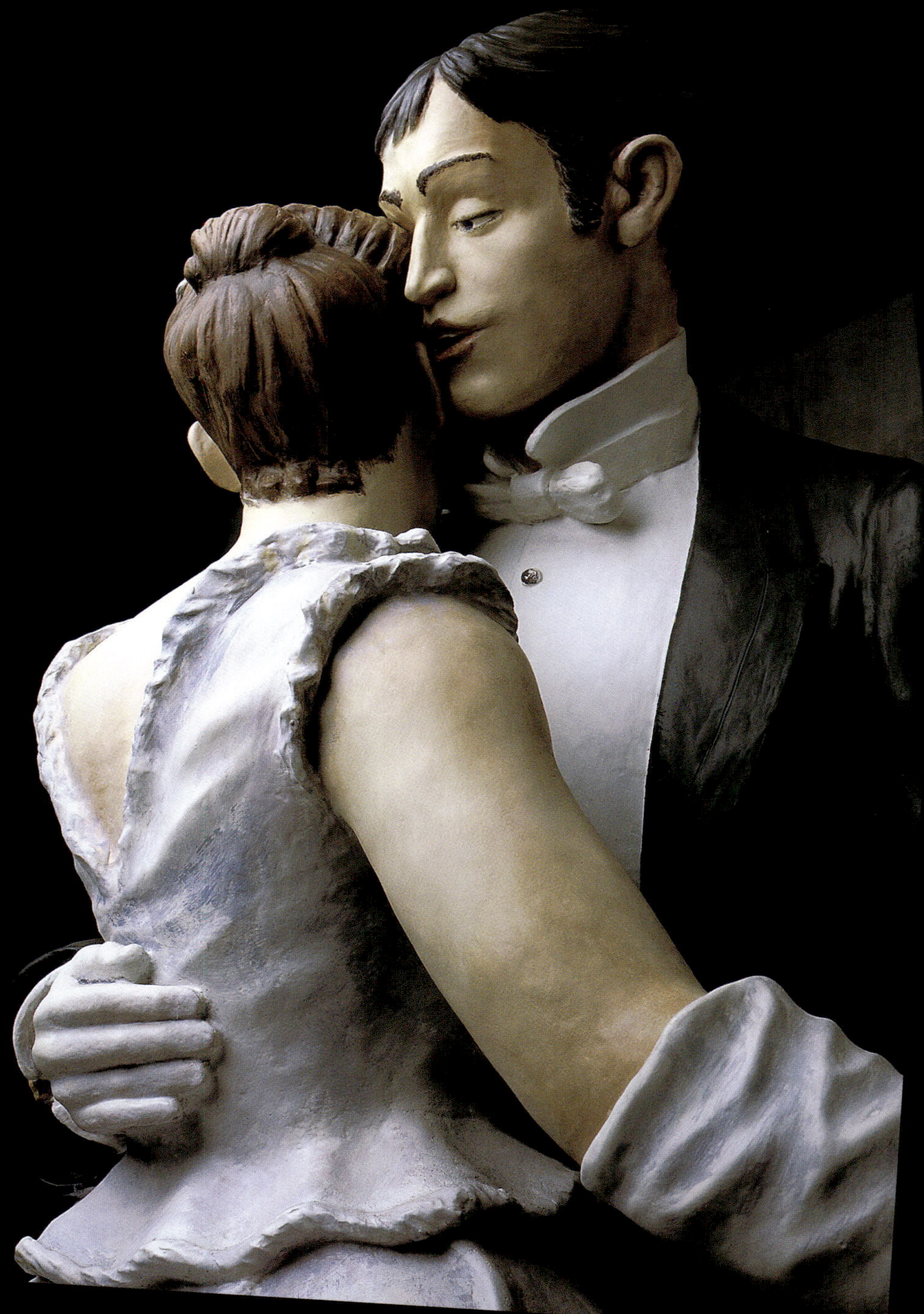

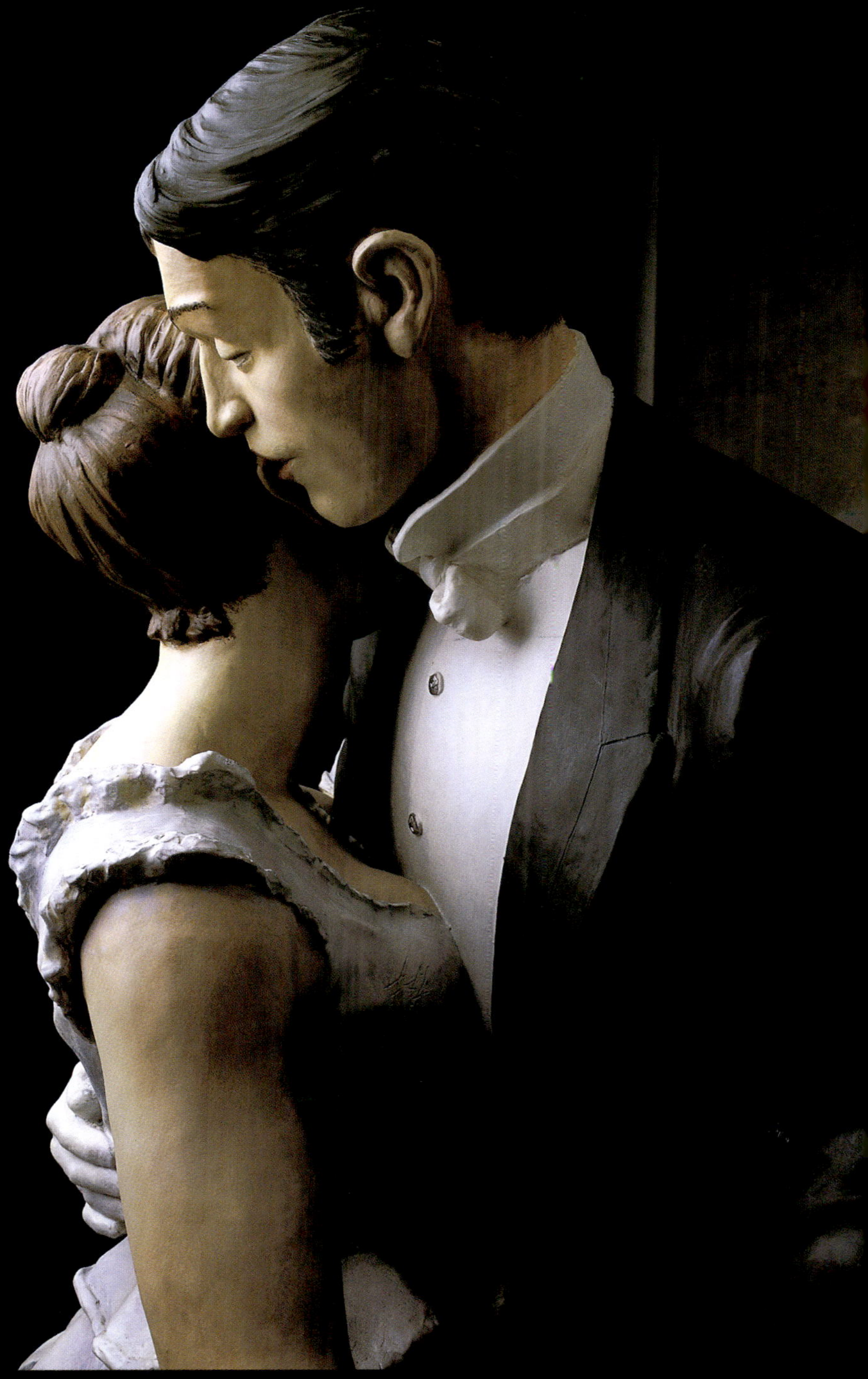

A Turn of the Century

J. Seward Johnson, Jr.

after

Dance at Bougival 1883

Pierre-Auguste Renoir

Museum of Fine Arts, Boston

> "A drawing for the composition bears Renior's inscription: 'She was waltzing, deliciously abandoned in the arms of a fair headed man with the air of an oarsman'."

—Beverly Fazio

> "*Dance at Bougival* creates a mood, rather than telling a story. The girl, wearing a ring on her wedding finger, seems momentarily to turn away from her companion's attentions, but we know no more of their relations."

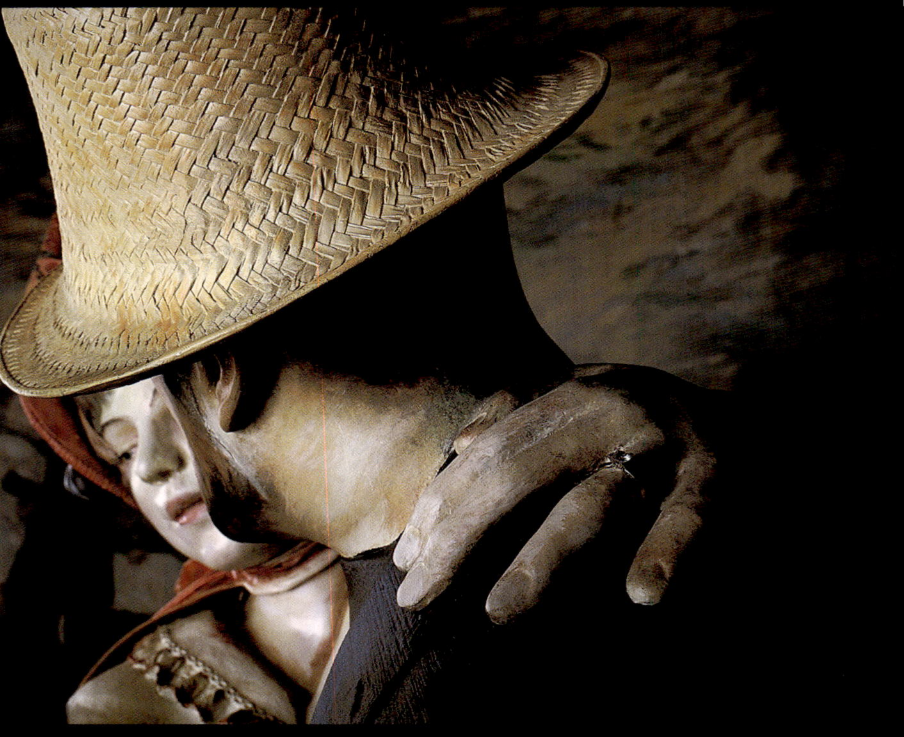

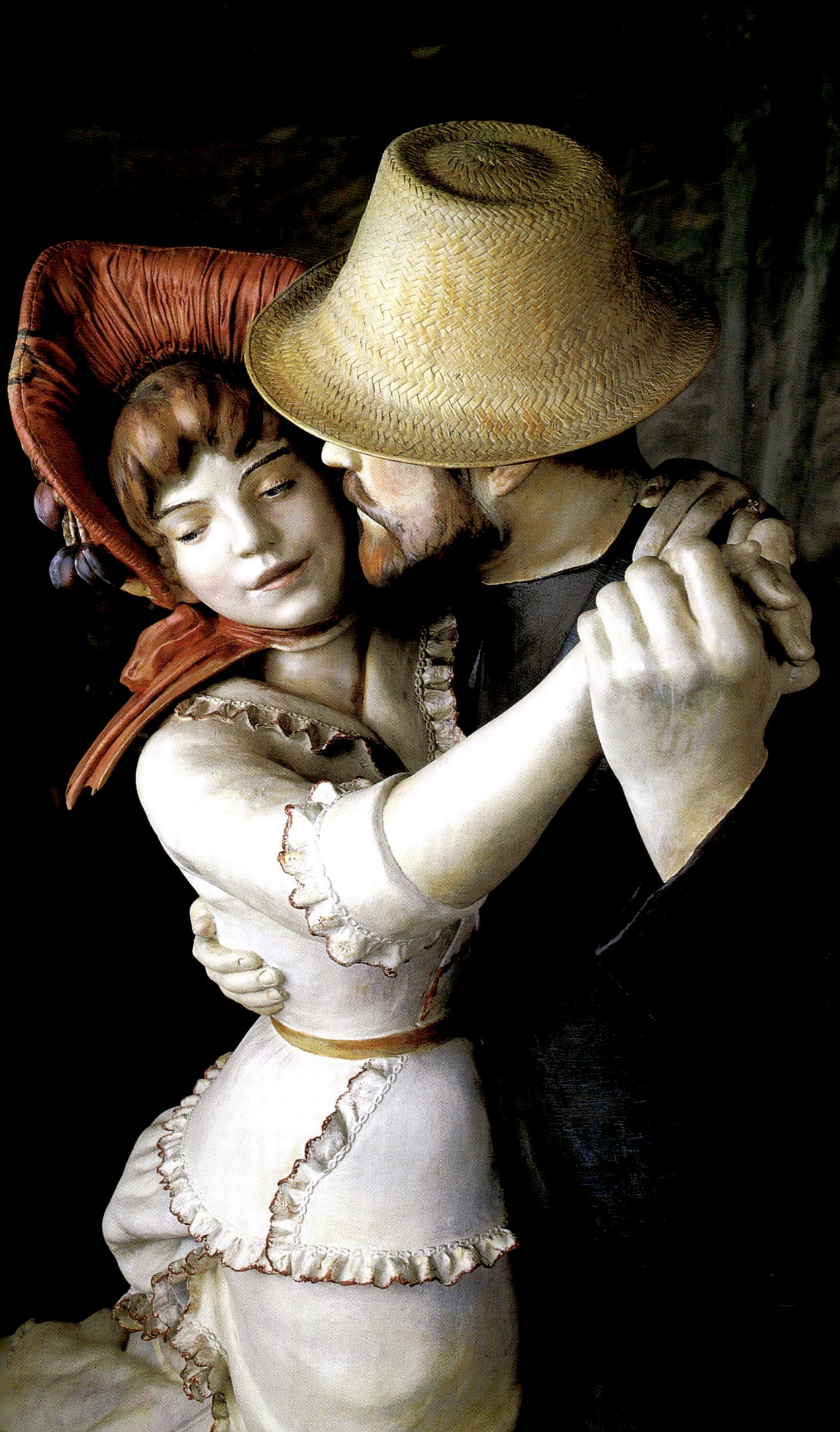

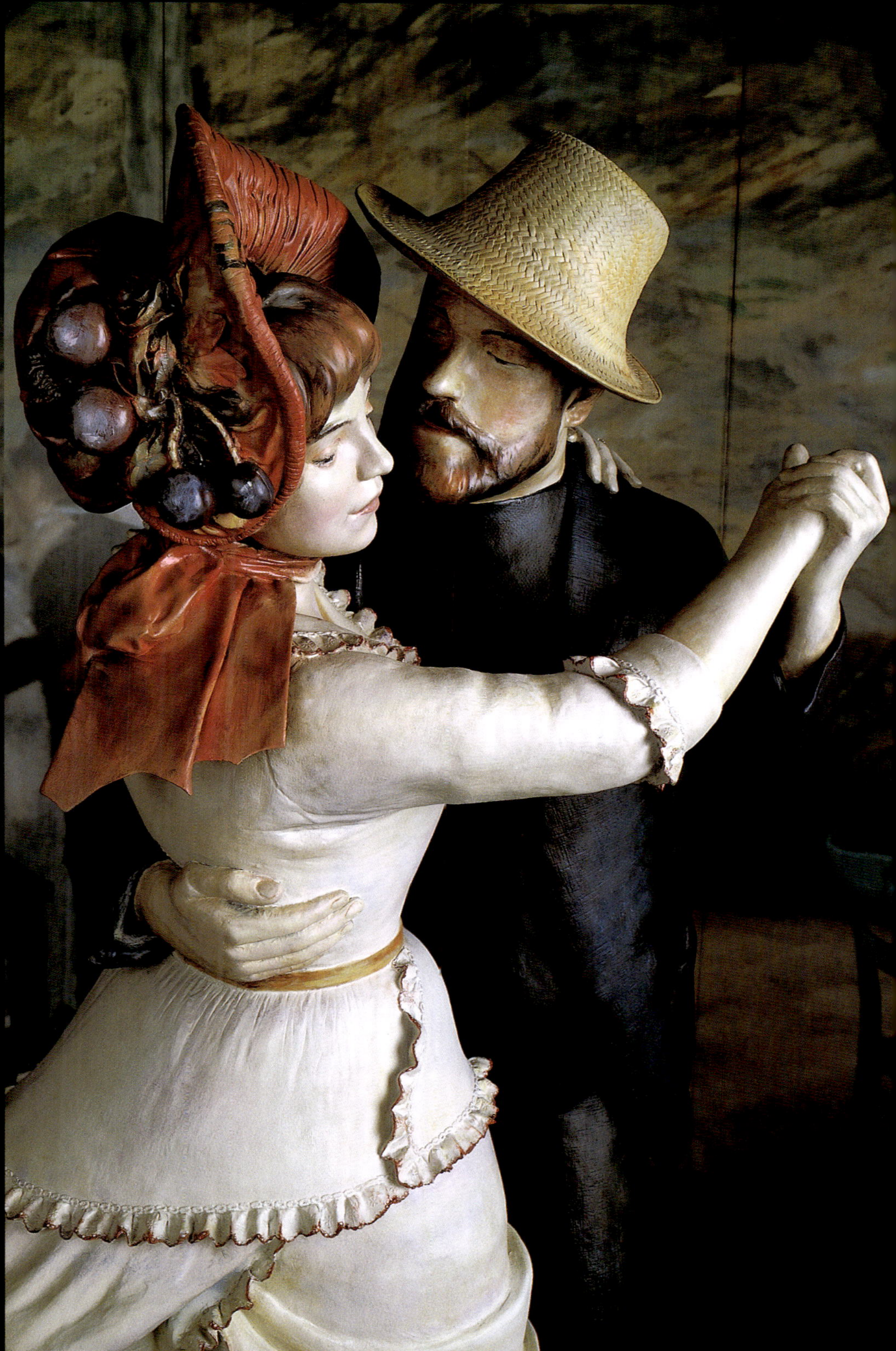

On Poppied Hill

J. Seward Johnson, Jr.

after

Woman with a Parasol—Madame Monet and Her Son 1875

Claude Monet

National Gallery of Art, Washington, DC

and

Poppies 1873

Claude Monet

Musée d'Orsay, Paris

> "I am working as never before, and at new projects, figures in the open air as I understand them, done as landscapes. It is an old dream that still haunts me."

—Claude Monet

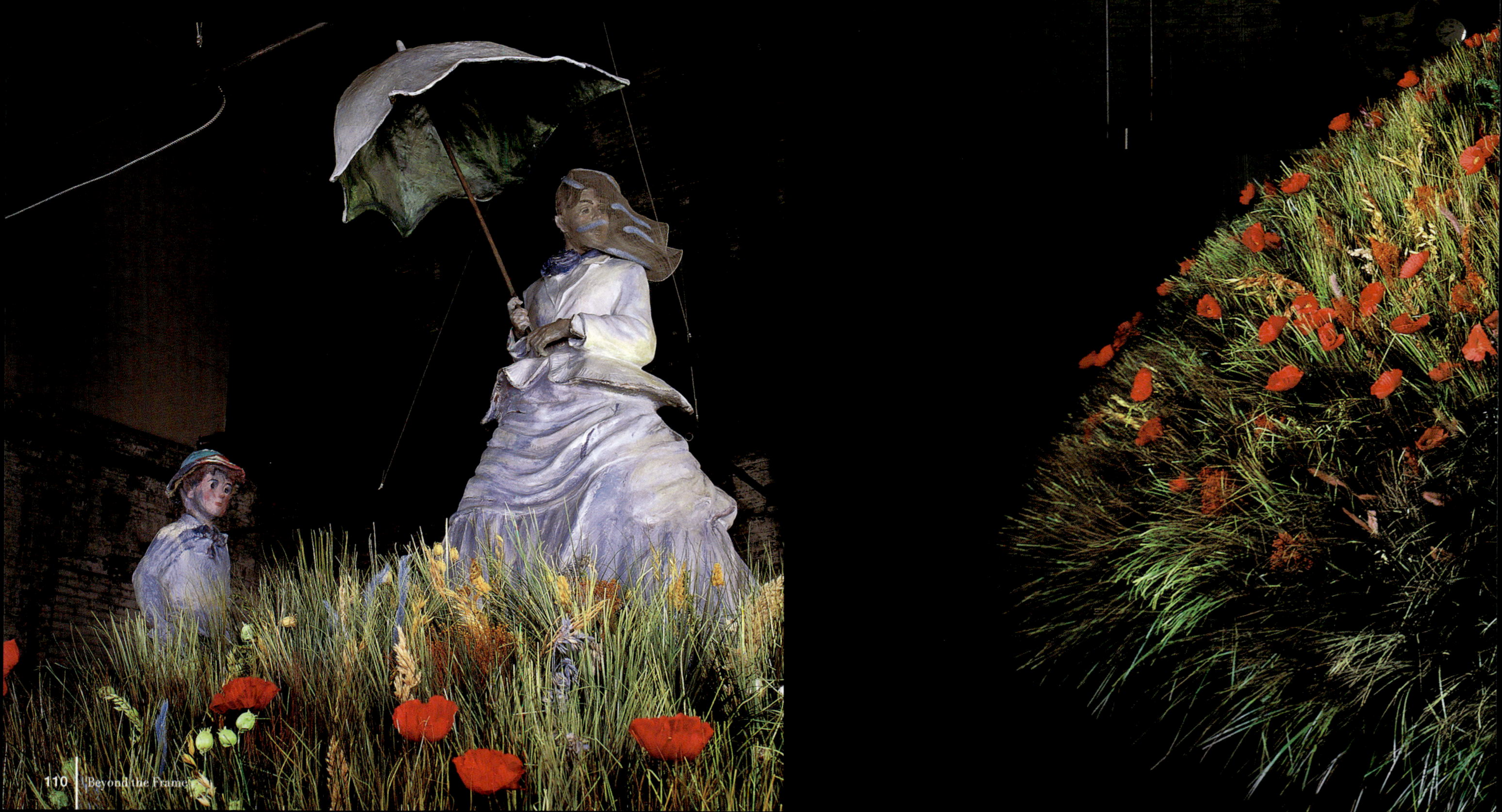

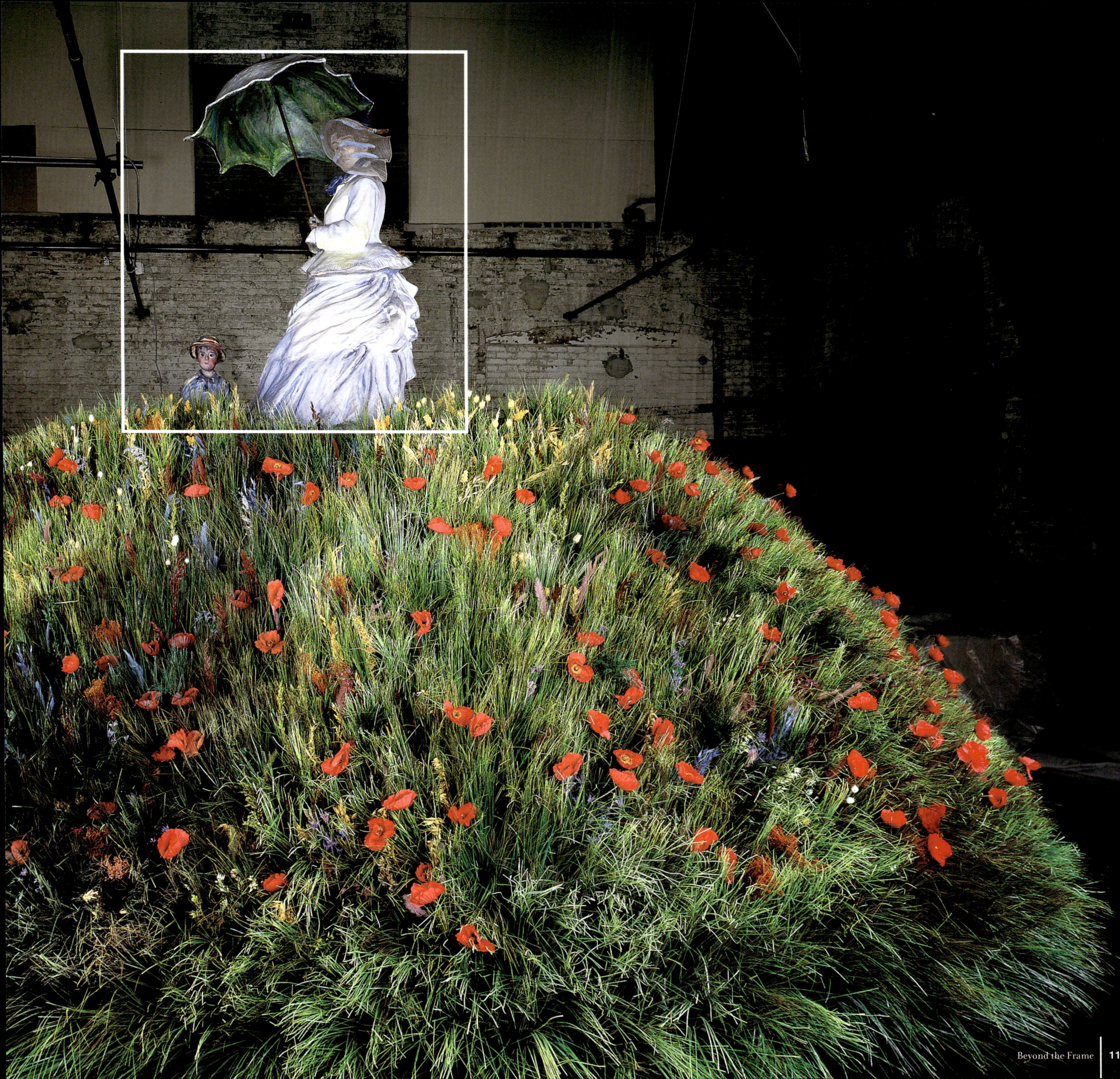

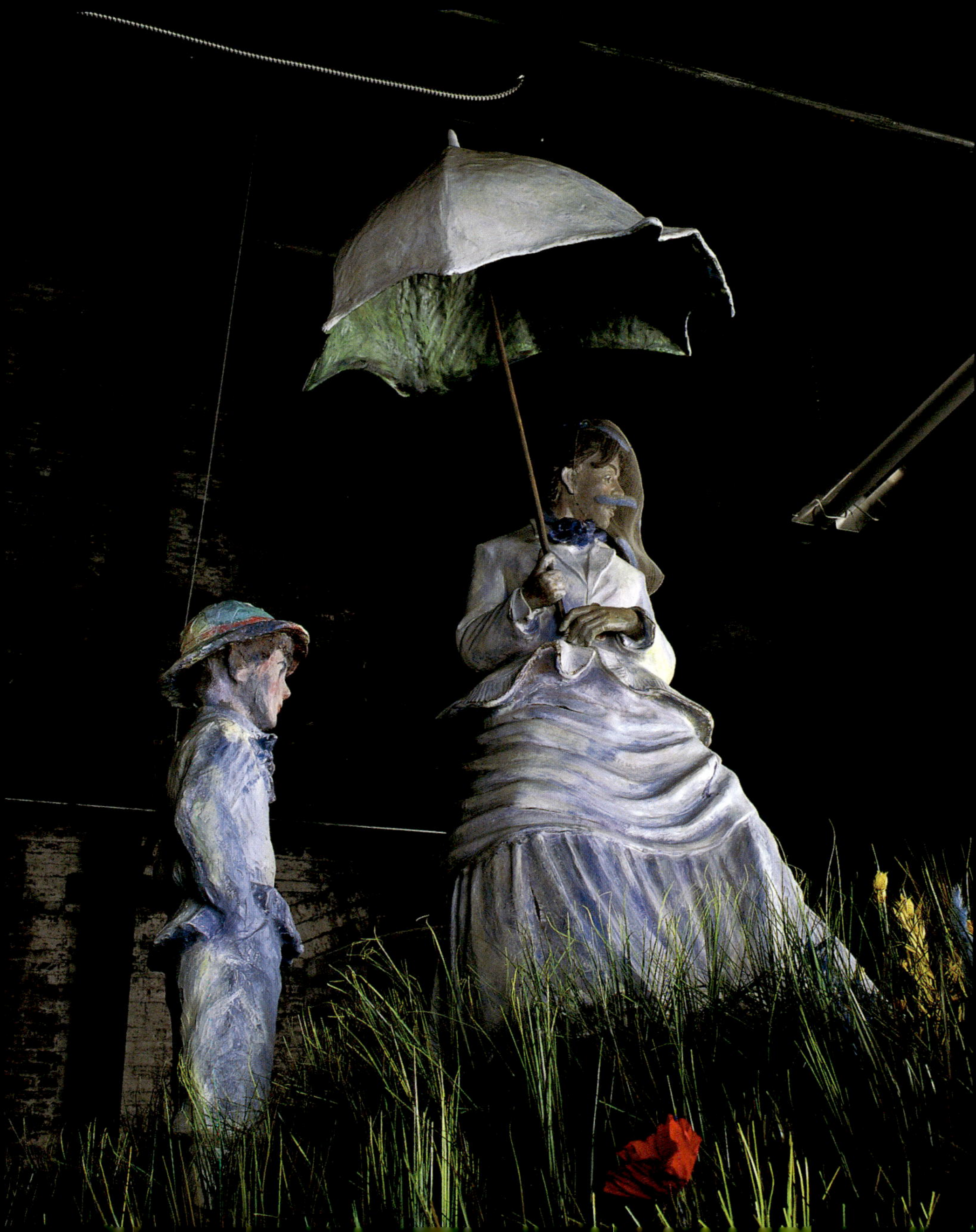

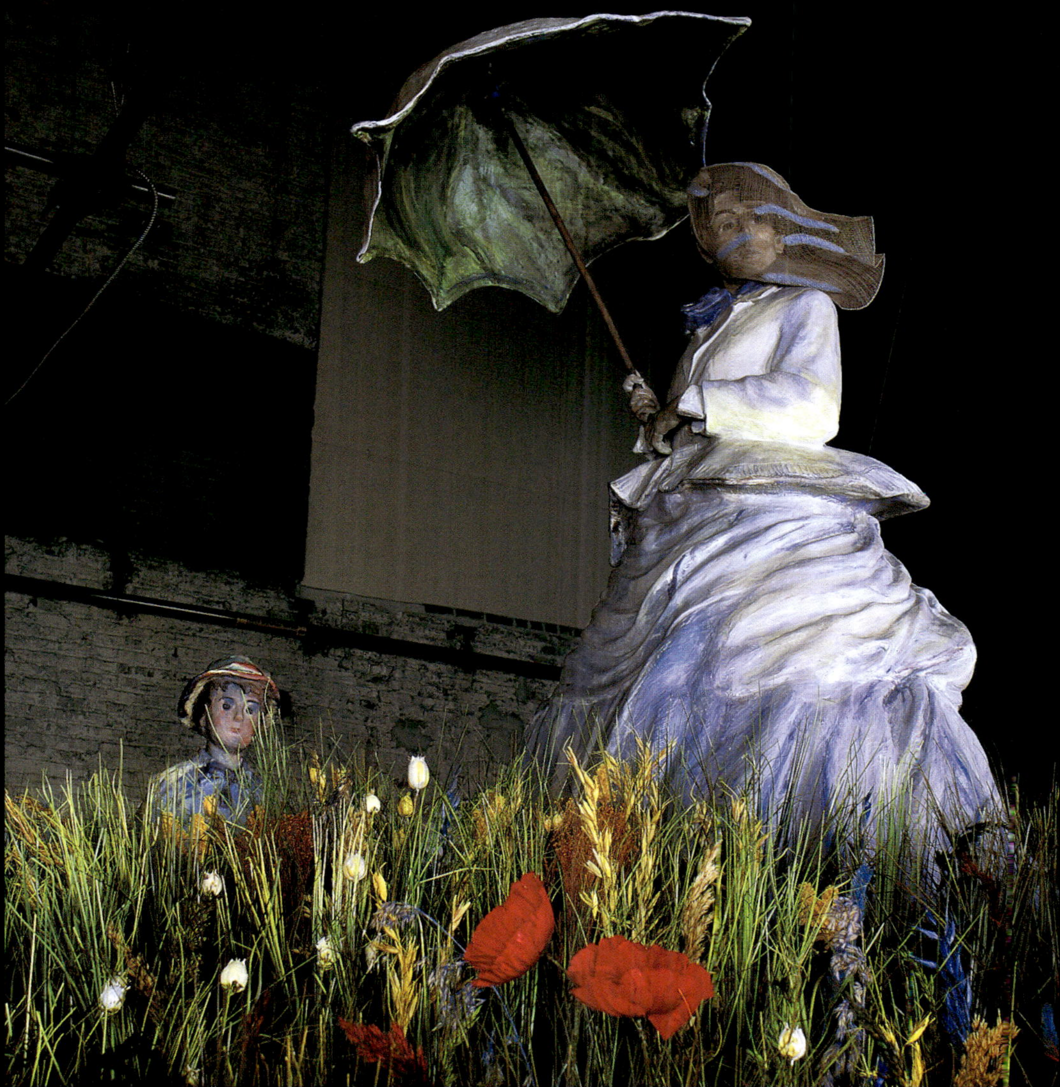

On Poppied Hill is a combination of two of Monet's paintings, one in a field of poppies and one on a hill. I didn't want to give up the poppies, so I put them on the hill.

—J. Seward Johnson, Jr.

Modeling Perspective: The Creative Process and Technology of J. Seward Johnson, Jr.

Jan Rothschild

Inspired when he saw a Japanese garden with plywood silhouettes against a forest landscape, J. Seward Johnson, Jr. sculpted a three-dimensional version of Manet's famous *Déjeuner sur l'herbe* and installed it in his public garden, Grounds for Sculpture, in Hamilton, New Jersey. Grappling with the perennial notions of allusion and illusion, Johnson began playing with other iconic nineteenth century works of art, transforming them into distinctly modern objects. Inevitably, the question arises, "How does he make them?"

"Viewers recognize the original painting as they first approach," reflects Johnson. "Then they walk into it and experience it as life-size sculpture. It's a kind of mind game." Making the sculptures is both simple and complex: Johnson uses ancient techniques and contemporary technology, but his thinking is rooted in the history of art.

Since the Renaissance, painters have used perspective to show three dimensions in two. "I am making two dimensions into three, so I use the painterly tricks of perspective to turn perspective on its head," Johnson admits. "I lie to tell the truth of the painting."

As a preliminary step for each piece, Johnson extensively researches the artist, the period, and the setting of the original painting. "I am re-creating the artist's subject, not his work," he explains. "The artist painted only part of what he saw. What is beyond his frame is my territory, and I have a tremendous amount of fun deciding what else to include." Often Johnson's additions are based on his historical research, as in his series of dancers whose costumes and attitudes match Renoir's paintings. At other times, Johnson adds a touch of humor. In his sculpture *Sailing the Seine*, inspired by Manet's *Argenteuil*, an amorous sailor strokes the derrière of his date, perhaps suggesting a bawdy moment that Manet did not record. Johnson sometimes even adds whole scenes as in *Were You Invited?* where he sculpted portraits of himself and some friends crashing Renoir's *Luncheon of the Boating Party* and drinking most of the wine. The additions can only be discovered when a visitor enters the setting.

From sculpting the figures to designing the backdrops, creating these artworks is an intricate and time-consuming process. To begin, Johnson carefully photographs the original painting, using both full-frame and close-up shots to capture the figures, brushstrokes, and color choices. Next, he traces the photograph onto a transparency and places it in a view box, a kind of frame on a tripod. Looking through the transparency, Johnson decides which forms to cast as sculpture and which to include either as props or illusionistic painted backdrops. Throughout the process, Johnson and his team look through the view box to check the alignment of the sculptural or painted components as they are added to the tableau.

A critical step in Johnson's process occurs when he determines the scale of the sculptures and the "sweet spot," the vantage point corresponding to the perspective of the original. All other decisions about the work of art flow from this initial decision. The vantage point for the work is carefully calculated and marked on the floor. From this spot, mathematical perspective helps plot the composition. Complications often arise, however. "I put myself in the world of the painting and defer to the painter, but sometimes the perspective is all wrong," Johnson laughs. "Van Gogh isn't even trying to use correct perspective," he adds ruefully. "And look at the chairs in *Eye of the Beholder*! [A work based on Manet's *At Père Lathuille's*] They look like they were designed by Salvador Dalí to confuse you. Manet made a pretense of realism, but with his own agenda. That is the world I have given myself over to."

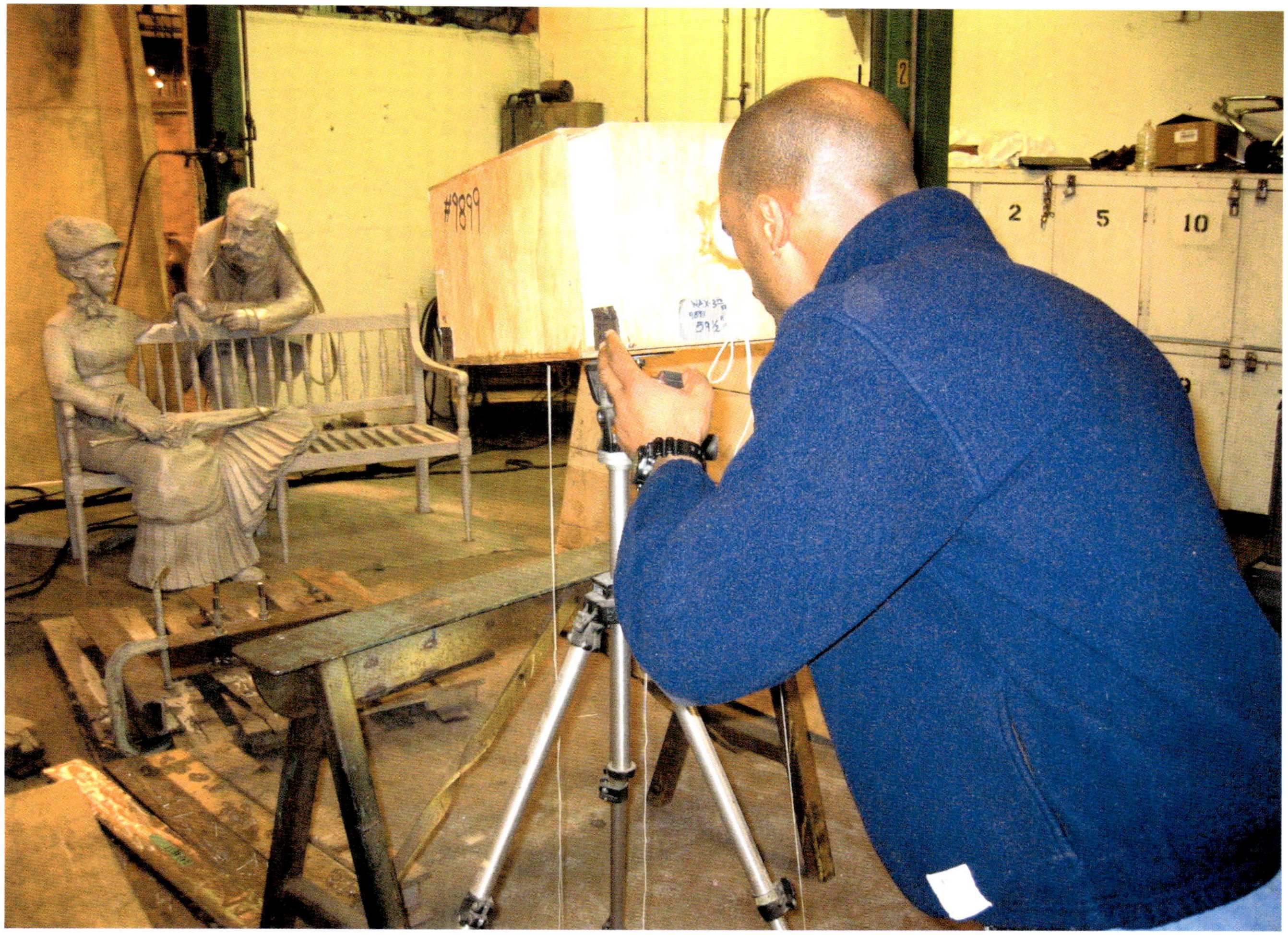

Using the view box to check alignment

View through the transparency

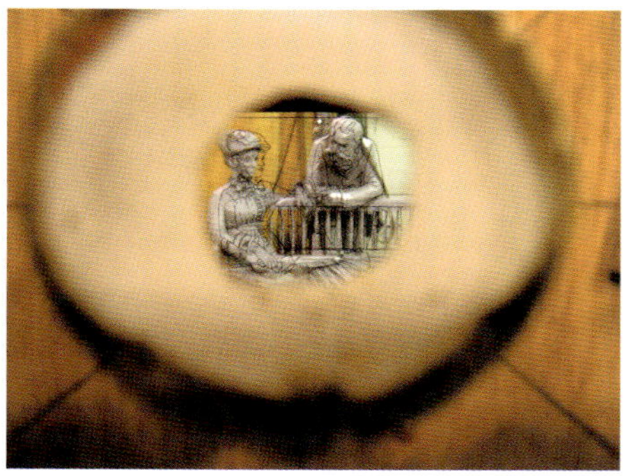

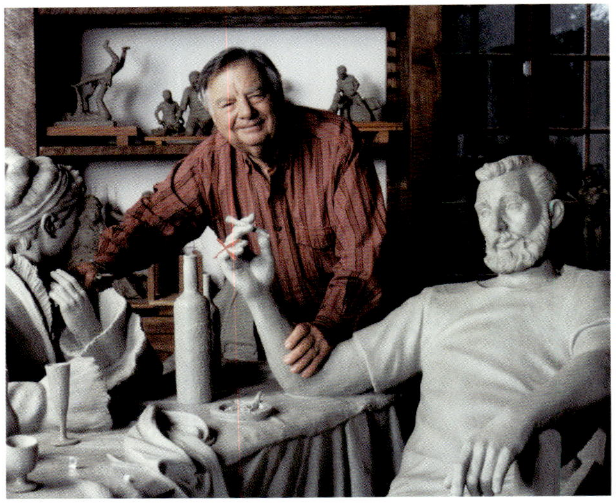

Plasteline model

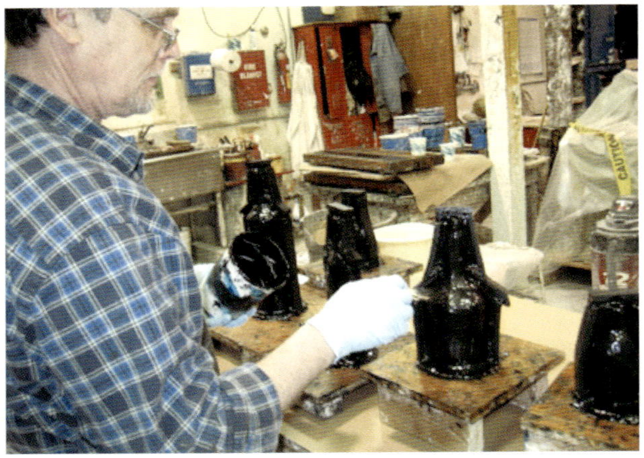

Applying the rubber mold

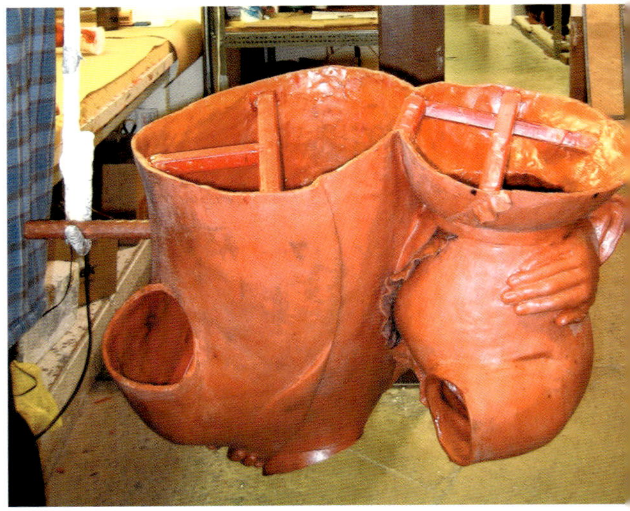

Wax model with sprues

CASTING THE FIGURES

Johnson builds metal armatures that serve as skeletons for the figures he will later sculpt. With plasteline, a synthetic clay-like substance that is easy to model, he builds the figures to scale, being careful to keep them in their exact positions when viewed through the view box. It is during this phase of the creative process that Johnson adds his famous touches. He uses the view box to ensure that none of his additions can be seen from the sweet spot.

The sculpted figures are then cast using the lost wax technique, an ancient process that Johnson has perfected in his atelier near Grounds for Sculpture. Once a plasteline figure is complete, assistants carefully cut it into sections and coat each piece with liquid rubber to form a flexible mold. This is the most exacting phase of the casting process. The quality of the rubber molds is paramount as they are used to duplicate the original sculpture. They must preserve every detail of the model, including minute surface textures and patterns. Next, the molds are pulled away from the plasteline (the rubber is stiff enough to retain its shape) and filled with molten wax. When the wax cools, the sections are reassembled to create a wax replica of the plasteline model. Imperfections are carefully removed or "chased" until the wax cast is virtually identical to the original.

Before casting, a network of wax rods is attached to the wax figure, forming a kind of external trusswork. These rods or "sprues" help distribute molten metal throughout the mold during the casting process. A sprue cup is added to act as a funnel for the molten metal, and the replica is dipped several times into a ceramic slurry that dries to form a hard shell. This shell functions as the mold for the molten metal. Once it has hardened for several days, the replica in its shell is baked in a kiln, further hardening the ceramic and causing the wax inside to melt and burn away, leaving a hollow mold—thus, the name "lost wax process."

The ceramic mold can now receive the molten metal, usually bronze or aluminum in Johnson's work. Heated to temperatures as high as 2,000 degrees Fahrenheit, the metal glows orange like coals in a barbecue. "This part of the process is the most beautiful to me," says Michelle Post, a sculptor who is Johnson's primary assistant for the Impressionist project. "It looks like we are pouring the most beautiful sunset in the world." The red-hot liquid goes into the sprue cup and courses down through the network of channels that

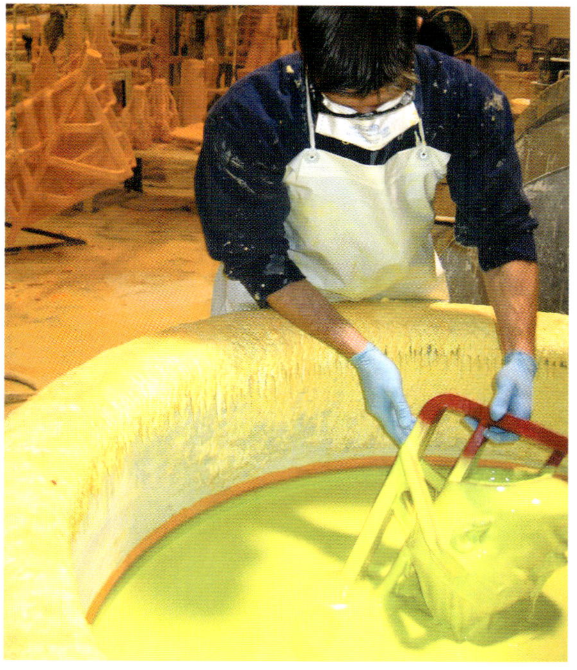
Dipping the wax model into ceramic slurry

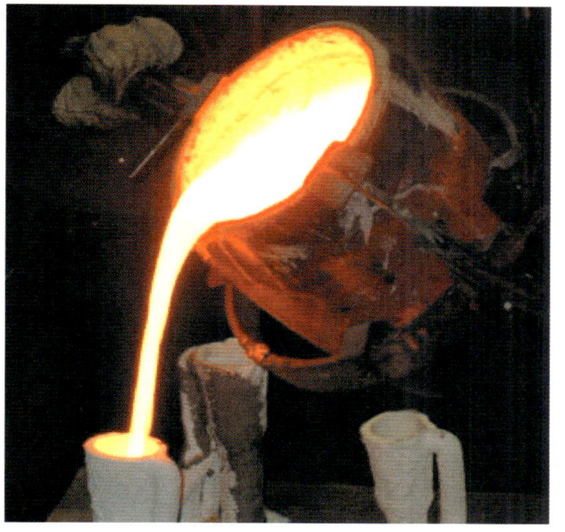
Pouring the metal

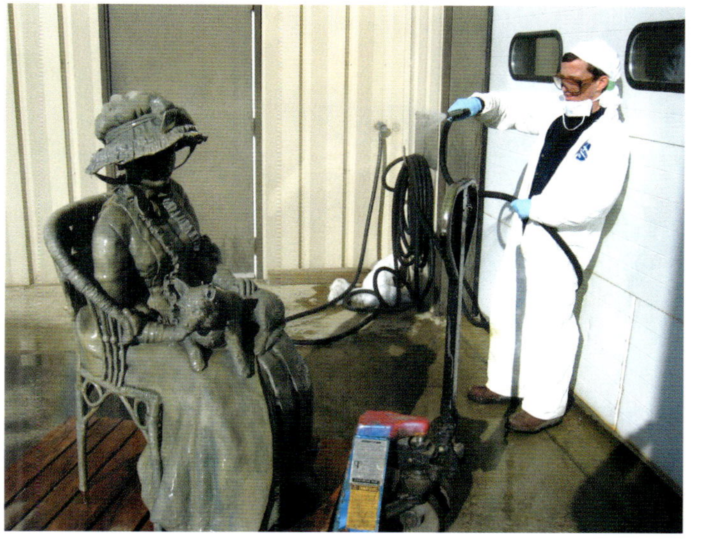
Spraying on the primer paint

allow trapped air and gas to escape upward as the mold slowly fills. After the metal cools, the ceramic shell is broken away revealing the cast inside. The sprues are cut off and the sections of the figure welded together. After the surface is meticulously chased (refined as in the wax chasing process), the metal sculpture exactly matches the original plasteline figure.

Painting the figures is arguably the most demanding part of the process. Johnson uses the colors and brush strokes of the original artist, reproducing the memorable effect of each individual painting. Johnson explains that, "most of the time I have to be painterly like the Impressionists, using layered color and visible brush strokes. But the 'crashers' added to The Boating Party are modern, so I used a more realist approach for them."

Johnson first sprays several layers of primer onto the figure to help the paint adhere. After this undercoat dries, each sculpture is hand painted, following the original painting as exactly as possible. "No reproduction can show the true colors," remarks Johnson. "My assistants and I have had to go back to the museums with books of paint samples to try to find the right colors. We hold the chips up to the painting to find a match, and guards have never shooed us off. It's a miracle!"

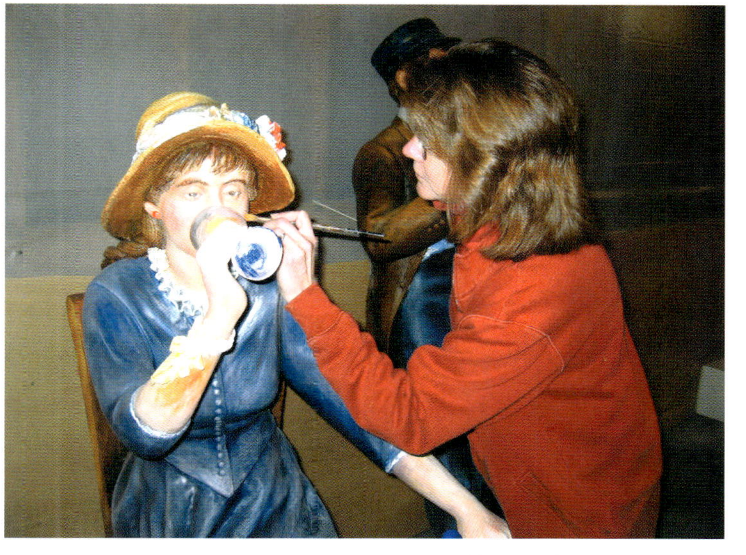
Hand-painting the details

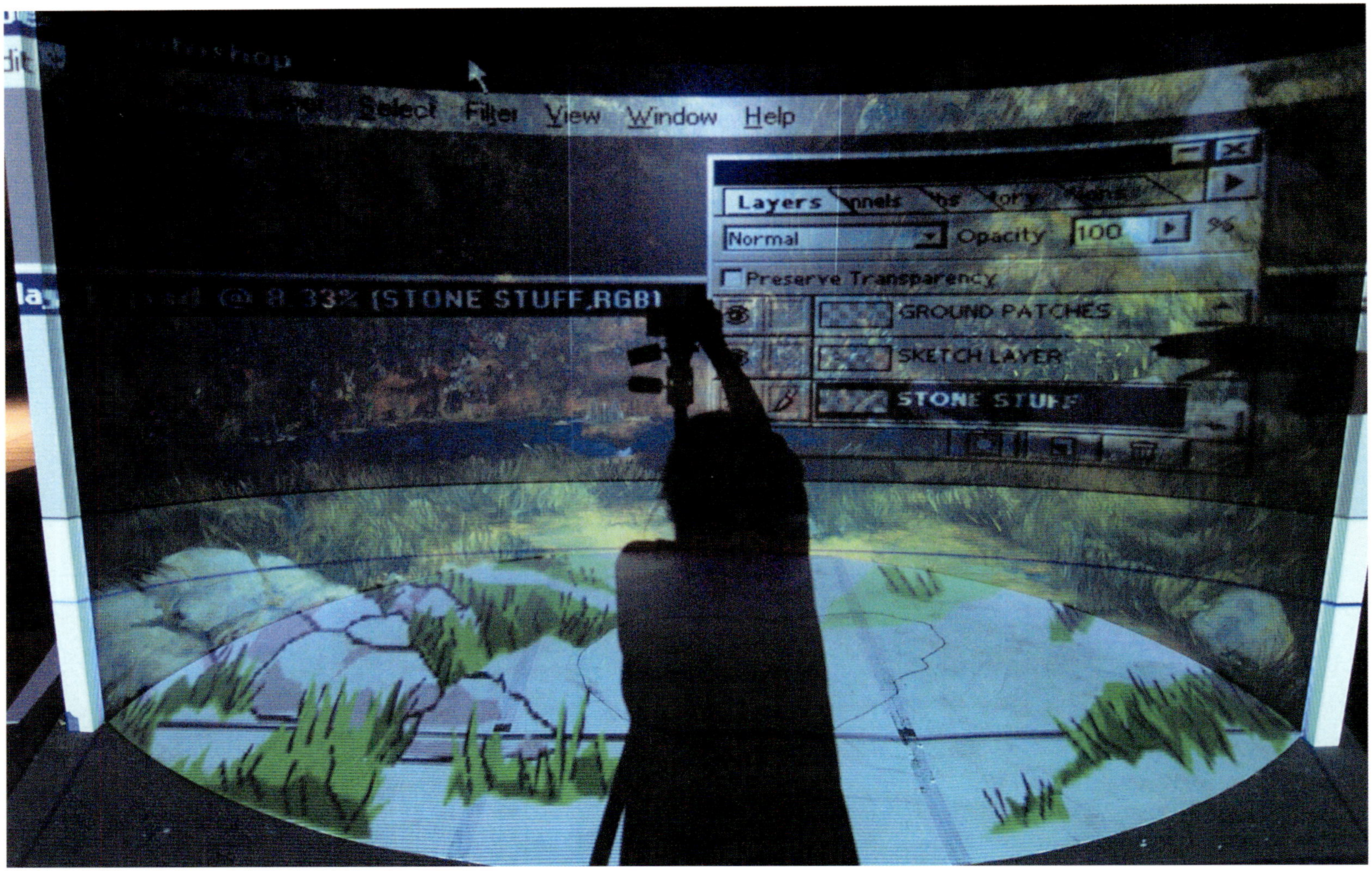

Projecting the painting onto the diorama floor

CREATING THE BACKGROUNDS

Once the figures are finished, the final step is to recreate the background of the painting to complete the illusion. For the Corcoran exhibition, Johnson decided to put each sculpture into an individual setting that includes both computer-generated backdrops and actual objects made of plastic, silk, and fabric. "I want the visitors to be surrounded by the paintings and to experience each work separately," Johnson says, "so for most of the sculptures we made dioramas with curved walls." This presented a formidable challenge. His solution to making the painting look flat against the curved backdrop is to use a perspective technique called anamorphosis, first developed in the Renaissance to create paintings that fool the eye. "Using anamorphosis preserves my sweet spot and adds elements of discovery and surprise," remarks Johnson.

Artists including Leonardo da Vinci and Hans Holbein used anamorphosis to include objects in their paintings that could be seen properly only from one vantage point and are distorted from everywhere else. To achieve this effect, they morphed the image using complicated perspective formulas that today can be duplicated by computers. "Many artists have been working with computers to play with perspective," says David Dempewolf, a Philadelphia artist who helped Johnson devise the techniques he ultimately adopted to create the museum settings for the exhibition. "But to create the impression of

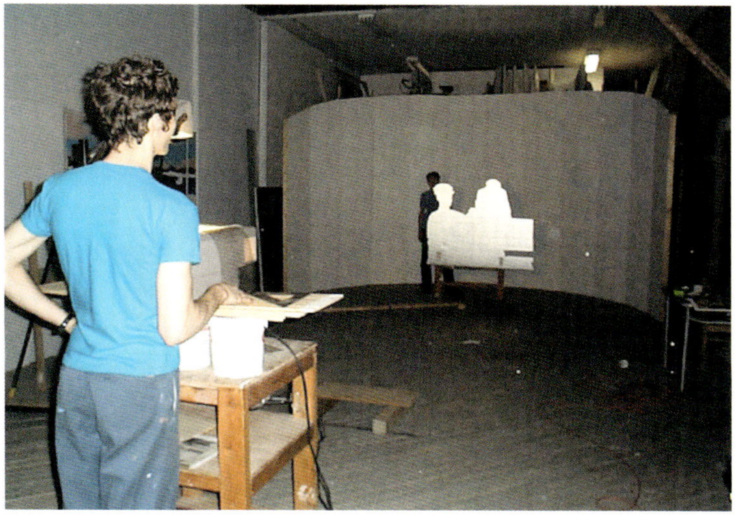

Adjusting the cardboard cutouts

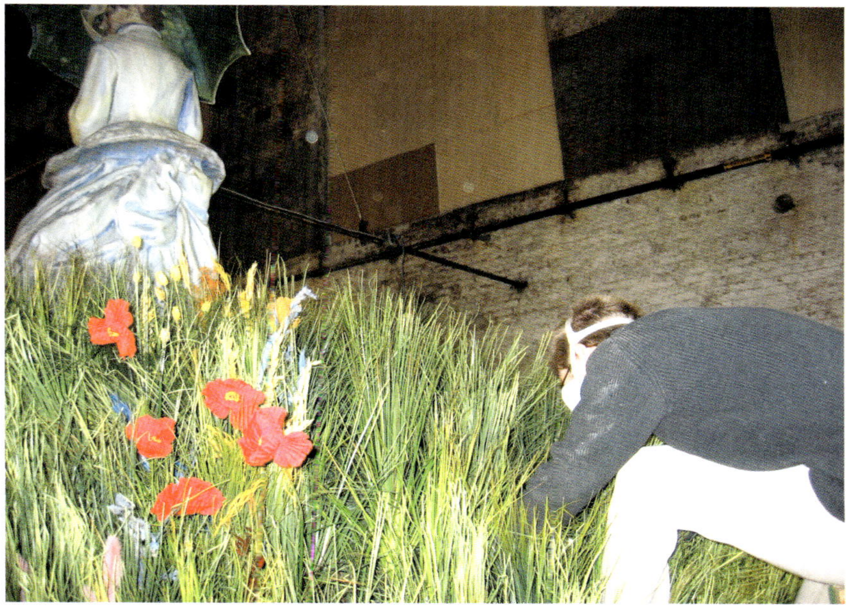

Adding botanical elements

two-dimensional space using three-dimensional objects before a curved background required us to start from scratch." Dempewolf and his team developed a process using computers, view boxes, cameras, and multiple projections, enabling the diorama images to appear true from the vantage point and in precise relation to the sculptures within them.

To create this illusion, Johnson projects a photograph of the painting through the original tracing into the curved diorama. Cardboard cutouts of the sculptures are placed into the space and aligned with the tracing. In most cases, the original artworks do not occupy the entire backdrop when everything is enlarged to life size. In order to expand the painting, Johnson creates a sketch for the additional sections and assistants use his outline to paint a new canvas in the style of the original. This newly enlarged painting is digitally photographed and projected onto the curving surfaces of the diorama. It is in this projection that the distortions appear that create the effect of anamorphosis. Digital photographs are taken to record the distortions; these become the template for the final design. The new photograph is again projected into the diorama and adjusted using a television camera to match the appearance of the painting from a single viewpoint. Once everything lines up properly and the distortions seem authentic, the computer file is finalized and used for the background.

Since the floors are flat, Johnson expected that they would be easier to construct than the walls. Because there is a small amount of information stretched over a large space, the distortions on the floor are much more pronounced than those on the walls. The transition from vertical to horizontal is difficult as well. The distortions are more extreme when the viewer moves into the diorama or views it from other angles. "The floors get really weird," laughs Johnson. "That's part of the fun of entering the work."

At the Corcoran, many of the installations will be shown with the sweet spot marked and the original tracing in place in its view box. This will allow viewers to better understand Johnson's creative process and technology without interrupting the pleasure of the experience. "It is supposed to be surprising and even a little strange," Johnson confesses. "After all, just like the Impressionists, I am playing with reality."

Original Impressionist Paintings and Quotes

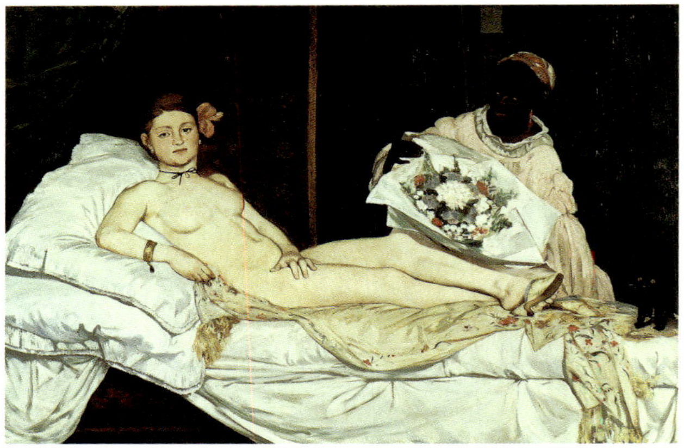

OLYMPIA
Edouard Manet

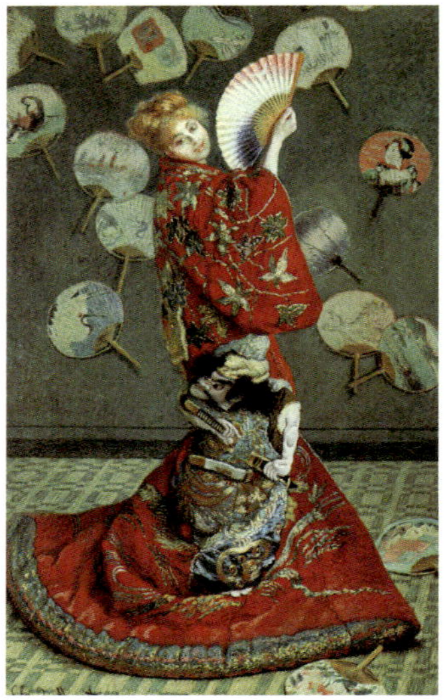

LA JAPONAISE (CAMILLE MONET IN JAPANESE COSTUME)
Claude Monet

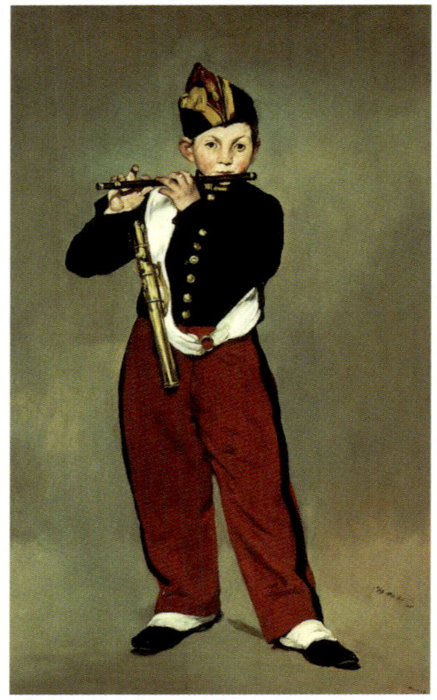

THE FIFER
Edouard Manet

> "*Olympia*; that wan, wasted courtesan, showing to the public, for the first time, the nontraditional, unconventional nude .... Rarely has any modern work been more applauded by so few, or more deeply damned by the many, than was that of this innovator."

— Stephen Mallarmé, *The Art Monthly Review*, September 30, 1876.

> "Manet's distinctly modern 'Old Master' is a sophisticated mixture of ambiguity, tease, and homage, and these are the reasons why the painting continues to challenge and confound.

—Alan Krell, *Manet and the Painters of Contemporary Life*, London: Thames and Hudson Ltd, 1996, p. 34.

> "Olympia's black choker and fashionable slipper make it clear that she is not a mythical being, but a mercenary love goddess of the nineteenth century."

—Petra ten-Doesschate Chu, *Nineteenth-Century European Art*, New York: Harry N. Abrams, Inc., 2003, p. 286.

> "I myself worry very little about what could have been said on art. But if I had to give an opinion, I would formulate one in this way: everything that has the soul of humanity, everything that has the soul of contemporaneity is interesting. Everything that is deprived of it is worthless."

—Edouard Manet, as recalled by Antonin Proust, from Francoise Cachin, *Manet: Painter of Modern Life*, London: Thames and Hudson/New Horizons, 1995, p. 142

> "*La Japonaise* was Monet's only venture into a popular genre subject. He was in desperate financial straits, and he probably conceived *La Japonaise* as a potboiler, an illusionistic tour-de-force in a flamboyant style that would be successful with the public. It did in fact sell quickly and at quite a high price."

—Virginia Spate, et al., *Monet & Japan*, Canberra: National Gallery of Australia; Seattle, University of Washington Press, 2001, p. 23.

> "*La Japonaise* is not a Japanese woman, but a Parisienne dressed as a Japanese. It's my first wife who posed."

—Claude Monet, quoted in Spate, et al., *Monet & Japan*, Canberra: National Gallery of Australia; Seattle, University of Washington Press, 2001, p. 24.

> "[Manet] lends an unforgettable grace, both bizarre and naïve, to this gamin disguised as a warrior, planted on his feet in oversized shoes and white spats."

—Paul Jamot, cited in Beth Archer Brombert, *Edouard Manet: Rebel in a Frock Coat*, New York: Little, Brown & Company, 1996, p. 185.

> "Manet made no attempt to suggest perspective; only the short shadows behind the boy's heels indicate a source of light and depth."

—Beth Archer Brombert, *Edouard Manet: Rebel in a Frock Coat*, New York: Little, Brown & Company, 1996, p. 183.

> "Zola saw *The Fifer*, another work rejected by the Salon, as exemplifying Manet's artistic qualities: simplicity and perceptiveness, accuracy and energy, daring and truthfulness—superior qualities that he was sure would one day ensure the painter a well-deserved place in the Louvre."

—Hajo Düchting, *Edouard Manet: Images of Parisian Life*, Munich & New York: Prestel-Verlag, 1995, p. 46

> "Manet's talent lies in exactness and simplicity, and I was thinking in particular of the impression this canvas had made upon me."

—Emile Zola, *L'Evénement*, May 7 1866, from Francoise Cachin, *Manet: Painter of Modern Life*, London: Thames and Hudson/New Horizons, 1995, p. 69.

> "The artist [Manet], confronting any subject whatever, allows himself to be guided by his eyes, which perceive the subject in terms of broad tints that need to control each other. A head placed against a wall is but a more or less white spot against a more or less gray background, and the clothing next to the face becomes, for example, a more or less blue spot next to the more or less white spot. From this comes a great simplicity almost completely without details, an assembly of exact and delicate spots that at a short distance produce painting of striking relief."

— Emile Zola, *Edouard Manet*, 1867

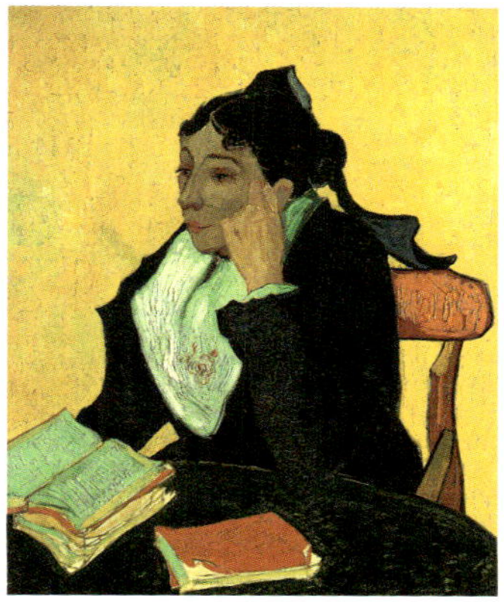

L'ARLÉSIENNE: MADAME JOSEPH-MICHEL GINOUX
Vincent van Gogh

> "Then I have an Arlésienne at last, a figure ... slashed on in an hour, background pale citron, the face gray, the clothes black, black, black, with perfectly raw Prussian blue. She is leaning on a green table and seated in an armchair of orange wood."

— Vincent van Gogh, letter from Arles to Theo van Gogh, c. November 6, 1888

> "The image has, through the books, connotations of modernity in which Mme Ginoux is given emblematic status as an ideal, literate modern woman."

—Lauren Soth, "Vincent van Gogh reads Harriet Beecher Stowe," *Work and Image*, vol. 10, no.2, (April–June 1994), p. 160.

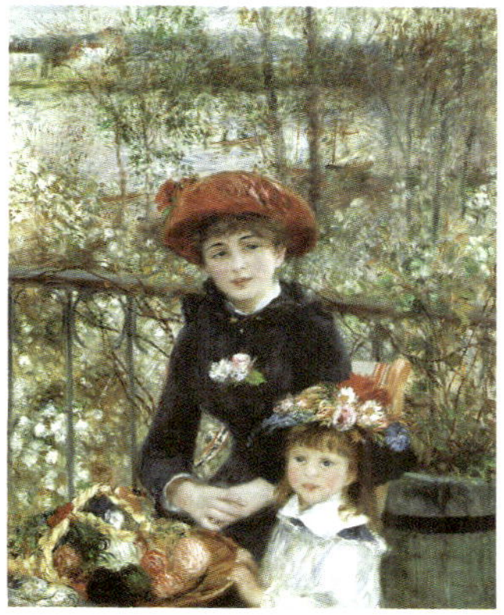

TWO SISTERS (ON THE TERRACE)
Pierre-Auguste Renoir

> "Originally called *Two Sisters*, this painting was dismissed by the critics with coarse jokes. It has since become one of the best known and best loved by Renoir. The models are sitting on the terrace of the Fournaise restaurant, and the work is now known more by the site than by the sisters."

—Anne Distel, *Renoir: A Sensuous Vision*, London: Thames and Hudson/New Horizons, 1995, p. 77.

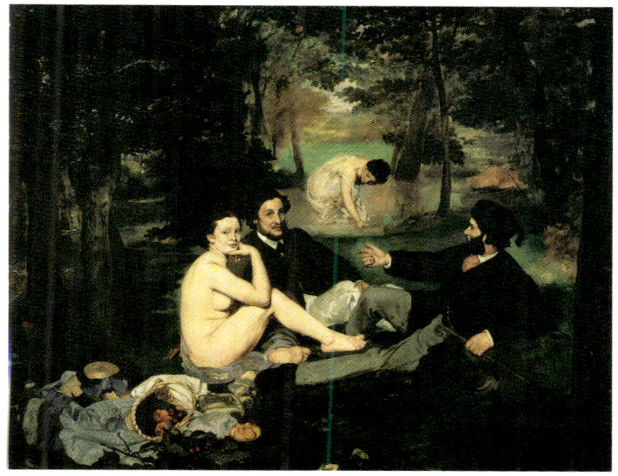

LE DÉJEUNER SUR L'HERBE
Edouard Manet

> "When I see *Le Dèjeuner sur l'herbe*, I say to myself: sorrows are for later."

—Pablo Picasso in 1932, cited in "Bonjour M. Manet," 1983, from Francoise Cachin, *Manet: Painter of Modern Life*, London: Thames and Hudson/New Horizons, 1995, p. 162.

> "First of all the famous *Déjeuner sur l'herbe*, rejected by the jury that stupidly did not understand that this is not a woman naked, but a women undressed, which is quite different."

—Fervacques, *Le Figaro*, December 27, 1873, from Francoise Cachin, *Manet: Painter of Modern Life*, London: Thames and Hudson/New Horizons, 1995, p. 150

> "To exhibit is to find friends and allies for the struggle."

—Eduoard Manet, "Preface" to his exhibition catalogue, May 1867.

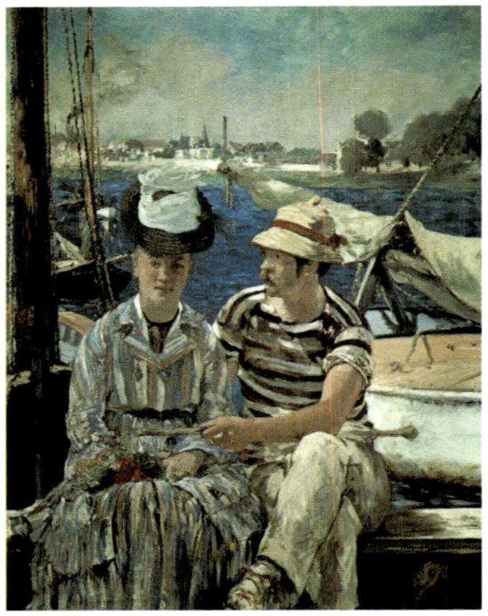

ARGENTEUIL
Edouard Manet

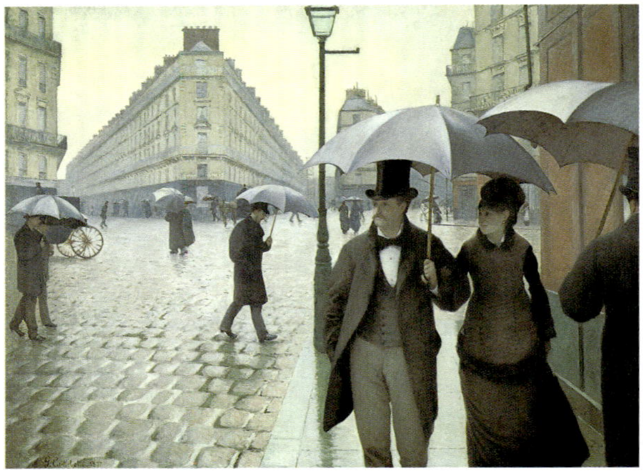

PARIS STREET; RAINY DAY
Gustave Caillebotte

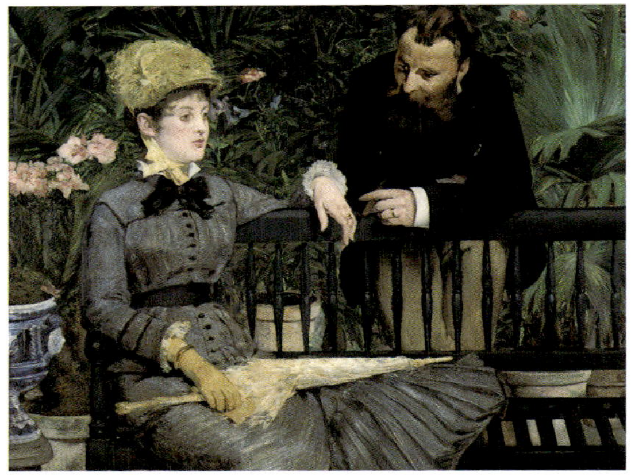

IN THE WINTER GARDEN
Edouard Manet

> "Boatmen came from various walks of life, but the women they brought with them all belonged to the class of second-rate ladies of pleasure. Such as the one in Argenteuil."

—Théodore Duret, quoted in Hajo Düchting, *Edouard Manet: Images of Parisian Life*, Munich and New York: Prestel-Verlag, 1995, p.133.

> "These anonymous figures, almost uniformly dressed in grey or black, are as monotonous as the street itself. They appear listless, spiritless, without direction, aptly described by Varnedoe as strolling somnambulants."

—Anne Distel, "The Street" in *Gustave Caillebotte: the Unknown Impressionist*. London: Royal Academy of Arts in association with Ludion Press, 1996, p.71.

> "Manet's men and women live imprisoned in their respective inner monologues; even when people share the same spot, the same space, there is an invisible barrier between them."

—Werner Hofmann, "Glances," unpublished lecture given at "Manet: A Symposium," The Metropolitan Museum of Art, New York, October 22, 1983, quoted in B. Collins, "Manet's *In the Conservatory and Chez Le Père Lathuille*," *Art Journal*, vol. 45, (Spring 1985), p. 60.

> "Figures in Manet's work are lonely in crowds, disconnected in pairs, totally oblivious to each other, or subtly detached."

—B. Collins, "Manet's *In the Conservatory and Chez Le Père Lathuille*," *Art Journal*, vol. 45 (Spring 1985), p. 60.

> "She is self-possessed, lost in thought. There is not a hint of flirtation anywhere. In fact, during the moment of the painting, the woman ignores her companion, who, it turns out, is her husband."

—E. Lipton, "Manet: A Radicalized Female Imagery," *Artforum*, vol. 13, (March 1975), p. 53.

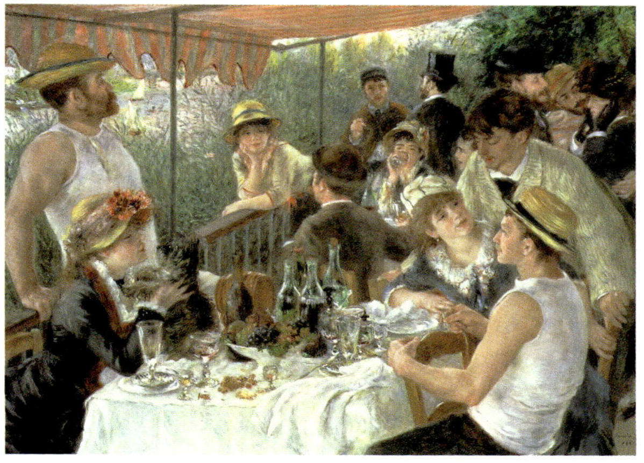

LUNCHEON OF THE
BOATING PARTY
Pierre-Auguste Renoir

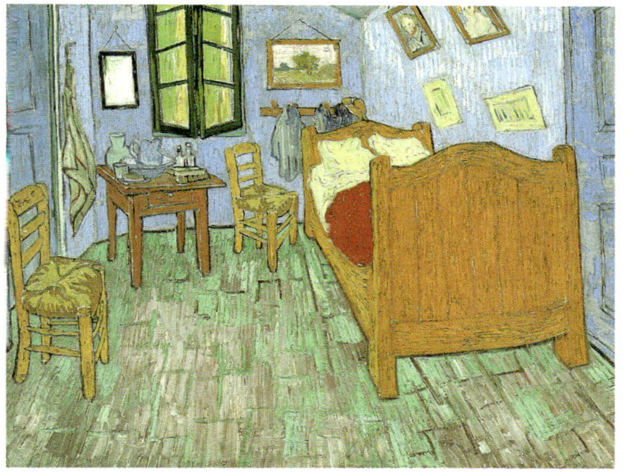

THE BEDROOM
Vincent van Gogh

> "On his own terms Renoir compresses into one image the example of the past and vitality of the present. This duality is the foundation of Renoir's best work and is nowhere more eloquently and successfully expressed than in *Luncheon of the Boating Party*."

—Elizabeth Steele, "Achieving Composition in *Luncheon of the Boating Party*," in *Impressionism on the Seine: A Celebration of Renoir's Luncheon of the Boating Party*. Washington, D.C.: Counterpoint in association with the Phillips Collection, 1996, p. 222.

> "Much of the painting's success lies in the convincing interaction that Renoir creates among his sitters. Their arrangement in twos and threes leads the eye back and forth across the table and through the composition to the rear of the balcony. It is the complexity of the scene that makes the painting so intriguing, and it demonstrates the painter's mastery of strong compositional skills."

—Elizabeth Steele, "Achieving Composition in *Luncheon of the Boating Party*," in *Impressionism on the Seine: A Celebration of Renoir's Luncheon of the Boating Party*. Washington, D.C: Counterpoint in association with the Phillips Collection, 1996, p. 221.

> "*Un déjeuner à Bougival* [*Luncheon of the Boating Party*] is a charming work, full of gaiety and spirit, its wild youth caught in the act, radiant and lively, frolicking at high noon in the sun, laughing at everything, seeing only today and mocking tomorrow. For them eternity is in their glass, in their boat, and in their songs. It is fresh and free without being too bawdy."

— Paul de Charry, *Le Pays*, March 10, 1882

> "In real life views of things and people are manifested in a thousand unexpected ways. Our vantage point is not always located in the center of a room whose two side walls converge toward the back wall; the lines of sight and angles of cornices do not always join with mathematical regularity and symmetry. Nor does our point of view always exclude the large expanse of ground or floor in the immediate foreground. Sometimes our viewpoint is very high, and sometimes very low; as a result we lose sight of the ceiling, and everything crowds into our immediate field of vision …"

— Louis Emile Edmond Duranty, *La Nouvelle Peinture*, 1876.

> "Who can deny that *The Bedroom*, painted by Van Gogh… is a kind of wooden womb, a warm room for having pleasant dreams in?"

—Waldemar Januskczak, "With a Handshake: Van Gogh and Bevan," *Modern Painters*, vol. 3, (Summer 1990), p. 39.

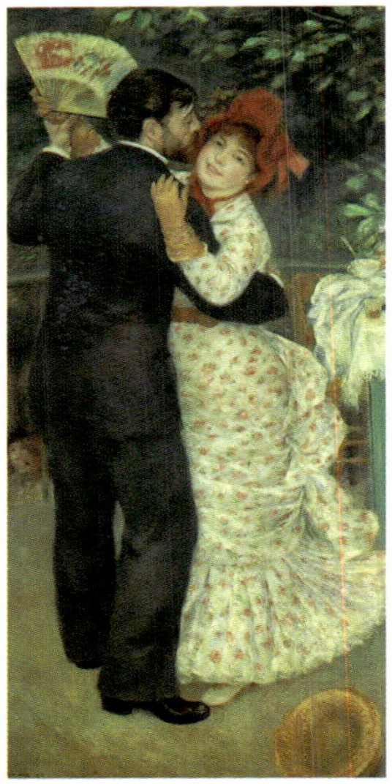

DANCE IN THE COUNTRY
Pierre-Auguste Renoir

> "One could add to the dancers the literary commentary so dear to the French imagination, but I can see in them only an art that is skilled at painting faces flushed with pleasure, relaxed by delicious fatigue, an art which makes clothing that is cut well and worn well seem elegant and distinguished."

—Philippe Burty, 1883, quoted in *Renoir*, London: The Arts Council of Great Britain in collaboration with the Réunion des musées nationaux and the Museum of Fine Arts, Boston, 1985, p. 237.

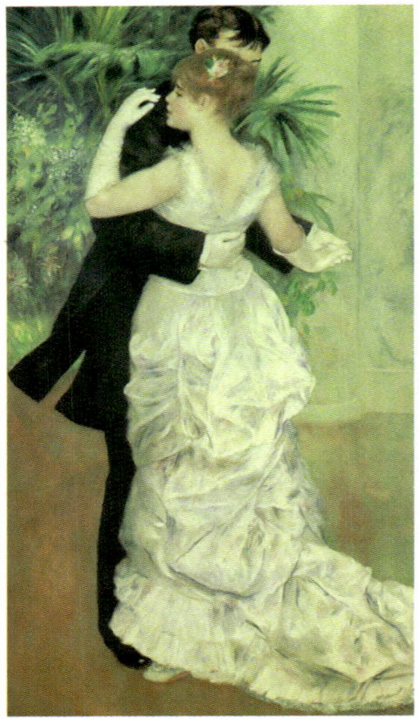

DANCE IN THE CITY
Pierre-Auguste Renoir

> "The model is only there to set me going. She enables me to dare things that I couldn't invent without her, also to help me back on course if I go too far."

—Renoir on his models, 1919, trans. In *Renoir: A Retrospective*, ed. Nicholas Wadley, 1987, from Anne Distel, *Renoir: A Sensuous Vision*, London: Thames and Hudson/New Horizons, 1995, p. 143.

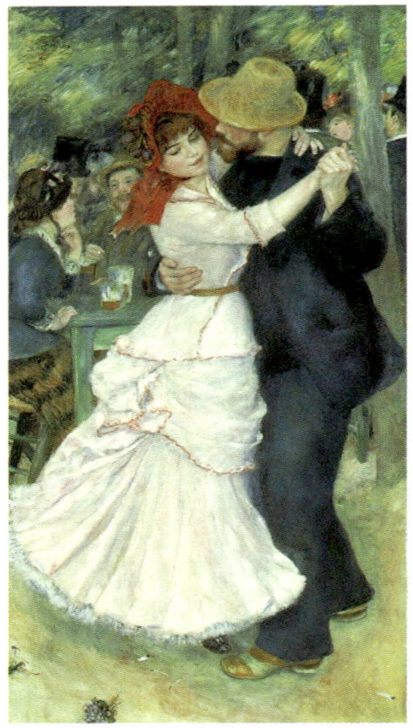

DANCE AT BOUGIVAL
Pierre-Auguste Renoir

> "A drawing for the composition bears Renior's inscription: 'She was waltzing, deliciously abandoned in the arms of a fair headed man with the air of an oarsman'."

—*Masterpiece Paintings from the Museum of Fine Arts, Boston*, Beverly Fazio ed., Boston: Museum of Fine Arts, Boston in association with Harry N. Abrams, Inc., New York, 1986, p. 72.

> "*Dance at Bougival* creates a mood, rather than telling a story. The girl, wearing a ring on her wedding finger, seems momentarily to turn away from her companion's attentions, but we know no more of their relations."

—*Renoir*, London: The Arts Council of Great Britain in collaboration with the Réunion des musées nationaux and the Museum of Fine Arts, Boston, 1985, p. 237.

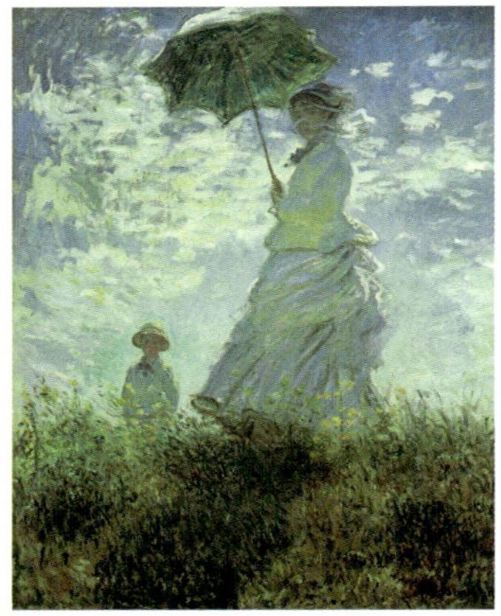

WOMAN WITH A PARASOL —MADAME MONET AND HER SON *AND* POPPIES
Claude Monet

> "I am working as never before, and at new projects, figures in the open air as I understand them, done as landscapes. It is an old dream that still haunts me."

—Claude Monet in a letter to Duret, August 13, 1887, from Sylvie Théodore Patin, *Monet: The Ultimate Impressionist*, London: Thames and Hudson/New Horizons, p. 98.

Acknowledgments

David Levy and I first conceived of this exhibition on a trip to Grounds for Sculpture in 2000. An enchanted encounter with several of the Impressionist tableaux in the garden made us wonder if we could achieve a similar experience for the visitor in a museum setting. The subsequent discussions with J. Seward Johnson, Jr. and his team convinced us that individual environments could be created for the sculptures that would evoke a comparable sense of awe and discovery.

Soon afterwards, Johnson and his assistants went to work producing the plastiline models and subsequent casts of the many figures and props, while also developing the complicated technology required to produce the settings and backdrops for sixteen Impressionist-inspired works in three dimensions. The results are astonishing. How else would you know who lurked beneath Monet's *La Japonaise*, or what the seated figures look like in *Garden at Sainte-Adresse* since Monet's original painting only shows their backs? Surely we will all enjoy visiting Olympia in her boudoir where we can see what kind of furniture she might have chosen, or what kind of liqueur her amoureux preferred.

To accomplish this grand undertaking required the devotion and hard work of many individuals. Michelle Post, Johnson's project manager for the Impressionist series and an artist in her own right, and Paula Stoeke, long-time curator of Johnson's work, are two of the most important.

Under Post's supervision Technical Engineer Tim Abbott, Construction Supervisor Kent DeCardenas, and staff carpenters Eric Schultz, George Dubinski, and Jeremy Eustice provided essential expertise in bringing these great pictures to life. The impressive skills of computer graphics expert David Dempewolf and his staff members Eric McDade, Scott Rigby, Vickie Schlegel, and Jason Browning made possible the remarkable settings with floors and backdrops that evoke the original canvases. The painstaking details applied to the figures, props, still-life elements, and landscape embellishments owe their elegant effects to Lindsey Young-Lockett, Joni Fitzgerald-Alyea, Patti Quigley, Rob Quigley, Marc Robinson, and Lori Young-Lockett, while Helen Uger executed the gallery-sized mural painting that sets the stage for *If It Were Time*, Johnson's irresistible reinterpretation of Monet's celebrated picture, *Garden at Sainte-Adresse*, as well as the backdrops for *Were You Invited?* and many of the diorama backgrounds. Jackie and John Nicolai flawlessly executed the sculpture installations. Finally, Portnoy DeCardenas provided encouragement and comic relief as the project mascot.

Credit for the publication of this beautiful book accompanying the exhibition goes to Michael Sand, executive editor at Bulfinch Press, and to Jim Trulove, CEO of Grayson Publishing, and his chief designer, James Pittman. Wyatt Gallery, principal photographer for the publication, embraced the enormous challenges involved in photographing these complex works with grace and ingenuity. The resulting photographs are not only beautiful, but magical in their evocation of the works of art. We have the Corcoran's long-time friend, Zach Morfogen, to thank for bringing the project to the attention of the publishers. And we owe the irresistible pop-up of *Déjeuner Déjà Vu* to the generosity of Sarah Hood Solomon.

David C. Levy, always a great enthusiast of Johnson and this body of work, has written a wonderful homage to the artist as both a sculptor and a stalwart supporter of his fellow artists whose works enliven the studios and open spaces at Grounds for Sculpture.

Professor ten-Doesschate Chu, a well-known scholar and expert on nineteenth-century European art, has provided the perfect context for our understanding of Johnson's works and the icons that inspired them. Her informed discussion and analysis extend our knowledge while also enhancing our enjoyment as we revisit the Impressionist enterprise.

At the Corcoran, Jan Rothschild, chief communications officer, played a major role in coordinating the preparation of the book, working with Michelle Post, Jim Trulove, and Wyatt Gallery to make sure the various elements would come together perfectly. In addition, she applied her journalistic talents to the essay describing the complex techniques and disciplines involved in realizing Johnson's Impressionist tableaux. Her able staff members, consisting of public affairs associate Susan Kenney, assistant Hilary Allard, and web master Robert Tobin have made invaluable contributions to the public presentation of the project.

On the Museum side, the Curatorial Department has enthusiastically devoted itself to planning and executing the project beginning with the earliest meetings with Michelle Post here at the museum. Lauren Harry, assistant to the chief curator, handled many aspects of the project, doing substantive research as well as collaborating on installation decisions and editing the texts for the book. Laura Coyle, curator of European art, drew on her knowledge of the nineteenth-century artists in preparing the informative labels and wall texts. Corcoran intern Rachel Leverenz sacrificed some of her research time with curator Eric Denker to gather information on the individual works.

The presentation of the educational materials was especially complex, and Susan Badder demonstrated her many skills in collaborating with Paula Stoeke to organize and exhibit the didactic content in the most interesting and effective way possible. We are grateful also to Martin Huberman, who created the entertaining and informative video for the education gallery. In conjunction with Reading is Fundamental, members of the Education Department staff, including Diane Arkin, Sarah Loffman, Laura Pasquini, and Emilie Johnson, produced one of our best Family Days ever with the Johnson exhibition as the centerpiece.

Elizabeth Parr, exhibitions director, coordinated the overall planning for the museum's presentation, while Kimberly Davis, formerly the Corcoran's registrar, and her associate registrar, Rebekah Sobel, handled all the shipping and advance preparation. Lighting specialist Michael Parker used his theater experience to enhance the make-believe atmosphere. Our current registrar, Nancy Swallow, has supervised the on-site installation. Chief preparator Clyde Paton and assistant preparator David Jung, artists in their own right, brought their usual considerable skills to bear in realizing this large installation.

Kelly Baker, rights and reproductions coordinator, performed brilliantly in locating and procuring the wide-ranging photographic material needed for the book—reproducing works by artists as varied as Titian, Picasso, Larry Rivers, and Jean Michel Basquiat. We are grateful to photographer Mea Jambroes-ten Doessschate Ameling for her images on site at Grounds for Sculpture.

Past Chairman of the Board of Trustees Ronald Abramson, and the present Chairman, Otto Ruesch, have been enormously supportive in helping us to realize this unusual exhibition. Trustee and Chair of the Museum Board of Overseers Anne Barnett Hazel has generously shared her wisdom and practical advice all along the way. Paul Frazer, chair of the Museum Board's Exhibition and Audience Committee, contributed much-appreciated guidance as well, along with committee members Steven Phillips, Jeannette Petite, Nina Herrick, Bernie Koteen, Anne Murphy, Felix Sanchez, Sigita Naujokaitis, Carlotta Miles, Susan Firestone, and David Schwartz.

Special thanks are due to Olga Hirshhorn, an active member of the Corcoran's College Board of Overseers, a generous donor to our permanent collection, and someone who early on understood the fairy-tale element of Johnson's work. It was she who shared the enchanting passage from Vladimir Nabokov's autobiography, and suggested the parallels between Johnson's tableaux and the stage sets for the recent Kennedy Center production of Stephen Sondheim's *Sunday in the Park with George*.

Finally, we must all express our deeply felt appreciation to J. Seward Johnson, Jr. for the vision and conviction that produced this current body of work. With his special mix of fantasy, reality, and illusion, Johnson has created a new world of experiences that simultaneously immerse us in the past while also reminding us of our capacity for joy and discovery in the present.

JACQUELYN DAYS SERWER
Chief Curator
Corcoran Gallery of Art

Illustration and Photo Credits

PHOTOS BY WYATT GALLERY

Cover, half title, full title, 32-37, 38, 41-45, 52-57, 60-65, 67, 68-71, 72-77, 78-83, 84-91, 92-95, 96-101, 102-107, 108, 109, 110-113

IMAGES OF ORIGINAL IMPRESSIONIST PAINTINGS

Page 10, 123: Gustave Caillebotte (French, 1848–1894) *Paris Street: Rainy Day*, 1877, oil on canvas, 212.2 x 276.2 cm, Charles H. and Mary F.S. Worcester Collection, 1964.336. The Art Institute of Chicago.

Page 120: Edouard Manet (1832–1883). *The Fifer*. Oil on canvas. © Eric Lessing/Art Resource, New York. Musée d'Orsay, Paris, France.

Page 124: Pierre Auguste Renoir (French, 1841–1919) *Two Sisters (On the Terrace)*, 1881, oil on canvas, 100.5 x 81 cm, Mr. and Mrs. Lewis Larned Coburn Memorial Collection, 1933.455. The Art Institute of Chicago.

Page 10, 123: Vincent van Gogh (Dutch, 1853–1890) *The Bedroom*, 1889, oil on canvas, 73.6 x 92.3 cm, Helen Birch Bartlett Memorial Collection, 1926.417. The Art Institute of Chicago.

Page 121: Vincent van Gogh (Dutch, 1853–1890) *L'Arlésienne: Madame Joseph-Michel Ginoux* (Marie Julien, 1848–1911), 1888 or 1889, oil on canvas; 36 x 29 in., The Metropolitan Museum of Art, bequest of Sam A. Lewisohn, 1951 (51.112.3). Photo by Malcolm Varon. Photo © 1979 The Metropolitan Museum of Art.

Page 10, 122: Edouard Manet (1832–1883). *Olympia*, 1863, oil on canvas. Photo by Hervé Lewandowski. © Réunion des Musées Nationaux/Art Resource, New York, Musée d'Orsay, Paris, France.

Page 14, 124: Edouard Manet (1832–1883). *Dejeuner sur l'herbe* (Luncheon on the Grass), 1863. © Erich Lessing/Art Resource, New York, Musée d'Orsay, Paris, France.

Page 16, 121: Pierre Auguste Renoir, *Luncheon of the Boating Party*, 1880–81, Oil on canvas, 51 1/4 x 69 1/8 in., acquired 1923. The Phillips Collection, Washington D.C.

Page 120: Claude Monet (French, 1840–1926), *La Japonaise (Camille Monet in Japanese Costume)*, 1876, Oil on canvas, 231.8 x 142.3 cm, Museum of Fine Arts, Boston, 1951 Purchase Fund: 56.147. © 2003 Museum of Fine Arts, Boston.

Page 124: Pierre-Auguste Renoir (French, 1841–1919), *Dance at Bougival*, 1883, Oil on canvas, 181.9 x 98.1 cm, Museum of Fine Arts, Boston, Picture Fund: 37.375. © 2003 Museum of Fine Arts, Boston.

Page 123: Pierre-Auguste Renoir (French, 1841–1919), *Dance in the Country*, 1883, Oil on canvas, 180 x 90 cm, © Eric Lessing / Art Resource, New York, Musée d'Orsay, Paris, France.

Page 120: Pierre-Auguste Renoir (French, 1841–1919), *Dance in the City*, 1883, Oil on canvas, 180 x 90 cm, © Eric Lessing / Art Resource, New York, Musée d'Orsay, Paris, France.

Page 121: Edouard Manet (1832–1883), *Sunday on the Seine (Argenteuil)*, 1874. Oil on canvas. © Eric Lessing / Art Resource, New York, Musée des Beaux-Arts, Tournai, Belgium.

Page 124: Claude Monet, *Woman with a Parasol—Madame Monet and Her Son*, 1875, oil on canvas, Collection of Mr. and Mrs. Paul Mellon, Image © 2003 Board of Trustees, National Gallery of Art, Washington, D.C.

ADDITIONAL ILLUSTRATIONS AND IMAGES

Page 6: Photo by Keith Meyer/*The New York Times*.

Page 10: Claude Monet (French, 1840–1926) *Garden at Sainte-Adresse*, 1867, oil on canvas; 38 5/8 x 51 1/8 in., The Metropolitan Museum of Art, Purchase, special contributions, and funds given or bequeathed by friends of the Museum, 1967 (67.241). Photo © 1989 The Metropolitan Museum of Art.

Page 12: Grounds for Sculpture. Photo by Mea Jambroes-ten Doesschate.

Page 12, *Van Gogh's Bedroom: The Other End*, digital images created on an Acorn A3000 by Pete Clements, using *Illusionist* from Clares Micro Supplies.

Page 13: Titan (Tiziano Vecelli) (c.1488–1576). *The Venus of Urbino*. © Scala/Art Resource, New York, Uffizi, Florence, Italy.

Page 13: Marcantonio Raimondi (1840–1527/34). *The Judgment of Paris*, © Réunion des Musées Nationaux/Art Resource, New York, Louvre, Paris, France.

Page 14: Pablo Picasso (1881–1973). © 2003 Estate of Pablo Picasso/Artists Rights Society (ARS), New York. *Luncheon on the Grass (after Manet)*, Mougins, June 17, 1962. Colored pencil. © Réunion des Musées Nationaux / Art Resource, New York, Musée Picasso, Paris, France.

Page 15, Roy Lichtenstein, *Bedroom at Arles*, 1992. © The Estate of Roy Lichtenstein

Page 15: Larry Rivers (1923–2002), © VAGA, NY, *I Like Olympia in Blackface*, 1970. Photo by Jacqueline Hyde. © CNAC/MNAM/Dist. Réunion des Musées Nationaux / Art Resource, New York, Musée National d'Art Moderne, Centre Georges Pompidou, Paris, France.

Page 16, Jean-Michel Basquiat, *Arroz Con Pollo*, © 2003 Artists Rights Society (ARS), New York, ADAGP, Paris. Courtesy Tony Shafrazi Gallery, New York.

Page 18: *Van Gogh's Bedroom*, Diorama from The Palace of Living Art, San Francisco, CA. Photo courtesy Petra ten-Doesschate Chu.

Page 18: After Rembrandt, *The Storm on the Sea of Galilee*. Courtesy Unusual Films, Bob Jones University, Greenville, South Carolina.

Page 22: *Were You Invited? (Opening Gala)*, J. Seward Johnson, Jr. and Red Grooms. Photo courtesy of The Sculpture Foundation, info@TSFmail.com. Photo by © Michelle Post.

Page 22, Red Grooms, *Ruckus Manhattan*, Red Grooms with Mimi Gross and the Ruckus Construction Company, 1975–76. Courtesy of MTA and Marlborough Gallery, New York.

Page 23: *Designated Coachman*, The Sculpture Foundation, by J. Seward Johnson, Jr. Photo by Christopher Boas. Courtesy The Sculpture Foundation.

Page 24: *Déjeuner Déjà Vu* (detail), The Sculpture Foundation, by J. Seward Johnson, Jr. Photo courtesy of The Sculpture Foundation, info@TSFmail.com. Photo by © RicardoBarros.com.

Page 26: *Sunday in the Park with George*, The Kennedy Center, Washington, D.C. Photo © 2002 Joan Marcus.

Page 27, *La Grande Jatte II*, by Red Grooms. Photo courtesy Shark's Ink, Lyons, Colorado. Collection of Lysiane Grooms.

Page 115: View through the transparency. Using the view box to check alignment. Photos © Wyatt Gallery.

Page 116: Plasteline model. Photo courtesy The Sculpture Foundation. Photo by Christopher Boas. Applying the rubber mold. Photo © Michelle Post. Wax model with sprues. Photo © Wyatt Gallery.

Page 117: Dipping the wax model into ceramic slurry. Spraying on the primer paint. Hand-painting the details. Photos © Wyatt Gallery. Pouring the metal. Photo © Michelle Post.

Page 118: Projecting the painting onto the diorama floor. Photo courtesy The Sculpture Foundation.

Page 119: Adjusting the cardboard cutouts. Photo courtesy The Sculpture Foundation. Adding botanical elements. Photo © Wyatt Gallery.